Living in the Realm Of the MIRACULOUS

Laugh & Cry as You Read This Family's Amazing Journey!

Dr Michael & Kathleen Yeager

Living in the Realm of the Miraculous

2018 up dated Version

ISBN: 978-1-936578-29-0

Library of Congress Control Number: 2011945907

DEDICATION

We dedicate this book to those who hunger and yearn to live in the realm of the miraculous, and to those who have already tasted of the heavenly realm. We dedicate this to the bride of Christ, who are called tȯ go deeper, higher, and farther than they have yet experienced. It is only by the supernatural touch of God that we will be able to accomplish His will in this earth.

ENDORSEMENTS

This book is filled with wonderful experiences, healings, and signs and wonders. There is a strong anointing that will come upon you as you read this book. As you are reading these encounters with God, it is like reading a continuation of the book of Acts. I highly recommend this book, as it will radically change your life forever.
Joan Pearce, Channel of Love Ministries

This book will change your life! I've had the distinct privilege of meeting many of the Lord's servants in my travels, yet Mike Yeager stands out among all of them as a man of rare faith and insight. His passion for the lost caused him to pray a prayer few would dare to utter: "Lord, show me hell." This book is a brief glimpse of his remarkable, ongoing story that will both delight you and cause you to pause to look soberly at your own life. It is a must read for every believer in this hour—where apathy and a quasi-spiritual facade has masked the glaring reality of an eternity that awaits us all. **-Dr. Bruce Allen, Still Waters International Ministries**

This book teaches the believer how to live in Gods realm of glory. It is this glory that God wants His sons to fill the whole earth with. Dr. Mike is a man called to a divine assignment. It is evident by his life and the life of his family that they have stayed on course. Through the Yeager's lives God has brought to life that which is impossible, to the possible realm of God's glory. Thanks to the Yeager family's persistent faithfulness and unwavering faith, the hand of God has brought the realm of the miraculous into the world. - **Pastor Allen Mason, Solid Rock Ministries, North Carolina**

What Mike and Kathy share in this book, did not happen to them because they are special people, but because they chose to trust a supernatural God who was faithful in their lives. They made room for Him to move in their family and chose to trust His Word over their circumstances.

Gil Howard-Browne

CONTENTS

Preface: You Better Not Lie!

One day I picked up a book by a well-known author. This book had come highly recommended to me by one of my favorite preachers. The topic was about supernatural visitations. This was something I was interested in, because of my experience with having been taken into heaven.

As I began to read this book, there were experiences he said he had, which did not seem to line up with the Scriptures. I did not want to judge his heart, but we do have the responsibility to examine everything in the light of God's Word. As I was pondering upon the stories of this book, the Spirit of the Lord spoke to my heart. It was as if He was standing right there next to me, speaking audibly. What He spoke to me was rather shocking! God told me that the writer of this book would be dead in three months from a heart attack. I asked the Lord why He was telling me this. He said because the stories in the man's book were exaggerated, that judgment was coming. The Lord warned me that day that if I were ever to do the same thing, judgment would come to me. Please realize that God was not going to kill this man, but he had opened the door for the devil to take him out.

When the Spirit of the Lord spoke this to me, I turned and told my wife. I held the book up and said, in a very quiet whispering wavering voice, "Honey, the man who wrote this book will be dead in three months from a heart attack." Plus, I told her why the Lord told me this. I wish I had been wrong. However, three months later, the man died from a heart attack. The issue here is not the minister who died from a heart attack. The issue is the warning that God had spoken to me personally about judgment, if I exaggerated. That's why I'm striving to not exaggerate the retelling of the stories within this book about me, my wife, and my family's lives.

Dr. Michael & Kathleen Yeager

ACKNOWLEDGMENTS

To our heavenly Father, and His wonderful love.

To our Lord and Master, Jesus Christ, who saved us and set us free. To the Holy Spirit, who leads and guides us into the miraculous.

To all of those who had a part in helping us get this book ready for the publishers.

A special thanks to Mary Rockwell, Yu Catherine Li, and Cheryl Putnam who spent many hours fixing all the mistakes that was in this manuscript. Mary, you have helped beyond measure!

To our precious children, Michael, Daniel, Steven, Stephanie, and Naomi (who is now with the Lord).

Living in the Realm of the Miraculous

CHAPTER ONE

Our First Encounters with the Miraculous

Introduction

The miraculous happenings, heavenly visitations, and divine deliverances that you are about to read are all true, as they have happened personally to me and my family. These experiences are recalled and shared to the best of our ability.

By no means do the following stories account for all the visitations and miracles God has expressed in our lives. If we would recount every single answer to prayer and every wonderful miracle and blessing, there would be no end to this book! Both my wife and I, including our children, have had numerous supernatural dreams, visions, and experiences. In some of our heavenly encounters, God gave us specific information which has come to pass, as well as visions and dreams which have yet to be fulfilled.

What we are about to share with you in this book are simply some highlights of what we have experienced in the Lord. Some of these experiences will seem to be incredulous, however, they are true. This is not a testimony of how spiritual we are, but how wonderful and marvelous the Father, the Son, and the Holy Ghost are! We share these experiences to the best of our recollections and understanding. Not every conversation we share in these experiences are exactly word for word. We would love to name every person that was a part of these wonderful occurrences, but privacy laws do not allow this. If you are reading this book and you saw, experienced, or were a part of these events, please do not be offended because your names were not mentioned.

At the end of this book there will be a brief teaching on how you can enter a position where God will supernaturally begin to speak, lead and guide you in your life. It is God's will that all who follow Him would enter into this realm where all things are possible. What God has done for us, He will do for everyone. He is not a respecter of people.

From Kathleen:

This book is written primarily from my husband's perspective, as he's such a great storyteller. I have helped my husband recall the facts, changed a few things, and have added a few comments here and there.

Concerning myself, I have loved the Lord ever since I was a child. My father died when I was six years old, and I was molested at a young age. However, God rescued me and my family from abuse, shortly after I gave my life to Christ at the age of eight. I received the baptism of the Holy Ghost at the age of ten, and taught Sunday school from the age of twelve on. I have received my bachelors in theology, and have had the joy of teaching in our Christian academy. Mike and I have had five lovely children, and have had the privilege of helping several other children. God has been extremely good to us!

From Michael:

I was born prematurely on February 18, 1956. The inner bones of my ears were immobile, resulting in improper draining. This caused congestion and resulted in tremendous head pressure and hearing loss.

Like my older brother, Dennis, and sister, Debbie, I was born with my feet turned outward, so we all had to wear foot braces when we were little. I also suffered from a generational curse of weak lungs which caused me to end up in the hospital, placed in an oxygen tent, on numerous occasions. I was also born tongue-tied with my tongue grown to the bottom part of my mouth. They operated on my tongue in order to give me the ability to speak. It was almost impossible to move my tongue sufficiently to pronounce my words correctly.

2

I was raised in Catholicism, but our family was not very spiritual. My first experience with God took place when I was a baby, according to my mother. (she never told me about it until years later and I really don't know many of the details.)

Our First Encounters with the Miraculous

Kathee's Story:

1. Name's Sake

I was born on October 14th, 1958. My mother named me Kathleen after one of her previous siblings which she never met, because Kathleen died when she was thirteen months old from pneumonia. Just like my name's sake, I developed pneumonia when I was thirteen months old. I developed a very high fever and could barely breathe.

Fearing the loss of her firstborn, and praying for God's healing mercy, my mother wrapped me in her heavy coat and rushed me to the hospital. Because I was wrapped in a heavy coat, the long wait in the emergency room caused me to sweat until my fever broke. My mother said that according to the doctor, my life was spared because of what she had done.

Nevertheless he saved them for his name's sake, that he might make his mighty power to be known (Psalm 106:8).

3

2. Tragedy Strikes and a Change of Heart

My mother had drifted from the Lord after she got married. Her mother, my grandmother, was a godly prayer warrior and she constantly lifted her children and their families before God in intercession.

My Mom repented and decided to live for Christ. Nevertheless, my father wanted nothing to do with Jesus Christ; he blasphemed and swore that he would never serve God. He was only twenty-nine years old when his life was tragically taken in a terrible automobile accident.

My mother was forced to rear her three small children alone after the death of her husband. I was the oldest child at the time, being only six years old. My brother was three, and my sister was barely two years old. I can remember how my mother drew nearer to God, and prayed fervently for her little family.

My heart was softened by my heavenly Father's love and care, and I accepted Christ as my Savior at the age of eight.

A father of the fatherless, and a judge of the widows, is God in his holy habitation (Psalm 68:5).

3. A Trap

It wasn't long after the death of my father that another relative stepped in to be our dad, and my mom's new husband.

At first this seemed to be a good thing; however, it proved to be a grave mistake: Our stepfather was a wonderful person, except for the vice of alcohol. Our greatest joy was that mother had a son, and we gained a baby brother from the union.

My stepfather would beat us children, my mother, and molest my sister and me. I remember praying many nights that God would protect my mom, my new baby brother and us children, while I lay in bed hearing my stepfather fight with my precious mother. God became very real to me, during those dark times.

My mom would take us and run away, but our stepfather would seek us out, and take us all back home. Over and over, he promised that he would not beat Mom again, but never kept those promises. Mother knew nothing about the molestation, because he swore us to secrecy.

By the time I was ten years old, my mother broke away from all the abuse and brought us to Pennsylvania to live by her parents. God became our only Father and my mom's Husband.

Abba Father delivered me from all the pain and abuse, filling my heart with forgiveness and love.

God is our refuge and strength, a very present help in trouble (Psalm 46:1).

4. Spiritual Guidance

We were blessed by great Christians and family that watched over us. The pastor of the church was a tremendous influence in our lives, as well as a spiritual father. God wondrously provided for me to go to children's camp, where I received the baptism of the Holy Spirit at the age of ten.

At the age of twelve, our pastor asked me to teach Sunday school for those who were younger than I. That was the beginning of great spiritual growth in my life; which later led to me to go to Bible College. You will see how I met Michael in a later chapter (5).

And who knoweth whether thou art come to the kingdom for such a time as this? (Esther 4:14).

Michael's Life:

5. Touched as a Baby

Supposedly, Oral Roberts was conducting a large tent meeting in our area. My mother was desperate to get help for me, because of all my physical problems. She told me that Oral Roberts never laid hands on me. Yet, as she stood in the tent with all of the other masses of people, something began to happen to me. She said that I began to shake uncontrollably as she was standing in the service. She did not understand what was happening. I am convinced the Spirit of God came upon me in that service over fifty-five years ago. Never underestimate what God can do in the midst of a gathering of His saints!

Not forsaking the assembling of ourselves together, as the manner of some is; but exhorting one another: and so much the more, as ye see the day approaching (Hebrews 10:25).

6. Blood upon the Cross

I experienced a supernatural visitation when I was about seven years old. One cold winter night I had to get up to go to the restroom, so I went into our little bathroom. After I finished,

I washed my hands and turned off the lights. I noticed the moon reflecting off the bathroom mirror. The light was coming from the perforated, frosted-glass window. As I looked out the glass at the snow covered ground, I saw three crosses.

The two outer crosses seemed to be set back from the much-larger middle cross. My eyes were supernaturally drawn to the larger middle cross. As I looked at it, there appeared to be blood running down from it. My heart was smitten with great overwhelming sorrow when I looked at this cross and I began to weep uncontrollably. That experience radically changed my personality and attitude. I became helpful, kind, and caring. This transformation lasted for a brief time but soon dissipated.

No man can come to me, except the Father which hath sent me draw him: and I will raise him up at the last day (John 6:44).

*7. Blanket of Fear

Am I the devil? (1963)

If my mother was still alive, she could tell you all the heart aches that I caused her. I do remember as a young child being extremely tormented. I am sure that my parents loved me in whatever capacity they understood. I never heard my dad tell me that he loved me until I was approximately 23 years old. And that was after four years of me telling him every time that I spoke to him that I loved him. That began when I gave my heart to Jesus as a 19-year-old boy. He only once told me that he loved me and yet, to this day, I remember him speaking those words to me over the telephone. Tears rolled down my face when he said that to me.

As a very young child, I remember going out of my way to torment my older brother and sister. I just couldn't help myself. My mother was so exasperated on one occasion that she screamed at me, **"You Are the Devil Himself!"**

Those words were like a dagger to my heart. I do not think that we understand the power of our words. I remember going into our little bathroom in our two-bedroom house. I closed the door and climbed onto the sink where I could see my face in the mirror. Then I took my two little hands and began to rub them over the top of my head and, sure enough, to my shock and my amazement, there were two lumps on my head. I could feel a lump on my left side and a lump on my right side. I was the devil! And the horns were beginning to form on my head. I remember to this day weeping, knowing that I had no hope of salvation because I was the devil himself!

Matthew 15:22 And, behold, a woman of Canaan came out of the same coasts, and cried unto him, saying, Have mercy on me, O Lord, thou son of David; my daughter is grievously vexed with a devil.

Choking Cuddles & Peanuts

When a person who is tormented, of course, they will torment others. We can only reproduce from what we are or take people to where we live. If you are miserable and tormented, full of sin and wickedness, that's all you can produce. My parents used to have beagles as their number one choice of dogs. We would go rabbit hunting with them whenever the opportunity arose. I did eventually purchase a Redbone Coon hound puppy which I raised to hunt raccoons.

My mom had two small beagles which she kept in the house. Their names were Cuddles and Peanuts. I don't think my parents ever really understood how tormented I was. My heart and mind even as a young boy was twisted and sick. When no one else was around, I would call these two little beagles to me taking them one at a time. (I truly do not even want to share these stories, but I believe they will show you that there is hope for anyone and everyone.) I would take Cuddles into my lap, petting and cuddle her, and then I would put my hands on her throat and begin to choke her. Yes, I would begin to choke her with everything inside of me. I would choke poor little Cuddles until her tongue would hang out of her mouth until it seemed like there was no life left in her. Until her body went completely limp.

And then, when it would seem like she was almost dead, I would stop choking her. And then I would begin to cry and weep, begging her not to die, asking God to let her live. I would be shaking her trying to get her to breathe again. And, sure enough, she would begin to breathe and come back around. When she was completely recovered and was breathing normally again, I would start it all over. Yes, you heard correctly. My sick, tormented nature would grab her by the throat again, and I would repeat the cycle. Once again, I would begin to cry, asking her to live. And then I would start it all over again.

I not only did this to our dog Cuddles but also Peanut. I never did it where anybody could see me. Neither my mother, father, brother or sister ever suspected what I was doing. I was one little sick, tormented boy. These actions only reconfirmed to me that I was the Devil himself in human flesh.

Luke 9:42 And as he was yet a coming, the devil threw him down, and tare him. And Jesus rebuked the unclean spirit, and healed the child, and delivered him again to his father.

My Amazing Supernatural Salvation

It was my nineteenth birthday (February 18, 1975). I was in the Navy at the time and heavily involved in alcohol, drugs, and other ungodly activities. I had decided to commit suicide. I do not remember anyone ever sharing the gospel of Jesus Christ with me. No one ever took the time to warn me about eternal damnation for those who did not know God. Even to this day it amazes me that the government ever accepted me into the Navy (back in 1973 when I was 17 years old). At the time I had major mental, emotional and even physical problems which included hearing problems and a major speech impediment. I quit school at 15 years old, leaving home until I ended up in trouble with the law at 16.

I was given the option of being prosecuted or joining the military. I chose the military. However, for the military to accept me, I had to have my GED. Subsequently, I worked extremely hard to get it and I succeeded. At the time, I really believed that joining the Navy would take me out of the drugs, violence, immorality, and alcohol lifestyle that I had been living. That could not have been farther from the truth.

As soon as I graduated from basic training, Uncle Sam shipped me to San Diego, California for further training on repairing 16mm projectors. Upon accomplishing this training, I was sent to Adak, Alaska in the Aleutian Islands. I was assigned to the special services department. They provided all of the entertainment for the men on base. This included the movie theater, bowling alley, roller-skating rink, horse stables for taking men hunting and the cafeteria (not the chow hall).

I was extremely unreliable and incompetent, so much so that within the two years that I was there, I was transferred to every one of those facilities. My last job ended up being at the horse stables shoveling manure. During this time I was heavily involved in drugs, including selling them. I was drinking a lot of alcohol including ripple wine, vodka and tequila. I smoked an average of 3 1/2 packs of cigarettes per day, not including cigars. I used Brown Mule, Copenhagen, Beach Nut, and Skoal chewing tobaccos. My favorite singing groups were Dr. Hook and the Medicine Band, Pink Floyd, The Grateful Dead and America.

When I was off duty, my attire was extremely strange. First off, when I was younger, my older brother knocked out my front tooth. Of course, I had it replaced with a pegged tooth but while I was stationed in Adak, it got knocked out again. As a result, I picked up a ridiculous nickname. I was called "Tooth". I wanted to fit in with the cowboy crowd so I found an old cowboy hat which was way too large for me. In order to make it fit, I took an old military ski hat and sewed it on the inside in order that it would be snug on my head. (Of course, this old Stetson cowboy hat was way too large for me.) As I would walk around the base with this large cowboy hat, it would be flopping on top of my head, making me look extremely silly; especially with me missing one of my front teeth.

I did not want to just be a cowboy because I was also a hippie. So, with a bright new idea, I went to the cafeteria and asked for all of their chicken necks. I took these chicken necks and boiled them in a pot of hot vinegar water. Then I took these chicken bones after they were cleaned and strung them on a leather strand. I would wear these chicken bones as a necklace around my neck. It really stank! No wonder I was extremely depressed all of the time.

I think that you can begin to see what kind of a mess I was. **However, supernaturally one night, God stepped into my life, instantly and radically changing me forever!** My last three months of military life was so amazingly transformed that I was put in charge of working parties and details from time to time. God instantly delivered me from all of my devices including all of my foolish behaviors. I was a new creature in Christ! Christ had supernaturally set me free from the tormenting demonic powers that had possessed my life for so long!

On my **19th birthday** I was overwhelmed with self-pity and depression. I decided to end it all by slitting my wrist! I went into the bathroom with a large, survival hunting knife. I put the knife to my wrist with full intentions of slitting my artery. I was determined to kill myself. I held the knife firmly against my wrist and took one more last breath before I slid it across my wrist. Suddenly, an invisible presence came rushing down upon me like a blanket. It was a tangible, overwhelming presence of mind-boggling fear. It was the fear of God, and it overwhelmed me! Instantly, I realized with crystal-clear understanding that I was going to hell. I deserved hell; I belonged in hell, and hell had a right to me. Furthermore, I knew if I slit my wrist, I would be in hell forever.

And great fear came upon all the church, and upon as many as heard these things (Acts 5:11).

11

8. Overwhelming Love

I walked out of that little military bathroom to my bunk. I fell on my knees, reached my hands up toward heaven and cried out to Jesus with all of my heart. All of this was supernatural and strange. I did not ever recall any time when anyone ever shared with me how to become a Christian or how to be converted. Yet, I knew how to pray. I cried out to Jesus and told Him I believed He was the Son of God, had been raised from the dead, and I desperately needed Him.

I not only asked Him into my heart, but I gave Him my heart, soul, mind, and life. At that very instant, a love beyond description came rushing into my heart. I really knew what love was for the first time in my life. At the same time, I comprehended what I was placed on this earth for—I was here to follow, love, serve, and obey God. A deep love and hunger to know God grabbed my heart. I was filled with love from top to bottom, inside and out—inexpressibly beyond belief. Jesus had come to live inside of me!

Rivers of waters run down mine eyes, because they keep not thy law (Psalm 119:136).

9. Instantaneous Deliverance

I was instantly delivered: from over three packs of cigarettes a day, from worldly and satanic music, from chewing tobacco; from cussing and swearing, from drugs and alcohol, and from a filthy and dirty mind.

Some might ask why my conversion was so dramatic. I believe that it's because I had nothing to lose. I knew down deep that there was not one single thing worth saving in me. The only natural talent I ever possessed was the ability to mess things up. At the moment of salvation, I completely surrendered my heart and life to Jesus Christ.

I am crucified with Christ: nevertheless I live; yet not I, but Christ liveth in me: and the life which I now live in the flesh I live by the faith of the Son of God, who loved me, and gave himself for me (Galatians 2:20).

OBSESSED WITH A DEEP HUNGER for GOD'S WORD!

I remember after giving my heart to **Jesus Christ** that I got up from the floor born again, saved and delivered, I was a brand-new person. Immediately hunger and thirst for the Word of God took a hold of me. I began to devoured Matthew, Mark, Luke, and John. I just could not get enough of the word of God because of my love for **Jesus Christ** and his **Father**. **Jesus** became my hero in every area of my thoughts and daily life. He became my reason for getting up and going to work, eating, sleeping, and living.

I discovered that everything I did was based on the desire of wanting to please Him. I carried my little green military Bible with me wherever I went. Whenever I had an opportunity I would open it up and study it. It wasn't very long before I believed for a larger Bible. This larger Bible gave me much more room to make notes, highlight and circle certain Scriptures. The more I fed on the Scriptures, the greater my hunger became for them. I probably was not saved even for 2 months when I was asked to speak for the 1st time at a small Pentecostal church. I believe it was called Adak Full Gospel Church. As far as I know it was the only Pentecostal church on this military base situated on a Aleutian Island in Alaska. Since 1975 I have never lost my hunger, or my thirst for God's word. I can truly say even what the psalmist said!

Psalm 104:34 My meditation of him shall be sweet: I will be glad in the Lord.

*10. My Tongue Was Loosed

Healed Me of Being Tongue-Tied!

After I gave my heart to **Christ** a divine hunger and thirst for the Word of God began to possess me. I practically devoured Matthew, Mark, Luke, and John. **Jesus** became my hero in every sense of the word, in every area of my thoughts and daily living. He became my soul reason for getting up every day and going to work, eating, sleeping, and living. I discovered that everything I did was based on a desire of wanting to please Him.

One day I was reading my Bible and discovered where **Jesus** said that it was necessary for him to leave. That because when he would go back to the **Father**, he would send the promise of the Holy Ghost to make us a witness. Furthermore, I learned it was His will for me to be filled to overflowing with the Holy Ghost and that the Holy Ghost would empower and equip me to be a witness an ambassador for God. The Holy Ghost would also lead me and guide me into all truth.

With all my heart I desperately wanted to reach the lost for **Jesus Christ** in order for they could experience the same love and freedom that I was now walking in. I searched the Scriptures to confirm this experience. In the book of Joel, in the old covenant, the four Gospels and especially in the book of acts I discovered the will of God when it comes to this baptism. I perceived in my heart that I needed to receive this baptism the same way that I had received salvation.

I had to look to **Christ** and trust by faith that he would give to me this baptism of the Spirit. It declared in the book of acts that after they were baptized in the Holy Ghost they all began to speak in a heavenly language. I had not been around what we would call Pentecostal people, so I had never heard anybody else speak in this heavenly language. But that did not really matter to me, because it was within the Scriptures.

Acts 2:39 For the promise is unto you, and to your children, and to all that are afar off, even as many as the Lord our God shall call.

I remember getting on my knees next to my bunk bed where I cried out and asked God to fill me with the Holy Ghost, so I could be a witness. As I was crying out to God something began to happen on the inside of me. It literally felt like hot buckets of oil was beginning to be poured upon me and within me. Something then began to rise out of my innermost being. Before I knew what I was doing, a new language came out bubbling of my mouth which I had never heard before, or been taught to speak. I began to speak in a heavenly tongue.

Now up to this time I had a terrible speech impediment. You see I had been born tongue-tied. Yes, they had operated on me, and I had gone to speech therapy, and yet most people could not understand what I was saying. I could not even pronounce my own last name YEAGER properly. My tongue simply refused to move in a way in which I could pronounce my Rs.

After I was done praying in this new language, I discovered to my absolute surprise that my speech impediment was instantly and completely gone! From that time on, I have never stopped preaching **Jesus Christ**. For almost 40 years I have proclaimed the truth of **Jesus Christ** to as many as I can.

And they were all filled with the Holy Ghost, and began to speak with other tongues, as the Spirit gave them utterance (Acts 2:4).

\

*11. If I Was, I Am, If I Am, I Is!

While reading my Bible as a brand-new believer, (1975) I discovered that Jesus Christ went about healing **ALL** who were sick and oppressed of the devil. I began to search the Scriptures on this subject, and as I studied I discovered many Scriptures that support this:

Surely he hath borne our griefs, and carried our sorrows: yet we did esteem him stricken, smitten of God, and afflicted. But he was wounded for our transgressions, he was bruised for our iniquities: the chastisement of our peace was upon him; and with his stripes we are healed (Isaiah 53:4-5).

Who his own self bare our sins in his own body on the tree, that we, being dead to sins, should live unto righteousness: by whose stripes ye were healed.1 Peter 2:24

When the even was come, they brought unto him many that were possessed with devils: and he cast out the spirits with his word, and healed all that were sick: That it might be fulfilled which was spoken by Esaias the prophet, saying, Himself took our infirmities, and bare our sicknesses. Matthew 8:16-17

As I read and meditated upon these Scriptures, something wonderful happened within my heart. Great, overwhelming sorrow took a hold of me as I saw the pain and the agony that Jesus went through for my healing. In my heart and in my mind I saw that Jesus had taken my sicknesses and my diseases. I then experienced a great love for the son of God, and recognize the price he paid for my healing.

When God gave me this revelation, revealed to me by the Scriptures, I experienced a great an overwhelming love for the son of God, recognizing the price he had paid for my healing. It was like an open vision in which I saw my precious **Lord and Savior** tied to the whipping post. I saw the Roman soldiers striking, beating, and whipping the back of Jesus with the cat of nine tails. This was a Roman whip which had nine long strands, coated with oil, and covered with glass, metal shards, and sharp objects. In this vision I saw the flesh and the blood of my precious Savior splashing everything within a 10-foot radius, with each terrible stroke of the Romans soldier's whip hitting his body.

As I saw this open vision, (as I was on my knees in prayer) I wept because I knew that this horrendous beating he was enduring was for my healing, and my deliverance. To this day, even after 40 years, whenever I retell this story, great love, and sorrow still fills my heart for what Christ had to endure for me. This is the reason why I am so aggressive in my fight to receive healing. Still I have great joy, wonderful peace, and enthusiasm in this battle, because I know that by the **stripes of Jesus Christ I am healed**. This amazing price that he paid (God in the flesh) was not only for me, but for every believer who has received Christ as their Lord and Savior.

In this moment of this vision something exploded within my heart, an amazing faith possessed me with the knowledge that I no longer have to be sick. In the name of Jesus for over 40 years I have refused to allow what my precious Lord went through to be for nothing. I have refused to allow sickness and disease to dwell in my body, which is the temple of the Holy Ghost.

Jesus has taken my sicknesses and my diseases. No if, an, or butts, no matter what it looks like or how I feel, I know within my heart Jesus Christ has set me free from sicknesses and diseases. At the moment of this revelation great anger, yes great anger, rose up in my heart against the enemy of my Lord. The demonic world has no right to afflict me or any other believer, because Jesus took our sicknesses and bore our diseases.

Now I had been born with terrible physical infirmities, but now I found myself speaking aloud with authority to my ears, commanding them to be open and to be normal in the name of Jesus Christ of Nazareth. Then I spoke to my lungs, and commanded them to be healed in the name of Jesus Christ of

Nazareth. Next, I commanded my sinuses to be delivered, so I could smell normal scents in the name of Jesus Christ of Nazareth.

The minute I spoke the Word of God to my physical man, my ears popped completely open. Up to this moment I had a significant hearing loss, but now as I was listening to Christian music playing softly (at least I thought it was) the music became so loud that I had to turn it down. My lungs were clear, and I haven't experienced any lung congestion since in 40 years. I used to be so allergic to dust that my mother had to work extra hard to keep our house dust-free. I would literally end up in an oxygen tent in the hospital. From that moment to now dust, allergies, mold, or any such thing have never come back to torment me or cause me problems. Instantly my sense of smell returned! I had broken my nose about four times due to fights, accidents, and rough activities. I could barely smell anything.

Suddenly, I could smell a terrible odor. I tried to find out where it was coming from and then I looked at my feet and wondered if it could be them. I put my foot on a night stand and bent over toward it. I took a big sniff and nearly fell over. Man, did my feet stink! I went straight over to the bathroom and washed them in the sink.

The very 1st thing we must do to build a solid foundation for our lives is to let go of all our traditions, philosophies, doctrines, and experiences that contradict what is revealed to us through Jesus Christ. We must go back to Matthew, Mark, Luke and John rediscovering who Jesus Christ really is. Whatever Jesus said and did is what we agree with wholeheartedly. Any voice or teaching that contradicts Christ, and his redemptive work I immediately reject.

How God anointed Jesus of Nazareth with the Holy Ghost and with power: who went about doing good, and healing all that were oppressed of the devil; for God was with him (Acts 10:38).

12. The Circle Unbroken

My heart was quickened to gather with people of like-precious faith who loved Jesus Christ. I discovered a little full gospel church on our military base in Adak, Alaska, where I was stationed. When we began to worship the Lord in that little church, the Spirit of God would quicken within my heart. It felt like a Þre in my belly rising up within me. Something wanted to come forth out of my mouth. I didn't realize it was the Spirit of God, so I tried to resist it.

As I resisted this unction of the Holy Spirit, I began to shake uncontrollably. People right around me in the pews gathered in a circle and laid their hands upon me. As they were praying for me, I broke forth and spoke out in tongues. When I did this, the interpretation of what I had said came out in English. I did not realize at the time that this is what the Bible calls the diversity of tongues and interpretation.

Wherefore let him that speaketh in an unknown tongue pray that he may interpret (1 Corinthians 14:13).

*God, Where Are You? This Little Teaching Could Save Your Life!

In our walk with God, there are many things that we absolutely must learn. I wish that we could instantly learn them - just from reading the Bible. But … this is not the case. I had to learn a very hard lesson early in my Christian walk, one that many believers who have walked with God for years still have not learned.

I believe the reason that I had to learn this lesson was because of the amount of trials, tests, and hardships that I was to experience throughout my lifetime. I had to learn how to not live by feelings, or by the circumstances that surrounded me.

I gave my heart to Christ on February 18th, 1975

My whole life before this had been filled with pain, sorrow, depression, low self-esteem, physical disabilities, etc. You name it, I had it. But when I gave my heart to Christ, the presence of God instantly overwhelmed me. It was like electricity going through my body, twenty-four hours a day, seven days a week. This did not go away, but continued upon me.

I was instantly set free from all addictions, as well as emotional and mental problems. I was a brand-new creation in Christ Jesus. I fell in love with my Lord: head over heels. I immediately began devouring the Word of the Living God; specifically, the four Gospels. I got filled with the Holy Ghost, healed, and I preached my first sermon very shortly after I was saved. I think I took the presence and touch of God upon my life for granted, at that time, as if that was the normal, everyday experience, for every believer. I was soon to discover this was not true.

One morning I got up early to pray and read my Bible - as normal - but something was wrong. I had grown used to the very tangible presence and manifestation of God but, to my shock and horror, it was gone! I mean, to me, personally ... the presence of God was gone. Confusion suddenly clouded my heart and my mind. I cried out to God: "Lord, what's wrong? How have I offended you?" I did not hear any answer, which was, to me, also very strange. The Lord was constantly speaking to my heart. I examined myself to see if there was something I was doing that was against the will of God. I could not find anything wrong. I didn't know what else to do and I didn't really have anyone that I could go to, at that time, who was mature enough to help me.

So, I kept reading my Bible, kept on praying, worshipping, praising, and sharing Christ as I went along. I went to bed that night with no sense of God's presence. The next morning, I got up early, hoping that His presence had come back, but to my shock and sadness, God was not there. Once again, I went through the torment of examining my heart, crying out to Jesus and following my regular routine throughout the day. I went to bed that night in the same condition.

During the whole experience, I did not back off or give up but just kept pressing in.

This went on, day after day, after day. God just was not there in His tangible presence. Yes, I did get depressed, but I did not give up. I did not stop praying or reading my Bible. I never ceased worshiping and praising God. I did not stop sharing my faith with others and telling them the wonderful things Jesus had done for me. I think approximately two weeks went by with me in this spiritual desert —a no man's land— a dark and dry place in my daily walk. I did not know what was wrong, and there was nothing else I could do but keep pressing in closer. After about two weeks, I went to bed one night, praying and talking to God, even though He was not answering me in the same way as He did before.

The next morning, I got up early and began to pray ... when out of the blue God's presence came rushing in stronger than ever - like a mighty wind. It was like a powerful tsunami, a forceful flood of His presence and His Spirit. God's touch was upon me greatly. I began to laugh, to cry and to shout. Oh! It was so good to have God with me again.

I said to the Lord, when I was finally able to talk: "Lord, where were you?" There seemed to be a long pause, then He said to me, with what seemed to be a bit of amusement in His voice: **"I Was Here All Along."**

"You were, Lord?" **He replied: "Yes."** Then He said something that would forever change my life: **"I was teaching you how to live by faith."** He began to very specifically teach me out of the Scriptures, that man does not live by bread alone but by every word that comes out of the mouth of God.

Matthew 4:4 But he answered and said, It is written, Man shall not live by bread alone, but by every word that proceedeth out of the mouth of God.

I learned that our walk with Him does not depend upon our feelings, emotions, location, or circumstances. And that many of those who are believers are destroyed by the enemy because they do not understand nor believe this. Even the Apostle Paul had to learn how to be content in Christ, in whatever condition, trusting God, knowing that He is not a man that He should lie. Christ said that He would never leave us nor forsake us. We may call upon Christ with a sincere heart: knowing that He will be there for us, to answer us and show us great and mighty things which we know not!

Over forty years have come and gone since I learned this lesson. I now no longer allow the feelings of either His absence or His presence to affect me. Of course, I constantly examine my heart, but if I can find nothing wrong, I simply realize that I am flying by instruments and no longer operating by visual flight rules **(VFR).** Thank God, as the aviation industry would say, I am SFR rated! There are two sets of regulations governing all aspects of civilian aircraft operations: the first is Instrument flight rules **(IFR)** and the second is visual flight rules **(VFR)** defined as flying by sight and sensory input. All Christians are to be rated as (SFR) which would equate to Spiritual Flight Rules!

*13. His Hernia Was Instantly Gone! (1975)

One night I was at a fellowship gathering with other believers from our little church. Chief officer Lloyd and his wife, Bonnie, had invited us all to come to their house for fellowship.

Now as I was standing in their front room enjoying the fellowship, a kind of foggy image came floating up from my heart into my mind. In this semi-foggy vision, I saw a bulge in the lower stomach area of the man standing directly across from me. I did not know that this bulge was actually what they call a hernia. I had only been born again for about a month, and not yet been taught on the gifts of the Holy Ghost. This was the word of knowledge operating by a vision inspired by the Holy Ghost.

As I saw this image in my mind's eye, I said to the Lord in my heart: Lord, if this image is really of you then let that brother come over to me. The very moment this little prayer left my heart, this navy chief (Frank) looked up and walked over me. I then also walked toward him, and we both reached out our hands towards each other, shaking hands. He introduced himself as Frank. As we were making small talk, I brought up the image I just had.

He looked rather surprised and informed me that he was indeed having a terrible time with a hernia. The doctors had operated on it three times up to this point he informed me, but it had torn loose after each operation. I asked him if I could pray for him pertaining to this problem, and he gave me permission. I told him that I would like him to put his hand over this hernia and that I would place my hand over his.

Then I simply prayed but not a long prayer. I simply spoke very quietly to this hernia telling it to go away in the name of Jesus Christ, and for his stomach muscles to be healed. The moment I finished praying, it disappeared. The hernia was instantly and literally sucked back into his abdomen; it was gone!

We both stood there, being wonderfully surprised, and

rejoicing in the miracle that God had just performed. How this miracle came to pass is that God had given me "a word of knowledge and operating with the gift of faith and healing." Frank and I became good friends afterwards. At times we would go fishing out on the Bering Sea for halibut, but that's a whole another story.

For to one is given by the Spirit the word of wisdom; to another the word of knowledge by the same Spirit; to another faith by the same Spirit; to another the gifts of healing by the same Spirit (1 Corinthians 12:8-9).

14. Very First Sermon

The moment I gave my heart to Jesus, there was this unspoken knowledge within my heart: that I was called to proclaim the good news of Jesus Christ. With this knowledge came a supernatural boldness and urge to preach. I was saved for approximately two months before I ministered my first message. It was at the same small Pentecostal church where the Spirit of God moved upon me to speak in tongues and gave the interpretation.

Even though this church did not have a pastor, those who were on the board recognized the call of God upon my life. They approached me and asked me to minister in one of their services. Even though it's been over thirty-six years, I still remember my first sermon. It came out of the book of Proverbs and the book of Daniel: **He that winneth souls is wise, and will shine like stars throughout eternity.**

And they that be wise shall shine as the brightness of the firmament; and they that turn many to righteousness as the stars forever and ever (Daniel 12:3).

CHAPTER TWO

Walking in the Miraculous

*15. Satanic Worshiper Delivered

My first encounter with a demon-possessed man was in 1975. I had only been a Christian for about two months, and I was in the Navy at the time. I was stationed on a military base on Adak, Alaska. One night (at about 8 p.m.) I was witnessing in my dormitory room to three men doing Bible study.

While sharing biblical truths with these three men, another man entered my room. We called him T.J. This individual had always been very different - and strange. He was kind of out there! I had never even spoken to him, up to that time, except one night when he showed a nasty movie to the guys in his dorm. I had walked out of his room, not being able to handle his level of filth!

When T.J. entered my room, he took over my Bible study and began to preach some weird, off-the-wall things about the devil. He said he was from California where he had been part of a satanic church. He showed us the ends of his fingers in which some of the ends were missing from the first joint out. He told us that he had eaten them for power, and he had drunk human blood at satanic worship services. As he spoke, there seemed to be an invisible power speaking through him. An evil and demonic darkness descended upon us in my dormitory. A visible, demonic power took him over, right in front of our eyes, and his eyes filled with a malevolent glow! One of the guys in my room, Hussein, (who was a Muslim) declared this was too much for him, and left the room. The other two, Bobby and Willie, sat and listened.

I had never encountered anything as sinister and evil as this ever before. I honestly didn't know what to do (at that time) so I went downstairs to the barracks right below me. There was a fellow Christian I'd had the opportunity of working with, who lived right below me. After I had given my heart to Jesus Christ, Willie, the cowboy, told me that he too was a born again, Spirit-filled Christian. I had yet to see the evidence of this in Willie's life, but I didn't know where else to go. I went down to his room and knocked on Willie's door. When he opened the door, I explained to him what was happening in my room.

I was able to get him to go to my room. Willie stepped into my dormitory and stopped. We both saw that T.J. was now up on a stool, made from a log, and he was preaching under the power of satanic spirits. At that very moment, cowboy Willie turned tail and ran out of my room. I went after him! He told me that he had no idea what to do and that he could not handle this. He left me standing outside my door alone.

I went back into my room and did the only thing I could do: I **Cried out to Jesus Christ**. The minute I cried out, looking up towards heaven, I'm telling you, a bright light from heaven shone right through my ceiling. It was a beam of light about three feet wide, an all glistening bright light, shining upon me. I do not know if anyone else in my room saw the bright light. All I know is that the Spirit of God rose up within me, and I was overwhelmed with God's presence.

My mouth was instantly filled with an amazingly powerful and Prophetic Word from Heaven. I began to preach Jesus Christ by the Power of the Spirit! As I began to speak by the Spirit, the power of God fell in that room. The next thing I knew, T.J. had dropped to the floor, like a rock. T.J. began squirming just like a snake; his body bending and twisting in an impossible way. There was no fear left in my heart as I watched this demonic activity. There was nothing but a Holy Ghost boldness and divine inspiration flowing through me at that time.

During this divine encounter of Heaven, both Willie and Bobby had fallen on their knees, crying out to Jesus to save them. At the same time, they gave their hearts to the Lord, and they were both instantly filled with the Holy Ghost! The next thing I knew, I found myself kneeling over the top of T.J. as he was squirming like a snake. I placed my hands upon him. Willie and Bobby came over and joined me, they also laid their hands upon T.J. With a voice of authority, inspired by the Spirit, I commanded the demons to come out of the man in the Name of Jesus Christ. As God is my witness, we all heard three to five different voices come screaming out of T.J.!

When the demons were gone, it was like T.J. breathed a last, long, breath, like that of a dying man, and he was completely still. After a while, he opened up his eyes - now filled with complete peace. At that very moment, he gave his heart to Jesus Christ. I led him into the baptism of the Holy Ghost. The presence of God overwhelmed all of us as we gave praise and thanks to the Lord. The next Sunday these three men went with me to church.

*16. Evil Personified

T.J. the man I had cast the demons out of, came to my room one night. His heart was filled with great fear, because he had been so deeply involved in the satanic realm. He was hearing satanic voices telling him that they were going to kill him. One night as I was sleeping, T.J. began to scream. He was yelling that the devil was there to kill him! I sat up in my bunk and looked around. From the position of my bed, I saw the light of the moon shining through our big plate glass window. There, on our wall, was a shadow of a large, demonic entity. I was not making this up. This entity moved across the room towards T.J. The very atmosphere of the room was filled with a terrible presence of evil. Fear tried to rise within my heart, but the Spirit of God quickened courage and boldness within me.

I rose up out of my bed, commanded this demonic power to leave our room and never return in the name of Jesus Christ of Nazareth. The minute I spoke to it in the name of Jesus, I heard a screeching voice, like fingernails scraping across a chalk board. The shadow was pulled out of the room, as if a gigantic vacuum cleaner had been turned on, and it was being sucked up by an invisible force. This demonic power never came back again.

Behold, I give unto you power to tread on serpents and scorpions, and over all the power of the enemy: and nothing shall by any means hurt you (Luke 10:19).

When the unclean spirit is gone out of a man, he walketh through dry places, seeking rest, and findeth none. Then he saith, I will return into my house from whence I came out; and when he is come, he findeth it empty, swept, and garnished. Then goeth he, and taketh with himself seven other spirits more wicked than himself, and they enter in and dwell there: and the last state of that man is worse than the first. Even so shall it be also unto this wicked generation (Matthew 12:43-45).

*17. Horrors of Hell

My journey to hell and to heaven took place even before I knew what the Bible had to say on either subject. If either one of these or any of the other experiences I have had through the years had been contrary to the teachings of Christ or the prophets, I would adamantly reject them, turn my back on them, and declare that they were not of God. A God-given vision of heaven or hell or any other visitation would never contradict Scriptures. I am not sharing with you something I made up out of the figment of my own imagination for the purpose of selling books or to make a name for myself. Please understand that when God gives visions, dreams, and divine encounters that many of these experiences could be revealed by shadows and illustrations of spiritual truths that He wants us to grasp and understand.

I began to cry out in prayer to God intensely, asking Him to allow me to have a supernatural experience of hell. I wanted this in order that I would have a greater and deeper compassion, a deeper love, a deeper understanding for the lost. I truly wanted to know the pains, the sorrows, the torments, the fears, and the agonies of those in hell.

I wanted to weep and wail, to travail with a broken heart over the unconverted to reach them more effectively. I did not realize at this time that it was the Holy Spirit who was putting this prayer in my mouth. The Spirit of the Lord began to take me into deep and **fervent intercessory prayer**. He began to teach me how to stand in the gap on behalf of others, to walk the floor for hours on end for souls.

He taught me how to lay upon my face in His presence until there was a breakthrough. He showed me how to submit my body as an instrument, a vessel He could **pray** through. Every believer, every child of God is called to intercede and travail for souls. It has been said that there is power in **prayer**. I know what people mean when they make that statement, but it's not exactly accurate. There are many religions in which people pray obsessively. But of course, it brings no good results. The power does not come from the **prayer**, but the power comes from the One that we are crying out to!

Now, one night I was **deep in prayer** with Willy, an African American brother in my barracks. I had the privilege of seeing Willie come back to Christ. At one time, previously he had walked with the Lord but had backslid. Before and after he was saved our nickname for him was "Willy Wine" because now he was filled with new wine. Now, as we were praying together, something very strange and very frightening began to happen to me. At the time of this event there was a gathering of some men in our battalion. They were having a party in the common area right outside our sleeping quarters where we were praying. The party they were having was quite loud with music and laughter, but it did not hinder us from crying out to God for souls.

As we were **praying**, I could sense that something was about to happen. The hair on the back of my arms and neck stood up on end. It was as if electricity was filling the very atmosphere around us. I sensed a strong tugging to go deeper in prayer. I gave myself completely over to the spirit of intercession, crying out to the Lord once again to experience the sorrows and agonies of hell. Please understand that I believe God put this desire, this **prayer**, into my heart for the love of souls. I began to **pray** in a realm that I had never been in before when suddenly an overwhelming and tangible darkness descended upon me.

"And when the sun was going down, a deep sleep fell upon Abram; and, lo, an horror of great darkness fell upon him" *(Gen. 15:12).*

A frightening darkness enveloped me. Everything around me disappeared. I no longer heard the music or the party that was taking place. Even though Willie was right there with me, I did not hear or see him. And it seemed as if time itself had come to a stop. To my utter shock, amazement, and horror, the floor and the building around me began to shake more violently than I had ever experienced before. Usually when we did get a quake (Adak Alaska) it would only last a matter of seconds. But in this situation the shaking did not stop as it normally did, rather it increased.

The Journey Begins

All I could do at this moment was to try to hug the floor and hang on for dear life. The darkness lifted, but I could not see Willie anywhere. Then a terrible ripping and grinding noise filled the air. I saw the floor of the barracks ripple like that of a wave on the sea. The very floor of the barracks that I was laying upon began to tear and rip apart. I watched in stunned amazement and horror as the floor tiles popped and stretched. The concrete and steel within the building began to twist and rip apart. And the floor I was laying on began to split and tear open right below me.

I immediately began to look for a way to get out of the building. Everything was shaking so violently that I could not get up off the floor to make a dash to escape. The dust and dirt in the room was so thick and heavy that I could hardly breathe. Now this rip in the floor began to enlarge and became an opening. I would call it more like a hole. I began to slip and fall into this hole; I tried desperately to reach for any kind of handhold that I could find. I began to scream and yell for help. But there was no one to help me. I became increasingly desperate trying to grab hold of something, anything that I could get my hands on. Objects around me began to fall through this hole in the floor. I watched as physical objects slipped past me into this hole. And I could feel myself sliding more and more.

No matter how desperately I was trying to cling to and hold on to items to prevent my falling, there was nothing that I could do. Finally, I slipped and fell backward as if falling off a ladder. As I was falling, everything seemed to go into slow motion like film that is slowed for a preview. I was falling with parts of the crumbling building all around me. I watched as I fell past twisted steel beams, concrete floors, walls ripped into pieces, plumbing and heating pipes, and sparking electric wires. I went past the underground tunnels that connected the buildings together. The floor of the barracks we were praying in ripped open and I fell into hell! This entire experience is revealed in another book I wrote called: Hell Is Real!

And in hell he lift up his eyes, being in torments, and seeth Abraham afar off, and Lazarus in his bosom. And he cried and said, Father Abraham, have mercy on me, and send Lazarus, that he may dip the tip of his finger in water, and cool my tongue; for I am tormented in this flame (Luke 16:23-24).

This experience is shared in my book:
Hell Is Real

18. Compassion for the Lost

After this particular experience, an overpowering love began to possess me! My heart was filled with immense concern for the lost and unsaved. I looked for men up and down the hallways and in the tunnels of our military facility.

One time when I witnessed to a man about the reality of heaven and hell, he basically said he did not want to hear it. God's love was so strong within me I instantly dropped to my knees and wrapped my arms around his legs. I begged him to give his heart to Jesus. I did not want to see him lose his soul and spend eternity in hell.

O Jerusalem, Jerusalem, thou that killest the prophets, and stonest them which are sent unto thee, how often would I have gathered thy children together, even as a hen gathereth her chickens under her wings, and ye would not! (Matthew 23:37).

19. Arrested for Preaching

The compassion of God was flowing in me like a mighty river. It was so strong that an overwhelming desire came upon me to reach as many people as I could at one time. The idea came to me that I could reach more men on that military base if I went to the movie theater we had on the island.

I remember going to the very front row of this movie theater. I sat down shaking and waiting, wondering if what I was about to do was right. I looked at my watch and knew the movie would begin any minute. Just before they started the movie, I stood up on the ledge where the movie screen was attached to the floor. I stood there shaking for a while, trying to get up enough nerve to open my mouth. The men in the theater began to yell for me to get off the stage and sit down. Instead, I opened my mouth and began to preach. As I preached, I could see the Holy Spirit was beginning to move upon the hearts of the audience.

It wasn't long before the military police showed up to arrest me. It was amazing that they did not take me by force, but instead waited for me to finish. When I finished what the Lord had told me to say, the police told me to come off the stage. The two of them grabbed my arms and dragged me out of the theater. They arrested me, put me in their military vehicle, and took me to jail. They asked what I was trying to do in the theater. I took the opportunity to share with them how Jesus had radically changed my life by saving my soul. I told them Jesus wanted to do the same for them. They released me without pressing charges.

For I am not ashamed of the gospel of Christ: for it is the power of God unto salvation to everyone that believeth; to the Jew first, and also to the Greek (Romans 1:16).

*20. Somebody's going to die

He Died Because He Did Not Heed My Warnings!

One night (back in 1975) while I was praying alone in my barracks, when a holy **unction**, and urgency came upon me to pray for a Muslim man that I knew. As I responded to this **unction** of the Holy Ghost I entered into deep travail for his soul. I began to weep almost uncontrollably for this man, whose name was Hussein. He was a military friend of mine that I used to do drugs with. As I prayed the Spirit of God spoke to my heart, telling me the devil was going to kill him in the very near future if he did not repent, and cry out to Jesus. The spirit of God told me that Hussein had only a very short period of time left on the earth before the enemy would snuff out his precious life.

This **unction**, this deep urgency of God was so strong within me that I got up off of the floor of my dorm room, where I had been praying. I immediately went to his room and knocked on his door. Hussein opened his door and saw me standing there weeping uncontrollably. I was so moved in my heart that I could not speak for a while. He asked what was wrong with great concern in his voice. "Mike, Mike, what's wrong?" I could barely speak in English because I was weeping so hard.

I finally was able to tell him that I had been in prayer in my room, when the Spirit of God literally told me that the devil was about to kill him. I told him that his time to get right with the Lord was running out. I explained that he was going to be dead in the very near future, and that he would end up in hell without Jesus. I began to plead with him with great urgency and compassion, with tears flowing down my face to get right with God. I encouraged him to cry out to God, repent for his sins, and give his heart to Jesus Christ.

It was obvious the Spirit of God was moving upon him in a very real way. He said that he believed what I was saying was true, but that he just was not ready to make that kind of commitment at this time. Soon after this experience I left the Navy, headed out to minister to the Yupik Indians. I kept in touch with some of the people that I knew on this military base.

It was approximately two months later that I was speaking to one of my friends on the base when he asked me if I had heard about what happened to Hussein. I informed him, no that I had not heard anything. He told me that they had discovered him dead, with his head in the toilet. They think that he had either gotten his hands on some bad drugs or he had simply overdosed. Oh how it must break the heart of God when souls are lost because they will not respond to his love and beckoning call.

(For he saith, I have heard thee in a time accepted, and in the day of salvation have I succoured thee: behold, now is the accepted time; behold, now is the day of salvation) (2 Corinthians 6:1-2).

*21. Pulverized for Jesus

Preaching Jesus was about to get me pulverized!

There was a big Texan I knew in the Navy who rode bulls in rodeos at one time. We called him Tuck, to this day I don't know why. After I gave my heart to **Jesus Christ**, I shared the gospel with him, his friends, and as many as I could. The Spirit of the Lord had begun to move upon one of Tuck's friends. Tuck was extremely irritated at me for causing this man to come under conviction. Up until the time I had given my heart to **Jesus**, tuck had been a good friend of mine. But now that I was in love with **Christ**, he did not want anything to do with me. Whenever he looked at me it was with great disdain.

One-night Tuck came into my room completely intoxicated with alcohol. He woke me up banging on my door like a madman. I went out to see what he wanted. When I entered the foyer he grabbed me by the neck with his large left hand. He literally picked me up off the floor by my neck and slammed me against the wall. He clenched his right hand into a fist right in front of my face pulling it back as if getting ready to hit me with all his might. His fist literally was as big as my face. He told me that he was going to pulverize me if I did not promise to leave one of his drinking friends alone. The man he was speaking about had taken an interest in the gospel.

In the natural, my heart should have been filled with great fear because without any doubt he could easily beat me to death. I could literally see, and feel the devil in him. His face was all red, and his steely blue eyes were bulging, but instead of fear what rose up in my heart was a great compassion for his soul. Right there on the spot as I was hanging from my neck with his hand pinning me against the wall I began to weep for him. I told him that he could do whatever he wanted to do to me, but I would never stop preaching and exalting **Jesus Christ**. I told him that I loved him and he needed to get right with God.

He began to shake violently like a leaf in a strong wind. His fist was moving back and forth in front of my face. His mouth was moving erratically with foam coming between his teeth and hanging on his lips. During this time the other men in my barracks had heard the commotion and were all standing around watching this event unfold. After what seemed a long time Tuck finally lowered his fist and put me down. He turned around without a word and walked away from me. From that moment up until I left the Navy he never spoke to me again.

Many years later I was talking with Willie, the cowboy. Willie had become a master chief in the Navy and his expertise was underwater demolition. I asked what had happened to Tuck. Right after that event with me he said, Tuck lost his mind. He literally took his Colt 44 magnum pistol and walked up to our militaries base commander and put the gun against his head.

Thank God, he did not shoot the man, but of course he was arrested and court-martialed. Tuck ended up being an alcoholic which caused him to lose his wife and family, and then he was diagnosed with cancer. Now the story does have a wonderful ending. Willie the cowboy told me that during his time in the Navy with me he really was not right with God. But the spirit of God had arrested him, and he had gotten right with **Jesus**.

Willy the cowboy had stayed in contact with Tuck all of those years and eventually had a chance to speak to him about the Lord. Before Tuck died Willie had the opportunity to lead Tuck to **Christ**, he was gloriously born again; shortly thereafter, Tuck died and went home to be with the Lord. Someday, Lord willing, I will see him again. Only this time we will have sweet fellowship.

Not by works of righteousness which we have done, but according to his mercy he saved us, by the washing of regeneration, and renewing of the Holy Ghost (Titus 3:5).

*22. Splendors of Heaven

My Journey to Heaven

My visitation from an angel and my journey to heaven took place even before I knew what the Bible had to say on the subject. If any of these experiences or any of the other experiences I have had through the years had been contrary to the teachings of Christ or the prophets, I would adamantly reject them, turn my back on them, and declare that they were not of God.

A God-given vision of heaven or hell or any other visitation would never contradict Scriptures. I am not sharing with you something I made up out of the figment of my own imagination for the purpose of selling books or to make a name for myself. What you are about to read truly happened to me. Please understand that when God gives visions, dreams, and divine encounters that many of these experiences could be revealed by shadows and illustrations of spiritual truths that He wants us to grasp and understand.

This divine, angelic visitation happened approximately one month after I had gone to hell. This time I was all alone once again **praying and crying out to God** in our dormitory. I had been walking around with my hands in the air **praying**, singing, and talking to the Lord. Suddenly, my room was filled with an overwhelming presence of the Lord. It was so real that I fell to my knees and tears began to flow freely from my eyes. I found myself lying flat upon my face totally caught up in this overwhelming presence. My face was buried into the floor. I was weeping, crying, and **praying**.

Suddenly, the room I was in was filled with an intense bright light. I lifted my head to see what was going on. There in front of me was a portal. It was like an opening into another world. It was not square like a regular door opening. This doorway was circular on the top like an archway. The light coming from this portal was so bright and brilliant that I could not look at it for very long.

I was completely petrified and did not know what to do. It felt as if I was frozen to the floor and unable even to move a muscle. A holy fear gripped my whole body. I could see that someone was walking toward me through this tunnel of light. Out of this glorious light stepped a figure of a man. This was no ordinary man. He was about seven feet tall with a broad chest and shoulders but a slender waist. His flesh blazed like the burning of an arch welder.

His face did not seem to have ever been shaved. In other words, there was no stubble on his face. He had the stature of a body builder only more solid and almost unearthly. He wore a glistening, brilliant, white gown with a slightly transparent belt around his waist that glowed of silver. I was not able to move or talk in his presence. When this angelic being finally spoke to me his voice seemed to fill the whole room. He told me not to. That he had come from the presence of the Lord to show me things that must come to pass."

I remember asking him, "What is your name?" He replied, "My name is of no importance. I am but a messenger sent to you with a message and a mission that is greater than I." Inwardly, I wondered what kind of purpose could there be in this visitation. As I reflect upon this experience, I will tell you that parts of it is missing from my memory. It's not that it was not real or substantial to me, but because it is sealed away in my heart.

The angel spoke to me and said, "Now you must come with me. For there are many things you must see." This angel stepped forward, leaned down, and took me by the hand. He lifted me to my feet. The way he lifted me up I must have been as light as a feather in his hands. It was as if he rippled with unlimited strength. I was like a little child in his hand. I knew in my heart that he could easily kill me without any effort. This was my first experience in a tangible way with an angelic being. From that time up to now I have been protected, provided by and helped by these amazing messengers of God. For instance, I'm convinced an angelic being drove my car for many hours once when I was totally caught up praising and worshiping God as I was driving down the road coming from northern Canada with my hands off the steering wheel.

I remember holding this angles hand with my right hand. There was tremendous heat coming from it. It was not the same type of heat I had experienced in hell. It is almost impossible to explain to you the sensations and feelings I was experiencing at that moment. The fire I felt in his hand was a holy fire. It seemed as if the heat was a living thing. Power radiated from his body. I cannot remember the color of his eyes. This angel was not Jesus. He was simply a messenger sent to take me into the heavens.

I knew a man in Christ above fourteen years ago, (whether in the body, I cannot tell; or whether out of the body, I cannot tell: God knoweth;) such an one caught up to the third heaven. And I knew such a man, (whether in the body, or out of the body, I cannot tell: God knoweth;) How that he was caught up into paradise, and heard unspeakable words, which it is not lawful for a man to utter (2 Corinthians 12:2-4).

This experience is shared in my book:
Heaven Is Real

CHAPTER THREE

Miracles beyond Comprehension

*23. Jesus Took the Wheel

Angels Drove My Vehicle

I realize how preposterous and insane this sounds, but it's the truth. None of the stories that I share with you about my life are fake or exaggerated. There is a Scripture that says all liars will go to hell.

Revelation 21:8 But the fearful, and unbelieving, and the abominable, and murderers, and whoremongers, and sorcerers, and idolaters, and all liars, shall have their part in the lake which burneth with fire and brimstone: which is the second death.

Personally, I would not blame people for not believing this story. Most of my testimonies there were others who were present to verify exactly what happened. Now in this situation, I was all by myself coming out of Canada, driving my sister's Maverick.

In May of 1975, I was driving my sister's 1973 red Maverick from Canada to Wisconsin. I had just been discharged from the Navy. I had completed most of my military service on an island called Adak Alaska. My sister was in the Air Force and was stationed in New Mexico. She asked me to drive her car from New Mexico to Anchorage, Alaska, which was her next tour of duty. I agreed since I had driven the Alcan Freeway during the onset of winter the previous year.

From Anchorage to Mukwonago Wisconsin is 3,500 miles long. (At the time I was only eighteen years old and not yet saved. I cover that amazing journey and experience in another book.) I was planning to return to Alaska to go out and minister to the Yupik Indians, so I agreed to drive her vehicle all the way to Anchorage.

I experienced heavy rains as I headed up through Canada on the dirt road which took me to Fairbanks. To my disappointment, the road to Alaska was blocked off. I had to stop and turn around because the bridges were all washed out. The authorities did not know when they would be able to open the roads that were washed out because of flooding rivers. The thought occurred to me about driving her car back to Wisconsin where my parents lived.

Looking back, I realize that God was in this event. You see I use to run with a gang right outside of Chicago Illinois. Since I had given my heart to Christ I had not been able to share the gospel with any of them. It was burning in my heart to go tell them, but I had committed myself to drive my sister's car up to Alaska. Now, he was my opportunity to share with them the gospel.

I came out of the mountains of Canada Praying, singing and worshiping God in the Spirit as the sun was at its peak in the sky above me. I'm guessing it was right around 11 o'clock in the morning. As I continue to pray and worship God I began to be filled with an overwhelming love for the Father, and Jesus Christ. It felt like my heart was going to come out of my chest because of the greatness of God's love for me and my gratitude.

I was weeping, **praying** and crying as I drove along so much so to where I could not really see where I was going any longer. Suddenly the car began to be filled with the tangible presence of the Lord. The inside of my car was filling with a light, glistening, sparkly, light blue, green, silver, gold mist. I was so caught up in the presence of the Lord that without even thinking I raised my hands toward heaven, taking them off of my steering wheel.

In this place of deep intimate worship time came to at stand still. Here I was in my sister's 1973 red maverick driving through the rugged back roads of Canada with my hands lifted towards heaven, weeping and crying, and worshiping God. I was ushered into a supernatural, incredible, mind-boggling realm of the Holy Ghost.

I remember that after what only seemed a short time my hands came back to the steering wheel as this divine mist, the Shekinah glory was dissipating. To my utter amazement, I noticed that the sun, which had been in the middle of the sky when I began to experience the overwhelming presence of God, was just now barely peeking over the horizon and it was beginning to get dark. At that time I did not check the mileage of the car, but I know my car had gone hundreds of miles without me driving it. Someone had driven my car as I was caught up in this intense realm of worship!

This total experience could've possibly been 5 to 7 hours long. It had to be Angelic beings that took complete control of my vehicle as I was lost in the Spirit! My heart was filled with joy unspeakable and full of glory at this amazing miracle. To this day as I think about this experience, I can hardly grasp its reality.

Then a cloud covered the tent of the congregation, and the glory of the LORD filled the tabernacle (Exodus 40:34).

*24. She Can Understand Me

For the First Time She Could Understand Me

About 4 months after I gave my heart to **Christ** I went back to my hometown, Mukwonago, Wisconsin, and I immediately went to see one of my best friends to share with him my conversion experience. It was his sister I had been dating for the last three years. I wrote her a letter telling her what happened to me, and how God gloriously had set me free from drugs, alcohol, and all of my worldly living. This caused her to cut me off completely, as if I had lost my mind. Praise God! I had lost my mind by receiving the mind of **Christ**. My friend's mother was listening while I was speaking to her son, and out of nowhere she said, **"Mike, what happened to you?"** I told her how I had been delivered from drugs and immorality because I gave my heart to **Jesus**. She said, "No, that's not what I'm talking about. After many years of knowing you, this is actually the **1st time I can fully understand what you are saying**."

You see, my speech was so garbled that it was very difficult for people to truly understand exactly what I was saying. Those who know me now would not have recognized the old me. Before I got baptized in the Holy Ghost you would not have been able to understand most of I said. I'm still trying to make up for the 1st nineteen years when I could not speak properly.

And Moses said unto the Lord, O my LORD, I am not eloquent, neither heretofore, nor since thou hast spoken unto thy servant: but I am slow of speech, and of a slow tongue. And the LORD said unto him, who hath made man's mouth? or who maketh the dumb, or deaf, or the seeing, or the blind? Have not I the LORD? Now therefore go, and I will be with thy mouth, and teach thee what thou shalt say (Exodus 4:10-12).

*25. A Knife for the Gut

A Gang Leader Kept Trying to Stab Me to Death

After being born again for a while, I perceived in my heart that I needed to reach out and witness to the gang I used to run with right outside of Chicago. We were not a gang in the sense that we had a name or any entrance rituals that we had to go through. We were just a group of young men who were constantly involved in corruption, drinking, fighting, using drugs, stripping cars, and doing other things to horrible that I will not mention. One day, I was sitting in a car between the two instigators of most of our shenanigans, Gary and Claire. Both of these men were very large and quite muscular.

I had fervently shared Christ with them and the others to let them know how much God had changed me. They sat around drinking, using dope, and cussing while I shared the good news with them. I explained I was on a heavenly high that drugs and the world could never take them to. Most of them just stared at me, not knowing how to respond. They all had known the old Mike Yeager. The crazy and ungodly stuff that I had done. They had seen me many times whacked out on drugs and alcohol. Now here I was a brand-new creation in Christ preaching Jesus with a deep and overwhelming zeal.

Now Gary who was one of the main leaders was different in many negative ways than the other guys. He was like a stick of dynamite ready to explode at any moment. He had been up to the big house already and spent some time behind the bars of justice. He never did like me, but now there was an unspoken, seething hatred for me under the surface, which eventually exploded. We were coming out of Racine, Illinois, as Gary was driving the car we were in. Claire was sitting against the door on the right side in the front seat, with me in the middle. At that moment I did not realize why they had put me in the middle, but it became very obvious.

Before I knew it, Gary reached up and grabbed a large knife from the dashboard of the car. I believe the vehicle was an old Impala that had the old-style steel dashboard. The heating and air conditioning were controlled by sliders in the dash. The knife had been shoved down into one of the slots. He pulled the knife out of the dashboard with his right hand, jabbed it high up into the air, and drove it down toward me very fast, trying to stab me in the gut with this knife. I saw him reach for the knife, and at that very moment I entered into the realm of the Spirit when time seems to come to a standstill. This has happened to me on numerous occasions in such dangerous situations.

When I enter this realm, time slows down while my speed or movement seems to increase. You could argue whether I speed up or time slows down. I really can't say, though; it just happens.

44

The knife came down toward my guts in slow motion, and I saw my hands reaching up towards the knife and grabbing Gary's wrist to prevent him from stabbing me through the gut. I could not prevent the knife from coming down, but I was able to cause it to plunge into the seat instead. His thrust had been so powerful that the knife literally pierced all the way down through the Springfield car seat. He immediately pulled it out of the car seat and tried to stab me again. He continued to try to stab me as he was driving down the road. Every time he tried to stab me, I was able to divert the stab just fractions of an inch away from my privates and for my legs.

During this entire event the peace of God was upon me in an overwhelming way. I was not shaking or breathing hard in the least; neither was my heart beating fast. It sounds unbelievable, I know, but it felt as if I were in heaven. The presence and the peace of God was upon me in a powerful supernatural way. I know this might sound extremely strange and weird, but I was actually kind of enjoying myself as I was watching God deliver me from this madman. During this entire time, it was like a slow-motion review of a movie. Up and down the knife came as he kept on trying to kill me.

This large muscular man was not able to kill a small 5'8" skinny guy. I just love how God does the supernatural miracles. There was not one thing in my life in which that I knew I was out of God's will. I believe if I had been out of the will of God most likely Gary would've succeeded in murdering me. He kept on trying to kill me until up ahead of us a police car came out from a side road. Gary's car window was open and when he saw the policeman he threw the knife out the window.

Gary continued to drive down the road without ever saying a word about what had just happened. In this whole situation Claire who I had thought was a friend of mine, did not in any way try to help me. No one said a word as we drove down the road, but the peace of God was upon me like I have the invisible blanket.

45

Thou wilt keep him in perfect peace, whose mind is stayed on thee: because he trusteth in thee. Trust ye in the LORD forever: for in the LORD JEHOVAH is everlasting strength (Isaiah 26:3-4).

*26. Shooting to Kill

About two days later I had to go to Gary's house. I really shouldn't have gone there, because there was just something satanic and evil about him. Just the day before, he tried to stab me to death! When I pulled up in my sister's red Maverick he was sitting on his porch. When he saw me get out of the car he grabbed a shotgun (I think it was a twelve gauge) which had been leaning against his house.

I walked toward him, and he aimed it right at my stomach. What was there about my gut that he was so enamored by it? There was no fear in my heart at the least. I just kept walking toward him. I was about twenty feet away from him when the barrel of the gun jerked slightly to the right as the gun went off. The sound of the gun echoed through the valley. Nothing happened to me! As I think back to that day, I firmly believe an angel nudged that gun barrel with his little finger. If there was bird shot in the gun, no pellets hit me, and if there was a deer slug in it, I did not feel it go by.

It must have missed me by a matter of inches, or God simply dissolved it. I was not shaking or breathing hard in the least; neither was my heart beating fast. It sounds unbelievable, I know, but once again it felt as if I was in heaven. I walked up the steps of the porch and walked up to Gary. I took the gun out of his hand, and leaned it back against the house. Gary just stared at me without saying a word. That was the last time I ever saw Gary. I have no idea what happened to him.

No weapon that is formed against thee shall prosper; and every tongue that shall rise against thee in judgment thou shalt condemn. This is the heritage of the servants of the LORD, and their righteousness is of me, saith the LORD (Isaiah 54:17).

27. Get on the Plane

A few days later I woke up having a sense I had done all I could to reach the gang I used to run with. I now knew in my heart it was not meant for me to drive the Alcan Freeway to Alaska. I had to come home and shared with those I knew and cared about how God had miraculously transformed and changed my life. Without a shadow of a doubt, the people I had lived with on a daily basis knew I was a different Mike Yeager.

That morning when I woke up, the Spirit of God impressed me to get on a plane and go to Anchorage, Alaska. The original plan was for me to meet a group of people who were going to Dillingham, Alaska. Because the roads had been flooded, I was not able to meet up with them. Of course we had no cell phones in those days and I had no idea where they were at. I had not spoken to them since I left New Mexico.

I bought a ticket at the Chicago O'Hare Airport that morning and caught the next available plane to Anchorage. I landed in Anchorage, Alaska at about 4:00 p.m. I knew I would have to stay in Anchorage that night because the plane that flew to Dillingham leaves in the early afternoon. As I exited the plane and entered the terminal, there standing in front of me were the very people I was to meet! It turned out the plane they were to take to Dillingham, Alaska, had been delayed due to mechanical problems. I bought my ticket to go to Dillingham with them. We got on the plane together and headed to Dillingham.

Not only had I met the people on the right day, but the right hour. God made it so I could witness to my friends, while He made all the important flight connections. God knows how to order our steps!

The steps of a good man are ordered by the LORD: and he delighteth in his way (Psalms 37:23).

CHAPTER FOUR

Miracles for Every Situation

28. Yupik Indians

As I (Michael) share some of my experiences living with the Yupik Indians, I do not want to paint a negative image of these precious people. My time with them was challenging, to say the least. I also saw that alcohol is a major tool of the devil being used to destroy their lives. There is much hurt and resentment among the Yupik Indians, due to what they perceive to be a robbery of their natural resources and land from the "white man." Here I was, a young "white man" trying to reach them for Jesus Christ.

I lived, fished, and hunted with them. My love and my faith was sorely tried and challenged by the young men. They treated me with total contempt and disdain. They would feed me the worst parts of their hunts. One time after we had finished hunting, they gave me duck head, duck feet, and duck guts, which I ate it with no complaints and a thankful heart.

At the time that I was with them, it didn't seem as if I had seen many results. However, the Word of God never returns void. I have been told by reliable sources that one of the young men I shared Jesus with is now an Assemblies of God pastor in the Dillingham area.

Shoot the Indians

As I share some of my experiences living with the Yupik Indians, I do not want to paint a negative image of these precious people. My time with them was challenging, to say the least. I also saw that alcohol is a major tool of the devil being used to destroy their lives. There is much hurt and resentment among the Yupik Indians due to what they perceive to be a robbery of their natural resources and land from the "white man". Here I was, a young "white man", trying to reach them for Jesus Christ.

I lived, fished and hunted with them. My love and my faith was sorely tried and challenged by the young men. They treated me with total contempt and disdain. They would feed me the worst parts of their hunts. One time, after we had finished hunting, they gave me duck head, duck feet and duck guts, which I ate with no complaints and a thankful heart.

Over and over God had protected me when, at times, the natives had gone out of their way to try to do me harm. I do not blame them. I truly believe they did not know what they were doing. One time I had gone up a very wild river with some of the men my age. This trip did not turn out very well because, as we were trying to advance beyond a set of rapids two days up the river, the prop hit some rocks. It sheared the prop right off of the motor shaft. The only option we had was to float down the river until we got back to the village. Two days later, as we were floating down the river, we came across a small graveyard of abandoned boats and engines.

I suggested that we paddle over to them and look just in case we might find an old propeller that would fit our engine. Amazingly, we found a four-prop blade with only one prop missing. It was the right blade to put on the boat engine. We fixed it and off we went, headed back to the village. A couple of hours later, we accidentally got too close to a sand bar and ended up stuck. They demanded that I get out of the boat and push them off the sandbar, which I did willingly. I was the only white man in their village besides a teacher.

The minute they were off the sandbar, the native who had control of the kicker (that's what they called the motor) revved the engine and took off leaving me behind. We were miles and miles from any habitation. Even their village was only accessible by river or by bush plane. My rifle was in the boat, so I had no protection from the grizzlies or any of the other critters that inhabited the wilderness. All I could do was cry out to God for his divine protection. Actually, I thank God, my gun was in the boat because, unbeknownst to them, I had come to the breaking point. I think that I might have been tempted to pop a couple holes in the hull of their boat with my rifle.

I followed the river for quite a distance walking back towards where I knew the village would be miles away. When I came around the corner of one bend, thank God, they were there waiting for me! They just kept pushing me to see if I would break, feeding me all of the filth from their killings, the parts of the animal that nobody in their right mind would eat. But I ate them by faith because I knew this was a test and their souls were more important to me than what my mind, stomach or taste buds were telling me. It was only the divine Spirit of God that caused me not to break under all of this pressure.

James 1:2-4[2] My brethren, count it all joy when ye fall into divers temptations; [3] knowing this, that the trying of your faith worketh patience. [4] But let patience have her perfect work, that ye may be perfect and entire, wanting nothing.

*29. Steamed Alive

Yupik Indians Tried to kill me! 1975

As I share this experience living with the Yupik Indians in Alaska, I do not want to paint a negative image of these precious people. My time with them was challenging, to say the least. I was only 19 years old at the time that I was doing missionary work among them. I can tell you that alcohol is a major tool of the devil being used to destroy their lives. There is much hurt and resentment among the Yupik Indians, due to what they perceive to be a robbery of their natural resources and land from the "white man." Here I was, a young "white man" trying to reach them for Jesus Christ.

I lived, fished, and hunted with them. My love and my faith was sorely tried and challenged by the young men. They treated me with total contempt and disdain. They would feed me the worst parts of their hunts. One time after we had finished hunting, they gave me duck head, duck feet, and duck guts, which I ate with no complaints and with a thankful heart.

At the time that I was with them, it didn't seem as if I had seen many results. However, the Word of God never returns void. I have been told by reliable sources that one of the young men I shared Jesus with is now an Assemblies of God pastor in the Dillingham area. When I was there, there was no Christian testimony in the community. But now there is an Assembly of God church right outside of Dillingham, Alaska. Now to the story of how I was almost teamed to death.

Steam baths were introduced to Yupik Indians by Russian fur traders and missionaries. The steam baths I experienced in the Bristol Bay area consisted of a dressing room, combination cooling room, and the hot room with very low ceilings that were only about four feet high. They were covered over with tundra to keep the steam and heat from escaping. These hot rooms were called a maqili or McQay.

The wood stove heater was an oil drum on its side with a chimney. Rocks were piled on top of the oil drum. There was half of a steel barrel full of water in the corner of the room next to the exit. They had about four-and-a-half-foot long piece of wood with a kitchen pan attached so they could scoop water out of the barrel, stretch the pan over the top of the oil barrel stove and dump it on the rocks. This sent forth a tremendous amount of heat and steam.

They packed the barrel completely full of wood for a steam bath. Steam baths seem to be an area of great pride for the Yupik men. They told stories how they would pass out trying to outdo each other. They were known to have fallen on the rocks and burned to death. They stayed in the steam bath as long as they could and then go out and roll in the snow or jump in the river. They also had a bench right outside where we would sit with nothing but a washcloth covering our loins.

One day they invited me to take a steam bath with them. On that particular day, there were three young Yupik Indians and an older man who looked like a walrus. The Spirit of the Lord spoke to my heart and told me not to be fearful and to **Pray**. They were going to try to steam me out of the maqili /McQay. God said not to be concerned because He was going to reveal Himself to them through this test. When we were all in the McQay and had closed the door they all stared at me, speaking in their native tongue to one another and laughing. Then they dumped water on the red-hot rocks.

The older gentleman had control of the scoop. As he continued to splash water on the rocks, it began to get extremely hot. I had a wet rag which they had given me, along with a pan of water at my feet. I dipped the cloth into the water and put it against my face and nostrils. I bowed my head and **prayed** quietly English and in tongues. I could hear the water hissing as more and more water was thrown on the red-hot rocks. I could feel their eyes staring at me. The heat was almost unbearable.

The minute I stopped thinking about Jesus and **praying** it would feel like I was being steamed alive. Finally, I heard the door of the McQay open and close three times. At this point I looked up and there was only the old Yupik Indian and myself. He smiled at me with a toothless grin.

I bowed my head once again and continued to **pray** knowing this was going to get extremely difficult. I knew this was a fight for their souls. I wanted the Spirit of God to reveal Himself to them. They needed to understand this was not a white man's religion but Jesus is the living God and Savior of all men. All at once I heard a very large splash. The old Yupik Indian threw a whole scoop of water upon the rocks and ran out the door of the McQay.

I panicked. It felt like my flesh was being melted from off my bones. I ran for the door to open it, but either it was locked or they were holding it shut from the outside. I pounded on the door and at that instant the Spirit of the Lord arrested me and told me to go back into **deep prayer**. I fell on my face directly on the wood plank floor and began to speak in tongues. The Spirit of God sent a cool breeze where there was no wind. A cold wind literally blew over the top of my bearskin. After what seemed to be a long time they let me out. I am sure they never understood how I could have beaten them at their own native hobby, or how I survived such tremendous heat. They never did ask me. They simply stared at me when I came out.

When thou passest through the waters, I will be with thee; and through the rivers, they shall not overflow thee: when thou walkest through the fire, thou shalt not be burned; neither shall the flame kindle upon thee (Isaiah 43:2).

30. Shekinah Glory

One Sunday while I was visiting Anchorage, Alaska, I decided to visit a church someone had told me about. I believe the name of it was Abbott Loop Fellowship. I arrived late because I had to hitchhike and walk my way there in twenty degrees below zero weather. You might ask, why in the world would I go through such trouble to get to that church? It's called being spiritually hungry and thirsty. I entered the sanctuary and found a chair all the way in the last row. The worship was wonderful, and I found myself being caught up in the Spirit. I smelled a beautiful fragrance in the air which I had never experienced before. It smelled like some type of beautiful flower.

My eyes were closed during this time, but as I smelled this beautiful aroma I opened them. The same glistening fog that had filled my car when I was driving through Canada began to descend upon me. Before I knew it, I could not see anyone else. I became totally lost in worshiping and praising God. To this day, I do not know if anyone else saw, or smelled what I experienced on that particular day.

It came even to pass, as the trumpeters and singers were as one, to make one sound to be heard in praising and thanking the

LORD; and when they lifted up their voice with the trumpets and cymbals and instruments of music, and praised the LORD, saying, For he is good; for his mercy endureth for ever: that then the house was filled with a cloud, even the house of the LORD; So that the priests could not stand to minister by reason of the cloud: for the glory of the LORD had filled the house of God (2 Chronicles 5:13-14).

*31. There's Power in That Name

My Mom's Hip Miraculously Healed (1975)

I was visiting my parent's home in Wisconsin. One day when I came home, my mother asked me to help her get her hip back into place where it belonged. For some reason her right hip would pop out of place which was extremely painful and difficult for her. When this happened, she would lay on the floor and grab onto something heavy and solid like the china hutch or the dining room table leg. Next, she would have one of us four boys grab her right ankle and pull with all our might with a heavy jerk until her hip would go back into place. She was just a little lady, so when we pulled her leg it would pull her whole body off the floor.

I told my mother I would help her. She laid down on her back on the dining room floor and grabbed the dining room table leg. I knelt on my knees and took a hold of her right ankle with both hands. She was waiting for me to jerk her leg with a powerful pull but Instead of pulling like I normally would, I whispered: "In the name of Jesus Christ of Nazareth I command this hip to go back into place."

The minute I whispered this a wonderful miracle transpired. Her leg instantly shot straight out. She was very surprised asked with a shocked voice, "Michael, what did you just do to me?" I told her what I had done. Then I shared the reality of Jesus with her. As far as I know until she went home to be with the Lord, for the next 25 years she never had another problem with that hip popping out of its socket.

And these signs shall follow them that believe; In my name shall they cast out devils; they shall speak with new tongues; They shall take up serpents; and if they drink any deadly thing, it shall not hurt them; they shall lay hands on the sick, and they shall recover (Mark 16:17-18)

*32. Divine Carpet Ride

Backslidden and Drunk on a motorcycle (1976)

Thank God for His wonderful mercy, kindness, and goodness. Even when we fall short, He's still there to help us, protect us and to keep us. There was a brief period in my life after I gave my heart to Christ that I backslid. I was like a yo-yo in my walk with God for maybe two months; messing up, repenting, walking with God, and then messing up again, just to start the cycle over.

Everything is a little bit foggy about those days. I had come back to Wisconsin from being in Alaska, doing missionary work with the Yupik Indians in the region of Dillingham. Before I left Alaska, deep depression began to hit me hard. I had experienced a lot of persecution while living with the Yupik Indians.

During that whole time of reaching out and evangelizing, I had no fellowship with other believers. I did not know one other believer, except for the local sheriff, who I had stayed with for a brief period. But now he and his wife had moved away, and I found myself all alone living on the mud flats in what had formally been a tent in the middle of winter.

I still remember laying in my goose down sleeping bag on a wooden platform in that tent. 40 below zero outside with the wind whipping and howling over my little structure. Hoping and believing I would make it through another night. I would wake up in the morning trying to get a fire going in my 30-gallon makeshift wood stove. And then I would have to head out into the snow and walk 3 miles to get to the gas station where I worked. God in his mercy had kept me alive.

There is no one my age (20 years old) or even close to my age that wanted anything to do with God that I knew of in that pioneer town. Another major problem I had is that I did not have enough of the **Word of God in my heart**. This is the main reason for many believers not being able to get victory over the devil, temptations, test and trials, sickness, and disease.

Kenneth Hagan (a minister used to work for) shares a personal story along this line: he said that he was having tremendous meetings where the power of God was falling. Many people were being touched, healed, laughing, crying, and shouting. And yet despite these amazing meetings many of these same people were living defeated lives and going back into sin. He asked the Lord: **Why this was happening?**

The Lord said to him that a person can continue to breathe, and still die. Breathing is symbolic of the moving of the spirit, but the physical body needs food. It is the same with the spirit and soul of man. It takes the word of God being digested daily in the believer's life to be able to overcome the test, trials, afflictions, and temptations that confront us all.

Psalm 119:11 Thy word have I hid in mine heart, that I might not sin against thee.

Not only did I not have enough of God word in my heart but I was not attending a good, Spirit-filled, Word church. There was no spirit filled church at that time available in Dillingham, Alaska.

(There is now an Assembly of God church there.) I began to go into deep depression out on the mud flats of Alaska. Now here I was, the middle of winter and 40° below with the wind and the snow whipping around my little wooden shack made from a tent frame. I found myself beginning to dabble back into drugs and alcohol. I knew that I was in big time trouble, so while I still had some money left, in about February 1976, I bought a ticket back to my hometown in Wisconsin.

When I got back to Mukwonago, I began to try to share my faith once again. I was able to get a job in Waukesha, Wisconsin at a company that built transformers for high voltage lines. It turned out to be a very well paying job, and yet I was spiritually miserable. I set enough money aside from this job to buy a 1973 Honda CB 750 touring bike.

MY Motorbike Sliding Down the Highway on its side, with me on it, On Black Ice!

Wintertime was just beginning to end, and the roads were clear of snow. I took my motorcycle out on the main highway and headed to work in Waukesha, Wisconsin one early morning. It was a CB 759.

(CB750: Was the most iconic of all Honda models and a game changer for the overall motorcycling industry. Introduced in 1969 after Honda introduced it as a race bike. The CB750 featured the first mass-produced transverse inline-four engine on a motorcycle, a front disc brake (almost unheard of at the time), big power, reliability and refinement that made high-performance bikes from Britain, America, and Europe suddenly look like relics of a bygone era.)

I was driving approximately fifty miles an hour when tragedy struck. For some reason, I had not noticed, that all of the vehicles on the highway were going extremely slow.

It was too late before I realized why. The whole highway was covered in nothing but black ice. My motorcycle began to slip out from underneath me; my wheels slid to the right while the top of the motorcycle swayed to the left. At that very moment, I entered a supernatural spiritual realm where everything begins to happen in slow motion. This realm is hard to explain to people. I am not exaggerating when I say time seems to come to a stop.

I have had this experience several times when God divinely intervened on my behalf. I can think of at least ten times this has happened to me. **#1** when a gang leader was trying to kill me by stabbing me to death while coming out of Chicago in his car. **#2** While saving a young man's life from a motorcycle accident. **#3** A large mule deer was going to slam into me on my motorcycle while I was headed through Canada. **#4** My wife and I rolling down a cliff in our car. My newborn son Michael was up in the air, as my wife reaches out and snatches him to her chest. **#5** My seventh-month pregnant wife, my son Michael and I on a 450 custom Honda. Headed for guardrails, telephone pole, and a pile of rocks. **#6** Supernaturally empowered while driving a motorcycle and communist infested lands. **#7** While flying my airplane through a set of high lines. **#8** Right before I slammed my Cadillac into a concrete bridge. **#9** Preventing a young lady from burning to death when her hair caught on fire. **#10** When I was engulfed in a gasoline fire.

Now as my motorcycle (in slow motion it seemed to me) slid on its left side, I began to move in rhythm with the falling bike. First I pulled my left foot up out of the way before it was smashed between the road and the bike. As it was falling over, I stepped up over the top of it. At this point, the bike was completely on its side against the asphalt still doing about fifty miles an hour or so. Thank God I had heavy duty crash bars on the front for the driver and on the back of the bike for the passenger.

They were designed to protect the rider and passenger but not to be used as skates on ice. Once the motorcycle was completely on its side, it kept on sliding down the road like it was on skates. I sat on it like it was a divine carpet ride. As I was perched on top of the motorcycle, I kept passing up cars. I slid down the highway never veering to the left or the right. It was like someone throwing a bowling ball down the middle of the lane for a strike. People were gaping at me as I passed them up. I'm sure they had never seen anything like this in their whole life. The black ice cause there to be very little friction between my crash bars in the highway. There were no sparks are screeching of rubbing steel against the asphalt.

Eventually, the motorcycle came to a complete stop, lying on its side in the middle of the highway still running. When the motorcycle had come to a completely stop, I jumped from it, grabbing its handlebars, and shoving it to its upright position. I remounted my bike, put it in gear (it was still running) and went on my way. During this whole experience, neither my breathing nor my heart rate increased even for one second. You see, I was no longer backslidden. I was in the perfect will of God. I had peace like a river. The kingdom of God is not in meat or drink, but in Righteousness, Peace, and the joy of the Holy Ghost!

Yes, I did quit my job because my soul was of much greater value to me than the pleasures of this world. I gave them a two-week notice, packed my bags, loaded my little bit of belongings into the saddlebags of my motorcycle, and headed out West. As I drove away from everyone I knew and loved, God once again took hold of my heart. I was on my way and thank God, I have never looked back!

And the peace of God, which passeth all understanding, shall keep your hearts and minds through Christ Jesus (Philippians 4:7).

*33. Holy Ghost Pig Farmer

Headed Back to Alaska On My Motorcycle

Spiritual growth does not come easy. It is a day by day process, Step-by-step, just putting one spiritual foot in front of the other. One thing I have learned through the years, whatever you do, do not ever run away from God no matter how bad you mess up but run to Him. Realize that the conviction of God is not your enemy, but it is a divine umbrella to save your soul. Run into it. Stay in it, live there.

As I prepared to head out on my motorbike, first to Oregon, and then to Alaska, I stayed in an attitude of prayer and reading Scripture. A verse that spoke to my heart was the one that said that God would not let you be tempted above what you are able and that the Lord would make a way of escape. My spiritual walk with God was way more important to me than making money or having a roof over my head.

As I got ready to leave for my trip, I filled my motorcycle saddlebags and backpack only with those items that were necessary and that which I could Carrie on my motorcycle. I packed my remaining clothes and belongings in some boxes the landlord had left in a crawl space in the ceiling, and left them at my parents' house.

By the end of the day, I had made the phone calls and arrangements that were necessary to fulfill my responsibilities before I left. It's amazing the favor that the Lord granted me. Even though I should have given a months' notice to my landlord, he said that he would not require me to pay the next month's rent. Also, I did not have to move any furniture because I had rented a furnished apartment.

The next morning, I went to the local outdoors outlet and bought a small one-man tent. I still had my compact goose-down sleeping bag that I used when I lived with the Yupik Indians in Alaska. I also made one last stop at the post office to pick up my mail and to fill out a change of address cards for the utility companies and other businesses. All my mail was going to be going to my parents' house.

By early afternoon, I arrived back at my apartment. Through part of the day, I finished the little things that were still left undone, including cleaning the apartment from top to bottom.

The rest of the day I worked on my motorcycle. He changed his oil, the air filter, checked the tire pressure, and adjusted the brakes. When everything had met my approval, I went back to my apartment. The phone was disconnected, so I had not received any phone calls that night.

The next morning, I woke up extremely early and crawled out of my sleeping bag, which I had slept in on the now stripped-down bed. After dressing and getting ready, I walked through the apartment to make sure everything was done. I picked up my sleeping bag, the packed one-man tent, and a small duffel bag of clothes and walked out the front door, locking it as I left.

As I stepped out on the porch, the sun was just beginning to peak over the eastern horizon. It was going to be a beautiful and glorious day. I walked off the porch around to the side of the building where I kept my bike in its designated spot. I strapped the tent and duffel bag to the passenger backrest, leaving the sleeping bag for last so I could use it to rest my back against. I placed the key in its ignition, swung his foot over the bike, and straddled it.

I sat there for a while, excitement bubbling inside of me. Once again, I felt the presence of the Lord in my life. Something significant was taking place. A chapter in my life had just closed, and a new one was just about to open.

As I sat there, a squirrel ran across the blacktop toward a tree with a mouth full of acorns. I heard birds singing somewhere in the distance. A robin was on the lawn looking for worms.

Well, I might as well start this journey the right way, I said to myself as I bowed my head to pray. Father God, thank you for this day and another chance. For a brief period, I was overwhelmed with the presence of the Lord as I communicated my love with human words to God. I knew that without the divine intervention of God, it would have all been over for me. I said: Lord, lead me in the path of righteousness for Your name's sake. And I thank You for Your angels that protect me in all ways. Amen.

He reached over on his right side, pulled the starting pedal out, put his foot on it, and kicked down hard. The engine roared to life with a loud rumble. He could have used the electric starter, but he preferred the old method. He flicked the car into first gear with his left foot, turned the accelerator with his right hand, released the clutch, and pulled away from the curb.

The sun was shining on my back as I headed west. Behind he was the past that included many glorious experiences and victories, but it also included shameful sins and defeat. Before me laid an endless horizon where all things are possible to those who believe.

On the Road

It was late in the afternoon, and the sun was shining brightly on my face. It had been two days since I had left my hometown in Wisconsin. I was headed northwest, not having any particular route in mind. I simply was trying to go by the leading in my heart. This may sound funny, but I felt like Abraham when God had called him out of the city of the Chaldeans to a land he did not know. It was a strange feeling to be free again from all-natural ties and to have God as the only source of security. Where I would end up after this trip, only God knew. But that was all right, for if God was for me, who could be against him?

The sun was setting as I pulled into a KOA campground. I went into the office and paid for a campsite for one night. Back outside I drove my bike around the campgrounds until I found myself a quiet, secluded spot. It was perfect; it even had large pine trees perched upon a rolling hillside looking down upon me in.

As I was driving my motorcycle out West, and I had acquired the address for a friend of mine whose name was Dale. While I was in the navy, Dale had Saved My Life Twice! He was my roommate, and he had a large painting of pigs over his bed.

As I was driving my motorcycle out West, and I had acquired the address for a friend of mine whose name was Dale. While I was in the navy, Dale had Saved My Life Twice! I would like to share these two experiences with you. I think it would be kind of entertaining.

I was still in the Navy in February of 1975. I had a roommate by the name of Dale who had a large painting of pigs over his bed. Now, I had approximately three months left in the Navy before I had fulfilled my military responsibilities. Dale and I were stationed on an island in the Bering Sea off the coast of Alaska called Adak, Alaska. What I did not realize at the time is that in a couple of days Dale was going to save my life not just once, but twice.

1st Time Dale Saved My Life

Dale and I decided to go fishing one day. It was the middle of winter in Alaska. Now, we are talking about being out there on the Aleutian chain. In retrospect, it probably was not too brilliant to be involved in such activities at that time of the year. We walked through deep snow in the tundra, working our way towards a small lake which we knew had trout. We finally pushed our way through the deep snow and made it to a stream which we were going to have to cross. Dale said we needed to find a place that we could jump over without stepping on the ice just in case it would not hold us. I told him that I thought the ice was more than thick enough to step on.

I told Dale that I was going to show him as I stepped out onto the ice in the stream. Dale immediately encouraged me to get off of the ice, but I told him that it was entirely frozen and okay to walk on. Standing in the middle of this stream, I started jumping up and down telling him, "See, it's solid." when suddenly, I broke through the ice; plunging into the freezing water. I was swallowed by the depths and dragged by the fast-moving stream. I ended up underneath the ice. I could not find the bottom of the stream. It was way over my head. The current began to pull me downstream. I was a goner —a dead man. I could not find my way back to the hole in the ice where I had broken through.

But then, I felt something grab hold of me, pulling me back through the hole in the ice. After my rescue, I discovered that it was Dale. It had to be supernatural because he had been at least 15 feet away from me when I fell in, but yet he was there so quick. Dale is a tall, lanky fellow. With his long arms, he had reached underneath the ice in the direction the current was taking me and grabbed me by my parka hood. God had used him to save my life.

2nd time that Dale Save My Life

The next day I was in my barracks working on some of my fishing equipment. My roommate, Dale, and I were going to go fishing again. I had purchased a small plastic box with all kinds of fishing lures in it. I went to open it, but no matter what I did, it would not open. That box was just downright stubborn. Then, a brilliant idea came to my mind (that was quite stupid). I went to my dresser, opened the top drawer and pulled out my survival knife. This was the same knife which I had bought previously with the intention of slitting my wrist to kill myself. Thank God the Spirit of the Lord fell upon me and gave me a revelation that I would go to hell. This caused me to fall to my knees and cry out to Jesus!

Picture this knife. It was approximately one foot long and, on the very end of the handle, there was a cap that you could screw off to store matches and other small, useful things for used for wilderness survival. Believe me when I tell you that this knife was extremely sharp. I had this brilliant idea that I could use the tip of this knife to pry open the lid of this stubborn, plastic box.

So, brilliant me held this box between my thumb and little finger. Immediately I perceived that I was going to get in trouble. The box was too close to my palm, so I moved it even further away, to the very tip of my thumb and my pinky. I began to apply pressure to the tip of the knife by pushing downward. This little box just did not want to open! I began to apply a lot more pressure and, as I did, the box slipped from between my pinky and my thumb. Now, here's the problem; the blade of the knife was aimed downwards towards my hand.

When the box slipped, the blade of the knife came down and sliced me from the wrist to the beginning of my thumb. It cut through my flesh like a hot knife through soft butter. It went so deep that it cut through an artery. If you opened an anatomy book that shows the human circulatory system, you would discover that near your wrist, on the thumb side, is a major artery called the radial artery. The instant that I cut through this artery, it seemed as if blood shot so high that it could have hit the 8-foot ceiling above my head.

This was back in 1975, so my memory is a little bit blurry. I'm not quite sure how high my bloodshot, but all I know is that the blood began to gush. I immediately applied pressure to the cut with my right hand. Thank God, that Dale was in the room doing something else. Remember, Dale had just rescued me from drowning the day before. I yelled out to him, "Dale, Dale!" causing him turn around. His face immediately turned an ashen white. I told him, "I need to get to the hospital!"

Our barracks were located on the top of a very high hill; the hospital was down in the valley. Here we were in Adak, Alaska with snow piled 5 feet deep everywhere. The roads were clear to some extent, but it was extremely slippery outside. There was no traffic on the road because there was a small blizzard blowing through. Dale's car was a little Volkswagen Beetle that was all beat up. The incident was somewhat hilarious, though because Dale was losing it like a newlywed husband whose wife was about ready to give birth to their first baby at any moment.

He put my winter coat on my shoulders because I could not stick my hand through the arm sleeve. There was blood beginning to spread everywhere. As I was keeping pressure to the severed artery, Dale opened up the car door for me to get in once we had gotten out to his vehicle. He then closed the door and ran to his side. He started that old Volkswagen beetle bug up. The engine was cold, causing it to clack away in close to 20° below zero weather. When the engine finally smoothed out to some extent, he put it in reverse, backing out of this parking space.

Then, off he went! I'll never forget that ride. It's a miracle we made it to the hospital. We were going down the mountain like a toboggan with a madman in the front. I kept telling him, "Dale, slow down, you're going to get us killed!" He would whip around those mountain curves, narrowly missing going over the edge. Thank God for the high snow banks because we hit them repeatedly. If you could have seen us, we looked like Laurel and Hardy. Dale was so tall and I was so short, but fortunately, I wasn't far. Miracles of miracles, we finally arrived at the hospital.

When I went into the emergency room, there was nobody in front of us, so they were able to see me right away. They had to use quite a number of stitches in my hand and wrist to seal up the artery. Because of this stupid accident, I now have a large scar on the palm of my hand, next to my thumb. To this day, I have a limited range of motion in my thumb, plus it certainly doesn't like the cold weather. But, believe you me, I am not complaining because I know that God rescued me once again from my stupidity. Thank God for his mercy!

The Pig Farmer with Two Hogs

Dale since the last time I had seen him had been discharged from the Navy. He now lived in South Dakota. I was never able to lead Dale to the Lord because he had wanted to be a pig farmer. In his mind, he felt that God was opposed to his desire to raise pigs. Over the top of his bunk, he had a huge Sow with its litter. I told him that he could be saved, love Jesus, and still have a hog farm. For some reason, he did not believe me. I had prayed earnestly for Dale many times since our time in the Navy.

As I followed the map to his house, I was going through heavy farm areas and cornfields everywhere. I finally found Dale's house. When I pulled into the yard, I discovered he had lots of pigs. He had his pig farm after all.

Outside of the old farmhouse there was sitting two Harley-Davidson motorcycles in the yard. I shut off my bike and parked it. I went up to the back door and knocked. As the door opened, I was met by a lady who probably was in her 60s. I asked her if Dale was home. She told me that this was his house, but that he was not home from work yet. She invited me in, telling me that Dale would be home any minute. There at the kitchen table were sitting two large, bearded, rough-looking men. I believe it was Dale's mother who had answered the door.

It turned out the motorcycles belonged to those two bearded, burly men. Somehow, they were related to Dale. While we were waiting for Dale to get home, I entered the conversation with these guys. After a while, we heard a vehicle pull into the yard.

I stepped out onto the back porch as an old blue Chevy Impala pulled into the driveway. Dale, who is tall and lanky, opened the door of his car and stepped out. He had this strange floppy cowboy hat on the top of his head. The minute Dale saw me a big old smile came upon his face. He began to shout, "Praise the Lord, Thank you, Jesus." I knew instantly that Dale had given his heart to the Lord since I had last seen him. I also discovered he was filled with the Holy Ghost. We had a wonderful reunion.

So shall my word be that goeth forth out of my mouth: it shall not return unto me void, but it shall accomplish that which I please, and it shall prosper in the thing whereto I sent it (Isaiah 55:11)

*34. Blood, Guts, and Flesh

Angel lifted a Mule Deer over the top of Me. (1977)

I remember one time when God's mercy came to me as I was driving a motorcycle through the mountains of Montana. I was a 21-year-old kid headed for Alaska on my motorcycle. It was early in the morning. Just a half an hour earlier I had broke camp, packed up my sleeping bag and a pup tent, jumped onto my motorcycle, and was headed into Oregon on a mountain road. My plan was to take the Alcan freeway all the way up to Alaska (which at the time was nothing but a dirt road), but 1st I was going to Oregon to visit some close friends of mine (Loyd & Bonnie Old's).

I was driving along early in the morning praising the Lord, meditating on the Scriptures. I was coming around a sharp corner, with a bank and trees on one side of the road. Just as I was at the sharpest point of the corner, I saw a flash of movement off to my right. Faster than I could possibly react, a very large mule deer, (a buck with a big set of antlers) leaped right into me.

In my heart, I knew that it was too late. I was going to be hit by this leaping buck. At about 40 miles per hour, I knew our bodies were going to be tangled together in blood, guts, skin, and hide. Mule deer flesh and human flesh was about to become as one. Everything went into slow motion at that moment! I saw his underside was headed right for my head and was only about two feet away from me. I could have reached out and grabbed this mule deer!

The mule deer is the larger of two species of deer on average, with a height of 31–42 in at the shoulders and a nose-to-tail length ranging from 4 to 6.9 ft. Adult bucks normally weigh 121–331 lb, averaging around 203 lb., although trophy specimens may weigh up to 460 lb.

Now I am telling you that something supernatural happened at that very moment. At the very last possible second, right there in front of my face, this mule deer was lifted higher up into the air, right over the top of my head and my Honda 750 motorcycle. It landed on the other side of the road and continued its way.

That is what I call the mercy of God! I was so overwhelmed by this act of God's mercy that without thinking my hands came off the steering bars of that motorcycle. I cannot tell you how long my hands were lifted in the air praising God, but I was lost in the Holy Ghost, overwhelmed by his love and his mercy.

What I imagined happened In the Realm of the Spirit

*In the realm of the spirit, I believe angels have names, but God does not share them with us because the emphasis is always upon the Father and upon his son Jesus Christ!) Let's have a little fun here and take a look at what possibly happened in the realm of the spirit in this situation. Let's give all these angels that maybe were involved. That way it will seem way more personal.

Angels Names with Greek Meanings: #1 Tabeal (God is good), #2 Tsaphah (watchman), #3 Nay-fo (sober and calm), #4 Saw-on (which means, "warrior, to trample"),   #5 Gil-bore (meaning, "mighty, valiant") #6 Sawkal (prudent and prosperous), #7 Leb'abreck (whose name means, "stout in heart and to kneel")

SCENARIO

As Michael drove down the highway, a small band of angels surrounded him. Tabeal and Tsaphah were in front of him; Nay-fo and Saw-on were in the rear, Gil-bore and Sawkal were to the left and to the right. Leb'abreck was immediately above him looking in every direction. Even though Mike was cruising at fifty-five miles per hour, it did not seem in the least to be putting pressures upon the angelic bodyguard. They had their swords were drawn and their eyes alert, ready for an attack of the enemy if he would show his face.

Mike rounded a sharp corner, leaning into the curve. There were high banks with trees on both sides. Just as Mike was at the sharpest point, he saw a flash off to his left. Faster than he could possibly react, a large mule deer, a buck, leaped in front of him. Mike knew that it was too late. He was going to hit the leaping deer. At fifty-five miles per hour, he knew their bodies would be tangled together in blood, guts, skin, and hide.

The hoofs of the deer were only inches from Mike's head as it leaped into the air. And then, at the very last possible moment, the deer seemed to be lifted higher into the air, right over Mike's head and his bike. The deer landed on the other side of the road and continued to run.

Gil-bore, though invisible to the naked eye of a mortal, had seen a number of demons frightening the mule deer in the woods and had seen it take off like a scared rabbit. As it leaped toward Mike's head, Gil-bore was there to lift the deer up and over Mike's head safely to the other side of the road. Sawkal went in pursuit of the devilish spirits who had frightened the deer in order to kill Mike. When he caught up with them, they would pay dearly for their mischief.

Mike was so totally overcome with praise. He knew it had to be a divine intervention. There was no way he could not have collided with that large deer. He was so overjoyed that, without thinking, he lifted both of his hands off of the handlebars. Leb'abreck swept down from above, grabbed the handles, and steered the cycle down the road as Mike was engrossed in worship.

For he shall give his angels charge over thee, to keep thee in all thy ways. They shall bear thee up in their hands, lest thou dash thy foot against a stone (Psalms 91:11-12).

*35. Stabbed in the Face

Stabbed In The Face With A Knife By A Demon Possessed Woman! (1977)

Back in 1977, I rode my 750 Honda motorcycle to Oregon to visit a good friend of mine, Judge Lloyd Olds, and his family. I stayed a while in Oregon, and ended up working on a fishing vessel. When it was time to leave Oregon, I rode my motorcycle up the Alcan Freeway, caught a ferry to Alaska, and rode on to Anchorage.

I arrived in Anchorage and the Lord quickened my heart to stop at a small, Full Gospel church that I used to visit. It just so happened that an evangelist I'd known when I was in the Navy (Adak, Alaska) was there too. We spent some time reminiscing about what had happened the previous year, and he shared how the Lord had laid upon his heart to go to Mount Union, Pennsylvania and open up an outreach center.

He invited me to go to Pennsylvania, with him and his wife, to open this Evangelistic Outreach Centre. I perceived in my heart that I needed to go with them. So, I made plans to fly back to Wisconsin, where he and his wife would pick me up as they went through. However, before I left Alaska, the Spirit of God had one more assignment for me: a precious woman needed to be set free.

One Sunday we decided to attend a small church along the road to Fairbanks. I was the first to enter this little, old, rustic church. When I went through the sanctuary doors, I immediately noticed a strange, little, elderly, lady across from me - sitting in the pews. She turned her head and stared right at me with the strangest look I have ever seen. I could sense immediately there was something demonic about her. Out of the blue, this little old lady jumped up, got out of the pew, and ran out of the church. At that moment I perceived that God wanted me to go and cast the devils out of her.

When the service was over, I asked the pastor who that elderly lady was. He said she was not a member of his church, but she came once in a great while. He also told me that she lived with her husband in a run-down house on a dirt road. I asked him if it would be okay to go and see her? **(I knew in my heart that God had sent me there to help bring deliverance)** He said he had no problems with this, especially since she wasn't a part of his church.

We followed the directions the pastor gave us, and when we arrived at the house it was exactly as the pastor had described it to us. It was run-down, and the yard was overflowing with old furniture and household items. It reminded me of the TV show

"Sanford and Son" - but it probably had ten-times more junk in the yard! I do not know how the old couple survived the winters in Alaska in such a poorly-built house. As we got out of the car, a little old man met us outside. It was her husband. He was thanking God as he walked toward us, and said he knew we were men of God, and that we had been sent by the Lord to help his poor, tormented wife. He informed us that his wife was in their kitchen.

So, we walked up to the house, having to go down the twisting and cluttered junk-filled path. We entered the house through a screen door that led into their summer kitchen. When we entered the kitchen, we could see his wife over at a large utility sink. Her back was to us, but we could see she was peeling carrots over her kitchen sink ... with a very large, scary-looking, butchers knife!! As I stood there, looking at the back of her head, I began to speak to her about Jesus. Out of the blue, she turned her head like it was on a swivel to look at me. I could hardly believe my eyes! It was like I was watching a horror movie! This little lady's eyes were glowing red on her swiveled head.

I rubbed my eyes at that moment; thinking that maybe I imagined this. No ... her head had swiveled - without her body moving - and her eyes were glowing red. Fear immediately filled my heart as she looked at me with the big knife ... a butcher's knife ... in her hand. Immediately, I came against the spirit of fear in my heart by quoting the holy Scriptures: **"For God hath not given me the spirit of fear; but of power, and of love, and of a sound mind"** *2 Timothy 1:7*. I shared with her about Jesus Christ.

The next thing I knew she was coming right at me - with her knife - as if she was filled with great rage. The knife was still in her right hand when she spun around and came at me. She leapt through the air onto me, wrapping her small skinny legs around my waist. How in the world she was able to do this - I do not know?! The next thing I knew, she was lifting up her right hand and hitting me in the face, very hard, multiple times. I could feel the pressure of her hitting me on the left side of my face. As she was hitting me in the face, out of my mouth came: "In the **Name of Jesus!**"

The minute I came against this attack "**In The Name of Jesus**" she was ripped off of me; picked up by an invisible power, and flung across the room about 10-feet or more. She slammed very hard against the bare wall of her kitchen, and slipped down to the floor. Amazingly when she hit the wall, she was not hurt! I went over to her, continuing to cast the demons out of her In the Name of Jesus. Once I perceived that she was free, and in her right mind, I asked her how she had become demon possessed? She told us her terrible story.

Her uncle had repeatedly molested and raped her when she was a very young girl. She thought she was free from him when he got sick and died. But then he began to visit her from the dead, continuing to molest and rape her at night. To her, it was physical and real. She did not know it was a familiar spirit disguised as her uncle. This had probably gone on for over fifty years! I led her to the Lord. Sweet, beautiful peace came upon her, completely changing her countenance. She was a brand-new person in Christ, finally free - after almost fifty years of torment. She and her husband began to go to church with us - until I left Alaska. I remember that we took them to see the Davis family at a local church, visiting Alaska on a missionary trip.

Years later, the evangelist who visited this lady with me, heard me retelling the story at a church; about how the woman kept punching me forcefully with her right hand. At the end of the service, he came and informed me that I was not telling the story correctly. I wondered if he thought I was exaggerating. He said that he was standing behind me when she jumped on top of me and began to hit me with her right fist.

But, he informed me, it wasn't her hand she was slapping me with … she still had the large butchers knife in her hand; and he saw her stabbing me in the face with this knife. Repeatedly!! He said he knew that I was a dead man, because nobody could survive being stabbed in the face repeatedly, with a large butcher knife. He expected to see nothing but blood, but instead of seeing my blood everywhere, he saw that there was not even one mark on my face where the knife was hitting me. I did feel something hit my face repeatedly, but I thought it was her hand! Instead, it was her knife, and it could not pierce my skin! Thank God for His love, His mercy, and His Supernatural Divine Protection.

I am convinced that if I had not been walking with God in His holiness and obedience, the devil in that little old lady would have stabbed me to death. Many people in the body of Christ are trying to deal with demonic powers when they are out of the father's will. When we are moving in the Holy Ghost, obedience, and absolute love for Jesus Christ - there is no power in hell that can hurt us!

My God hath sent his angel, and hath shut the lion's mouths, that they have not hurt me: forasmuch as before him innocence was found in me; and also before thee, O king, have I done no hurt (Daniel 6:22).

CHAPTER FIVE

Activating the Miraculous

36. Standing on the Word

In my earlier days, God was supernaturally quickening my mind to memorize scripture. The gifts of the Spirit were flowing with the word of knowledge, wisdom, prophecy, tongues, and interpretation. My life used to be filled with extreme depression and self-pity. This depression was trying to sneak its way back into my life in a strong way. I fought it constantly.

One morning I got up early to pray. I was fed up with the feelings and emotions of depression that were trying to overwhelm me. I took my large Bible (I know this sounds disrespectful but I was still young in the Lord) and put it on the floor. I physically stood upon the Word of God as an act of faith. I spoke to the depression and declared: "In the name of Jesus Christ of Nazareth, from this day forward I will not believe what my feelings or emotions are telling me. Let God's Word be true and everything else a lie."

I learned this lesson the first two months I was saved. I awoke one day with the total absence of God's presence. I did not know what to do in this particular situation. I examined my heart to make sure I was not out of God's will. I came to the conclusion there was nothing in my life I knowingly or willingly was doing to grieve the Father, Son, or Holy Ghost! I decided that regardless of how I felt, that I would continue to pray, read my Bible, share the gospel, and do God's will. This experience lasted for about two weeks. One day while I was in prayer, God's presence came flooding in. I asked the Lord "Where have you been?" The Spirit spoke to my heart saying: I never left you. I wanted you to learn how to live by faith and not by your feelings. God gave me glorious victory over depression the day I stood upon my Bible and declared I was free! I have continued to walk in that victory for over thirty years through the most difficult times one could ever imagine. Yes, depression tries to come back upon me, but I put it under my feet by faith every time

God forbid: yea, let God be true, but every man a liar; as it is written, That thou mightest be justiÞed in thy sayings, and mightest overcome when thou art judged (Romans 3:4).

37. Passing the Dope

The evangelist and I opened the outreach center in Mount Union Pennsylvania, known as "Little Chicago." One night I was ministering on the streets and walked down the back alleys behind an old movie theater. I saw ahead of me six young men standing in a circle passing something that looked like a cigarette to one another. Of course, I knew they were passing marijuana, what people refer to as "pot."

My heart was quickened to enter this circle. It was rather dark out, plus the Lord was working so they hadn't realized I had entered into this circle. It didn't hurt any that I looked like them with my bell bottom pants, jean jacket and natural afro-hairstyle. When the pot came to me I simply took it and held it in my hand. After a while they began to ask who had the dope. They looked around and saw me. I held the pot up in my right hand and began to preach under the unction of the Holy Ghost. When I finished speaking, I gave them an opportunity to get right with God. Three of them prayed with me that night and gave their hearts to Jesus Christ. *Behold, I send you forth as sheep in the midst of wolves: be ye therefore wise as serpents, and harmless as doves (Matthew 10:16).*

*38. A Preacher's Son Was Dying (1977)

One night I was fishing for souls in front of the old movie theater in Mount Union PA. Out of the darkness came the son of an African American minister I knew. I knew this minister's son was in a backslidden condition and was involved in heavy drugs and alcohol. The world had swallowed him up!

And here he was coming toward me. I could tell something drastic was wrong with him as he approached me. He was barely able to stand on his feet. He said, "Mike, help me. I'm dying." He had evidently gotten some bad drugs and asked if I would please pray and ask God to do a miracle and save him. I took him into the restroom on the second floor of that old movie theater, laid my hands upon him, and cried out to Jesus for mercy—that He would remove the drugs from his bloodstream.

I commanded the poisons, drugs, and alcohol to come out of his body right then in the name of Jesus Christ! The very minute I finished praying it was as if God snapped His fingers. All the chemicals and drugs came out of him instantly and he stood straight up. One minute he was a goner and the next minute he was absolutely straight, sober and healed. The preacher's son was completely mystified and told me that all the symptoms and effects of the drugs were completely gone.

Call unto me, and I will answer thee, and show thee great and mighty things, which thou knowest not (Jeremiah 33:3).

*39. Faceless Demon

Demonic power tried to kill me! (1977)

Here I was as a 21-year-old kid on-fire for God! I knew in my heart I was stirring things up in the satanic realm and the demonic world would try to find a way to destroy me. I did not have any fear in my heart because I had discovered the truth that *"greater is He that is in me, than he that is in the world!"*

Now I had a very realistic experience one night as I was sleeping. I saw this dark, faceless demon come running down the long hallway of the house I was staying in. It was just a tiny house that had been a chicken house converted into a small house with a guest quarters. I shared this house with an evangelist and his wife. I slept all the way down on the other side of this long narrow building.

I'm not complaining (faith never grumbles or gripes). I could handle it even if it was not heated or air conditioned. The particular night, I saw in a very tangible dream this demonic spirit come running down this long hallway through the door and into my bedroom. When it came into my bedroom, it immediately jumped on top of me and began choking me. I could not physically breathe at that moment. Panic and fear overwhelmed me! Then I heard the voice of God speak to my heart, telling me to be at peace.

The Lord's presence came flooding in upon me at that very moment. I cried out to Jesus with a whisper and rebuked this demon that was choking me, in the name of Jesus. At this point, I was fully awake by this time. As this dark image continued choking me, I saw a gigantic hand come down through the ceiling of my room. It grabbed this faceless, dark demonic power around the neck and ripped it off me. This gigantic hand shook it like a cat would a mouse and threw it out of the room. God's presence overwhelmed me as I was sitting up in my bed crying and weeping with joy and praising God! This experience was not just my imagination running wild, but it was literal and real!

And the seventy returned again with joy, saying, Lord, even the devils are subject unto us through thy name. And he said unto them, I beheld satan as lightning fall from heaven (Luke 10:17-18).

*40. Praising God at Midnight

I was working at Agape Camp farm, located in Shirleysburg, Pennsylvania, in the summer of 1977. Every year they have a very large Christian gathering. One night, instead of going back to Belleville, I stayed at one of the workers houses. They had three small children; I believe it was two boys and a little girl. We had a sweet time of fellowship as we all sat at the dinner table. I slept on their couch that night.

In the morning I could tell that something was different about how the children were looking at me. At breakfast the children just kept staring. I asked the father and mother if there was something wrong. They told me something strange had happened last night. They were all sleeping when all of a sudden they heard someone singing in a foreign language. It was so loud that they all had gotten up to see what was happening.

Supposedly they tip-toed down the stairs. They came down to see where the singing was coming from. They told me that they had discovered me with my eyes closed, and my hands were lifted up in the air singing in tongues. They could tell that I was not doing this in my own ability and that I was honestly and sincerely asleep! I can truly say I have no recollection of this happening.

..... God is a Spirit: and they that worship him must worship him in spirit and in truth (John 4:23-24).

*41. My Broken Back Healed (1977)

I share these stories, my personal experiences, hoping that they will give you an insight in how to receive healing, even in the most difficult situations. Now in the winter of 1977, I was working at the Belleville Feed & Grain Mill. My job was to pick up the corn, wheat, and oats from the farmers, and bring it to the mill. There it would be mixed and combined with other products for the farmers' livestock.

One cold, snowy day, the owner of the feed mill told me to deliver a load of cattle feed to an Amish farm. It was an extremely bad winter that year, with lots of snow. I was driving an International 1600 Lodestar. I backed up as far as I could to this Amish man's barn without getting stuck. The Amish never had their lanes plowed in those days, and they most likely still do not. I was approximately seventy-five feet away from his barn, which meant that I had to carry the bags at least seventy-five feet. I think there were about eighty bags of feed, with each bag weighing approximately one hundred pounds. During those years I only weighed about 130 pounds.

I would carry one bag on each of my shoulders, stumbling and pushing my way through the heavy, deep snow to get up the steep incline into the barn. Then I would stack the bags in a dry location. As usual, nobody came out to help me. Many a time when delivering things to the farms, the Amish would watch me work without lending a helping hand. About the third trip, something frightening happened to me as I was carrying two one-hundred-pound bags upon my shoulders. I felt the bones in my back snap. Something drastic just happened. I fell to the ground at that very moment almost completely crippled. I could barely move. I was filled with intense overwhelming pain.

I had been spending a lot of my time meditating in the Word of God. Every morning, I would get up about 5:00 a.m. to study. I

81

had one of those little bread baskets with memorization scriptures in it. I believe you can still buy them to this day at a Christian bookstore. Every morning I would memorize from three to five of them. It would not take me very long, so all day long I would be meditating on these verses.

The very minute I fell, immediately I cried out to Jesus, asking him to forgive me for my pride, and for being so stupid in carrying two hundred pounds on my little frame. After I asked Jesus to forgive me, I commanded my back to be healed in the name of Jesus Christ of Nazareth. Since I believed I was healed, I knew that I had to act now upon my faith. Please understand that I was full of tremendous pain, but I had declared that I was healed by the stripes of Jesus. The Word of God came out of my mouth as I tried to get up and then fell back down.

Even though the pain was more intense than I can express, I kept getting back up speaking the name of Jesus, then I would fall back down again. I fell more times than I can remember. After some time, I was able to take a couple steps, then I would fall again. This entire time I was saying, "In the name of Jesus, in the name of Jesus, in the name of Jesus."

I finally was able to get to the truck. I said to myself if I believe I'm healed then I will unload this truck in the name of Jesus. Of course, I did not have a cell phone in order to call for help and the Amish did not own any phones on their property. Now, even if they would have had a phone, I would not have called for help. I had already called upon my help, and His name was Jesus Christ. I knew in my heart that by the stripes of Jesus I was healed. I then pulled a bag off the back of the truck, with it falling on top of me. I would drag it a couple of feet, and then fall.

Tears were running down my face as I spoke the Word of God over and over. By the time I was done with all of the bags, the sun had already gone down. Maybe six or seven hours had gone by. I painstakingly pulled myself up into that big old 1600 Lodestar. It took everything within me to shift gears, pushing in the clutch, and driving it. I had to sit straight like a board all the way.

I finally got back to the feed mill late in the evening. Everybody had left for home a long time ago with the building being locked up. I struggled out of the Lodestar and stumbled and staggered over to my Ford pickup. I got into my pickup, and made it back to the converted chicken house. I went back to my cold, unheated, plywood floor room. It took everything in me to get my clothes off. It was a very rough and long night.

The next morning when I woke up, I was so stiff that I could not bend in the least. I was like a board. Of course, I was not going to miss work, because by the stripes of Jesus I was healed. To get out of bed, I had to literally roll off the bed, hitting the floor. Once I had hit the floor, it took everything for me to push myself back up into a sitting position. The tears were rolling down my face as I put my clothes and shoes on, which was a miracle. I did get to work on time, though every step was excruciatingly painful. Remember, I was only twenty-one at the time, but I knew what faith was and what it wasn't. I knew that I was healed no matter how it looked, that by the stripes of Jesus Christ I was healed.

When I got to work I did not tell my boss that I had been seriously hurt the day before. I walked into the office trying to keep the pain off of my face. For some reason he did not ask me what time I made it back to work. I did not tell him to change the time clock for me in order to be paid for all of the hours I was out on the job. They had me checked out at the normal quitting time. (The love of money is what causes a lot of people not to get healed.)

My boss gave me an order for feed that needed to be delivered to a local farmer. If you have ever been to a feed and grain mill, you know that there is a large shoot where the feed comes out. After it has been mixed, you have to take your feed bag, and hold it up until it's filled. It creates tremendous strain on your arms and your back, even if you're healthy.

As I was filling the bag, it almost felt like I was going to pass out, because I was in tremendous pain. Now, I'm simply saying, "In the name of Jesus, in the name of Jesus, in the name of Jesus" under my breath. The second bag was even more difficult than the first bag, but I kept on saying, "In the name of Jesus." I began on the third bag and as I was speaking the name of Jesus, the power of God hit my back and I was instantly and completely, totally healed from the top of my head, to the tip of my toes. I was healed as I went on my way. My place of employment never did know what had happened to me. That has been 38 years ago, and my back is still healed by the stripes of Christ to this day.

And from the days of John the Baptist until now the kingdom of heaven suffereth violence, and the violent take it by force (Matthew 11:12).

*42. Fired For My Good

One day, the transmission went out on my F- 250 Ford truck after I backed into the drain field of a septic system which I had not known was there. The engine in my truck basically needed an overhaul being a straight six 300. I still needed my truck because I was leaving my place of employment to go to a bible school in Broken Arrow, Oklahoma. I began to pray about this situation. As I prayed, I experience the peace and presence of God. It came into my heart to go to a salvage yard to try to find a transmission and an engine that would work in my truck.

I Located a 460 engine with a transmission in an old Ford Mercury. As I prayed the Spirit of the Lord quickened my heart that this engine would fit right into my Ford F-250 pickup. All the mechanics that I spoke to said that it would never work, but I had that inward witness. The engine and transmission was going to cost me four hundred dollars. I certainly didn't have the money and I had to get ready to go to bible school quick. I put it into the Lord's hands.

One day at work, my boss told me to back the Lodestar 1600 up to the grinding pit. I walked around the truck and got into the cab.

Unbeknownst to me, as I was getting into the cab, a farmer pulled up behind me in his pickup truck. It was so close to my vehicle that I could not see him in my side-view mirrors. I started the engine, put it into reverse and backed right up into this farmer's vehicle. When this happened, the boss said he really liked me but he would still have to let me go because of the accident.

The good news is that the truck had already been damaged previously and the farmer said his insurance would cover it because it really did not change what the body shop was going to have to do for his truck. I thanked my boss for letting me work for him. He did not know it, but I was about to give him my two week notice anyway. Before I left, he handed me an envelope. When I opened it up, there was the $400 that I needed to get my truck back on the road. Thank you, Jesus! Plus, the engine and transmission that came out of the Ford Mercury fit perfectly into my F-250 ford pickup.

And we know that all things work together for good to them that love God, to them who are the called according to his purpose (Romans 8:28).

43. She's the One

I was standing outside The Mount Union Christian Center, on a ladder one day, putting up new letters on the marquee, when I heard behind me the sweetest voice I had ever heard. The voice said, "Praise the Lord, Brother!" I turned around on the ladder. And there before me I saw a beautiful, blue-eyed blonde. I said back in return, "Praise God, Sister!" Immediately the Spirit of God spoke to my heart and said: she is your wife! All I could think at the moment was, wow! To be honest, I was quite overwhelmed.

This blue-eyed girl and I spoke for a little while. She told me that her name was Kathleen, and that she was home taking a break from college. She was one of the lead vocalists for a Christian college in Phoenixville, Pennsylvania. Actually, she was not even really supposed to be home. God had arranged it. (She will share her story with you after this little intermission.) I did not tell her what the Spirit of God had said to me, until after we were married.

Proverbs 29:11 says, "A fool uttereth all of his mind, but a wise man keeps it in till afterwards."

When Kathleen walked away, I got down from the ladder and I went into the old movie theater. I was so filled with the spirit of joy that I jumped up upon the back of the old, unstable, theater chairs. I ran on the back of these chairs all the way down to the front, spun around, and ran back to the rear of the theater on top of the chairs again. As I was running, I was shouting, "She's the one! She's the one!" Five months later we were gloriously married.

And Adam said, This is now bone of my bones, and flesh of my flesh: she shall be called Woman, because she was taken out of Man. Therefore shall a man leave his father and his mother, and shall cleave unto his wife: and they shall be one flesh (Genesis 2:23-24).

Kathleen's story:

When I met Michael (Mike), it was a God-arranged appointment, because I wasn't supposed to be there—I was supposed to be in college! We met while I was attending my second semester at a college in Valley Forge. It was the end of March 1978, the week classes were supposed to start after Spring break. I may have never met him, had not the Lord arranged for me to be home during that cherished week of destiny. I was only nineteen years old at the time.

During spring or Easter break, I was on tour with the school's choir. Our schedule had been quite grueling, and who ever set up the itinerary made it so we would have to travel during the night to make it to many of our next destinations.

Because of the excessive traveling, we did not sleep very well. Many of the choir members lost their voices, and I was one of them! However, when it would come to the time of my solos, the anointing of God would take over and I would miraculously be able to sing.

At the end of the tour, I was both exhausted and totally without a voice. School classes were scheduled to begin the following Tuesday, but I really wanted to go home and rest.

Seeking the dean of women's permission to go home and miss four days of classes was not going to be an easy task. Nonetheless, I was willing to try. When I entered the dean's office, I could tell that she had already had a bad day. She could tell that I had very little voice left, as I tried to squeak a whisper of my request to skip a few days of classes and go home to rest.

Perhaps, my squeaking only irritated her frayed nerves, but she let me have it! In her tirade, she told me in no certain terms that all we students were alike, and I could not go home!

Instead of getting angry, I felt compassion for her, and gave her a big hug. I told her that it was alright. I told her that I knew she was having a bad day, and prayed that the rest of her day would go better. I thanked her for her time, and let myself out of the room.

Not much later, my den mother came to me and asked what I had done to the dean of women! My den mother said that she had gone to see the dean of women shortly after I left, found the dean of women sitting in her chair, with her mouth open, and tears running down her face.

My den mother told me that all she could get out of the dean was, "I just chewed that girl up one side and down the other, and she came over, gave me a hug, thanked me, and wished me a good day!"

My act of kindness did not go unrewarded, because, apparently after the dean regained her composure, she determined to find me and talk to me privately. When I saw the dean coming, she called out to me. I wasn't sure what to expect when she grabbed my arm and drew me close to her. She whispered in my ear, "I am not even sure that I am allowed to do this, and I might get in trouble, so tell no one. You may go home for a few days." I gave her another big hug and thanked her. I was going home!

When I arrived home, little did I know that God was at work to bring Mike, my future husband, and I together.

The first day home I slept all day, but the next day my mother and I ended up in Mount Union to go shopping. Before we left the house, I decided that I didn't want to be bothered. I put my hair down around my face, put my glasses on, and dressed in a knit polyester pant suit. I certainly was not dressed to attract any male attention!

As God would have it, before we went grocery shopping, we passed by an old theatre called the Mount Union Christian Center. There was a young man on a ladder, putting "Jesus the Ultimate Trip" on the marquis. My voice had miraculously recovered, and I said, "Praise the Lord, Brother!" and he responded "Praise the Lord, Sister!"

This afro-haired young man, was cute and on fire for God! We spoke together for a little while about the goodness of God and of how the Lord had saved and touched lives during my choir tour. Michael spoke of God's goodness and wonders, too.

I liked Mike from the start, and was hoping to meet again before I returned to school. Little did I know that I would see him again that night and have lunch with him the next day.

I have to add here: After meeting Mike at the theater/Christian center, a young girl came running into the grocery store to find me. She was insistent on telling me that Mike really, really, liked me and asked if I liked him. She must have seen Mike running on the back of the theater chairs shouting, "She's the one! She's the one!" I told her that I barely knew him, how could I tell if I liked him?

Sure, he was nice, but I had not fallen for him—not yet!

However, she did spark a little more interest in me. So, that night, my mother, sister, and I came back to the center. Only this time I was dressed, perfumed, and ready for a little male attention— well one male's attention.

My mom was dating a man from the center, so I asked him to ask Mike if he'd like to go out with us, meaning my mom, my future step-father, and me. I was delighted when he accepted. This young man was beginning to win my heart.

Before I went back to college, Mike handed me a Laurel blossom; which I kept for years pressed within my college year book. The flower reminded me of the blossom of love that was beginning to bloom in my heart for this man of God.

Michael won my heart because he loved God. Our conversations were always centered on Jesus and God's Word. Had Michael been a forward person, I would have dropped interest in him immediately. I loved the Lord and only desired to serve Him. A man with any other desire would have turned me off instantly.

Consequently, by the time I went back to college to finish the semester, Mike was all I wanted to talk about, he had won my heart. The feeling must have been mutual, for I was back at school less than a day, when he called and spoke with me for over an hour. Michael wrote me long letters that were full of the Word of God. You could say, the Word of God within Mike's letters washed over me and made me one with him and God's Word.

I showed Mike's letters to my friends, because there was nothing embarrassing in them. They thought that he must be a baby Christian. I thought that to be a sad indictment on us "Bible" students! If it were only baby Christians who loved the Word of God and would fill their letters with scriptures, then we Bible students had lost our first love! When we lose our love for the Word of God, we are in trouble!

Mike and I kept in touch by phone calls and letters until I was to return home the first week of May. I had hoped to stay at the college to finish a short summer semester. (I reasoned that my feelings were better kept at a distance.) However, Mike was praying that God would bring me home, because he wanted to be with me!

I was stubborn, though. Had not my mom decided to get married May 6th, and wanted me there to sing and help her prepare for her wedding, I might have stayed at Valley Forge. My stubbornness to stay at college was not totally against Mike and spending the summer at home, but it was aimed at trying to make my mom wait to get married. I wasn't willing to give up my mom that easily to another man. My mom and I had been best friends for years, and while I was away at college she met a godly man and fell in love. For me, that was a hard pill to swallow. But God was in it!

Back home, our romance budded quickly, and by June we knew that we wanted to get married. Nonetheless, I wanted to go back to school for at least one more year. When Mike applied to go to a well-known Bible training center, I silently prayed that they would accept him for the following year, because I wanted to go along and attend too. Furthermore, I wanted to wait another year before getting married.

When Michael received his acceptance in July, I was torn. I wanted to go with Mike, but I wanted to wait! I only knew Mike three to four short months! I had earlier vowed that I would never get married unless I had dated at least two years! To add to my dilemma, we contacted this Bible school, and yes, they would accept me, too. They always tried to accept couples. I had some serious decisions to make.

Needless to say, we were married on August 19, 1978, and I had just met Mike around March 28! Besides accepting Jesus as my Lord and Savior, marrying Mike is the best thing I ever did. God had ordained that we would be together. Sure we've had rough times, but God has brought us through.

Looking back today, I believe that God had things go quickly, because I surely would have changed my mind if I had two years to think about it. Furthermore, the whirlwind of getting married, preparing for a wedding, and preparing to go to Oklahoma (which was far away from home) were only a foretaste of what the Lord had for me and Mike together.

If I couldn't take a fast-paced marriage, then I would never be prepared for the fast-paced life that we have lived!

I did not miss any of my college classes that spring when I came home and met my husband-to-be. Right after I left the school to come home for a rest, a snow storm hit Valley Forge and prevented classes from starting until the following week—the week I returned. God is a God of wonders! I did not have any classes to make up, and could sit starry-eyed, thinking about Mike, stress free!

Be kindly affectioned one to another with brotherly love; in honour preferring one another;...Bless them which persecute you: bless, and curse not......If it be possible, as much as lieth in you, live peaceably with all men.. (Romans 12:10, 14, 17,18, 21).

44. Suspended in the Air

When Kathleen returned home for the summer, she began to attend the services at the Mount Union Christian Center. We began spending time together in prayer and witnessing, attending different meetings together. Kathee went along the night I was to minister. As we were worshiping God, something very strange happened to me. I had been lifting my hands up in the air when all of a sudden it was like somebody grabbed my two hands and began to lift me up almost upon my toes. I knew it was God, but I did not know why this was happening. After the worship, my hands stayed up in the air. I could not bring them down. It was like somebody was holding my hands and pulling me up a little bit.

The minister made announcements, received the offering, and did whatever else needed to be done. My hands were stuck up in the air the whole time! People were staring at me as if there was something wrong with me. I was embarrassed, but I could not help it. The pastor of the church finally called for me to come and minister the Word to the people. Because I could not get my hands down, I asked Kathee if she would go with me on the stage, and hold my Bible while I preached. She agreed to do this. I went up front on the stage, and told the people that my hands were stuck up in the air, and I could not get them down, no matter how hard I tried. So, I would have to preach this way.

Kathleen held my Bible while I preached. I do not remember what I preached, but I think it was pretty good. My hands never came down until I had finished preaching and ministering. Then they just seemed to slowly descend on their own. My hands must have been stuck up in the air for nearly two hours. Go ahead and try it; see if you can do it. It was supernatural!

How great are his signs! And how mighty are his wonders! His kingdom is an everlasting kingdom, and his dominion is from generation to generation (Daniel 4:3).

CHAPTER SIX

School of the Holy Ghost

*45. Money Cometh

We were married On August 19, 1978. Three days after we were married we headed to Broken Arrow, Oklahoma to attend Bible school together. When Kathleen married me I did not have a penny to my name. She literally had to buy our wedding bands. Not only that, but she had lost her financial support which came from her deceased father's social security.

Her father had died when she was six years old in an automobile accident, but the government stopped the payments to her when she married. Of course, then I had to pay off her existing college tuition. It took all the faith in the world for her to marry me and head off to Bible school with someone she barely knew with no money or natural source of income.

When we arrived in Broken Arrow, Oklahoma, we ended up working at a fast-food restaurant for a brief period of time. We did not have enough money for both of us to go to the school, and she was going to drop out so I could go. However, I told her, no; we were both going together and that was that. To this day we really do not know where all the money came from, except that it was from God. With all the money we made, we were still short over five hundred dollars per month when paying our bills. Somehow God supernaturally kept bringing the finances in. To this day, our monthly expenses for the ministry come up short thousands of dollars a month, and somehow our bills are paid!

But my God shall supply all your need according to his riches in glory by Christ Jesus (Philippians 4:19).

*46. Out of Gas and Still Driving

The 460 engine that I had in my truck had a major problem: It loved to suck the gasoline like it was water; and man did it go through the gas! We ran into a situation where we had no money for gasoline. Because of this, we had no gas in our tank. I was driving one day and the needle on the gas gauge was way below empty. I said to my wife, "Kathee, let's lay our hands on the dash of the truck and command it to keep running."

So we laid our hands on the truck dash together and commanded the truck to keep on running. We drove without gas for a number of days. Every moment along the way we were praying in tongues and speaking the Word of God over our situation. The truck kept running until God provided money for gasoline.

On another day, the gas gauge was reading empty again. In this situation, I had money in my pocket for gasoline. My wife asked me if we were going to stop and get some gasoline. I told Kathee that we could believe God without putting gas in the tank like last time. About a mile later, the truck died with us pulling over to the side of the road. There was no gas in the tank. It is so easy to move from faith to foolishness. It's like people believing God for money when they already have money in their savings account.

And he commanded the multitude to sit down on the grass, and took the five loaves, and the two fishes, and looking up to heaven, he blessed, and brake, and gave the loaves to his disciples, and the disciples to the multitude. And they did all eat, and were filled: and they took up of the fragments that remained twelve baskets full (Matthew 14:19-20).

*47. Empty Cupboards Overflowing

November 1978 was our first Thanksgiving together as a couple. Things did not look too cheerful around our apartment. We had eaten the last bit of food left in the house. We had been surviving on pancakes and spaghetti for the longest time. Plus, we had no gas in the truck again. We had met a couple who lived in the same apartment complex who were going to the same Bible school as we were, so we would catch a ride with them to school and back. When he went to school that day, we decided to sow our last five dollar bill into the offering. We would never tell anybody our needs because God was our source.

After we got home from school, we sat back and rested a little bit. I was to leave for work about two o'clock. Kathleen and I sat together on the couch and held hands to agree in prayer for food and money. We were sitting on a miracle because when we had arrived in Broken Arrow, the only piece of furniture that we had with us was Kathleen's pink canopy bed. The Lord opened up this small apartment in which the last tenants left behind all of their furniture except the bed!

As we were praying, there came a knock at our door. I opened the door, and there was our next-door neighbor, who was a heavy pot smoking hippie. He and his wife's apartment was directly across from ours. Sometimes I would look over at their apartment and it looked like a "cloud of glory" was coming out of their window because of all the dope they smoked. I had shared the gospel with them many times.

When he had come to my door, I asked him what he needed. He told us that he and his wife were going away for Thanksgiving and they did not want to leave food in the house. He wanted to know if we could use some food. Praise the Lord! God had answered our prayers by using our next-door neighbor hippies. I told him "Yes we could use it!"

I thought he would bring one or two bags over to our apartment. Instead, he brought us bag after bag, and box after box of food. He brought so much food that it literally filled all of our kitchen cabinets! It did not make any natural sense because much of the food was in cans and jars, items that would not go bad for months, or even years. However, we did not argue with them; we simply thanked them with grateful hearts.

After they had left, we decided that we should bless someone else even as we had been blessed. We knew a single mother in the apartment complex that was really struggling. So we took a good portion of it to her apartment. I remember her crying with gratefulness. Right as I was getting ready to leave for work, there was another knock on the door.

I opened the door and there was a brother in Christ I knew standing there. He reached out his hand gave me a handshake, shoving a roll of money into the palm of my hand as he did so. This had to be God because Kathee and I did not tell anyone of our needs. I now had the money I needed to put gas in my truck to go to work!

Give, and it shall be given unto you; good measure, pressed down, and shaken together, and running over, shall men give into your bosom. For with the same measure that ye mete withal it shall be measured to you again (Luke 6:38).

*48. Who's the Turkey?

Kathleen and I had been attending bible college in Broken Arrow, Oklahoma. It was to be our first Thanksgiving together. We had just given away our last five dollars as an act of faith. When we arrived back at our apartment, to our wonderful amazement, God sent people to bless us with groceries and money. I had to go to work that night but before I walked out the door of our apartment, Kathleen said to me, "Let's **pray** and believe God for a turkey." I'm sorry to say that arrogance and pride rose in my heart. I very ignorantly raked her over the coals. I told her that I was doing all that I could do to believe God and if she wanted a turkey (at that moment she had one for a husband) she would have to believe God for one all by herself. She looked me straight in the eyes saying, "Okay, I will."

As I stood there, she **prayed crying out to God. "Lord, will you please give me a ten-pound Butterball turkey for Thanksgiving?** And now Lord, I thank you for that ten-pound Butterball turkey. Amen." I laughed at her, turned my back to her, got into my truck and went to work.

I thought in my heart that God was not going to answer her prayers because I was the man of faith. At this time, I was working for the Broken Arrow school district as a janitor. At About eight o'clock at night, I took my break for my meal. Kathleen had made me a bagged lunch so I had to go out to the truck to get it.

As I went to the parking lot and walked towards my truck, I noticed that there was something sitting on the hood. It was a cold, frosty night with the wind blowing slightly. As I got closer, I could see that it was a grocery bag. I grabbed it off the hood to look inside. I opened the bag, and, to my utter amazement, it was a turkey —not just any turkey but a ten-pound Butterball turkey! God had heard my wife's **prayers** and had someone put a turkey on my truck at work.

There were two turkeys out in the cold that November night. Was Kathleen ever elated when both of her turkeys came home that night. We ate one of the turkeys and the other still lives with her. We discovered later that a good friend of ours had a newspaper delivery route and he had recently obtained so many new customers that his company had given him an extra turkey.

As he was driving down the road, not knowing what to do with this extra turkey, he saw my pickup truck sitting at this elementary school. It was quickened in his heart to give us the turkey. The only problem was that my truck was locked. It was such a cold night that he knew that the turkey would be okay on the hood.

Now unto him that is able to do exceeding abundantly above all that we ask or think, according to the power that worketh in us (Ephesians 3:20).

*49. Rape and Murder (1979)

He Was Going to Rape & Murder My Wife! (1979)

I was working for the Broken Arrow school district as a janitor while my wife and I attended a Bible school in Oklahoma. One night at about 7:00 p.m. while I was waxing and buffing the floors in a classroom, the **unction's** of the Lord came upon me mightily. It was a divine urgency that overwhelmed my heart and my soul. Immediately I stopped what I was doing. I began to **pray fervently** in the spirit and in English. I asked the Lord what was going on. He spoke to me in an almost audible voice saying, there is a man at your house right now who is there to rape and murder your wife!

For the last couple months there had been a lot of rapes and murders going on in the Tulsa and Broken Arrow, Oklahoma area. There was literally a man hunt trying to find this man before he committed another atrocious crime. But up to this time they had been completely unsuccessful in finding him.

When I heard the voice of the Lord say this to me it shook me to the very core of my being. I did not have a phone to call her to see if she was okay. In those days, there is no such thing as cell phones. And we did not have a phone in our apartment. I knew it would be too late by the time I got in my truck and drove home. I did the only thing I could I began to cry out to God in prayer for her deliverance and safety.

I took authority over the demonic powers that were operating in this man. I kept praying and interceding. If you would have walked into that classroom at that moment you would've seen a man completely consumed in **prayer** on his knees, and in deep intercession. This continued for quite a while until all of a sudden, the peace of God that passes all understanding came upon me. At that moment, I knew that I knew in my heart God had divinely intervened, and that she was okay. The peace that passes all understanding had come upon my mind and my heart.

I do not get off work until after midnight, so it was rather late when I walked through the door of our apartment. When I came through the door the first thing I said to my wife was "Who came to the house tonight?" She looked at me a little surprised. She told me a man came by who said he was from children's services. I asked her what he wanted. He said they were doing a survey, and that he needed some questions to be answered. He began to ask her numerous questions about her life.

It turns out while that at that very moment he was asking my wife these personal questions, I was in deep intercessory prayer in the classroom where I was working. During that time, we had another couple staying with us temporarily in our apartment. The husband's wife, Pam, came out of the back room as the stranger was talking to my wife. Now Pam is just a very small petite woman that nobody in their right mind would be at all intimidated or concerned about. This man seemed to get extremely nervous and fearful at that moment. He said he needed to get some literature from his car, and that he would be right back. He quickly left through the door of our apartment. Thank God he never did come back. My wife said they saw him driving his car away.

The next day I called the children's services to investigate what had happened. I told them precisely what had happened. They adamantly declared that they never send anyone out after five o'clock. They also said that they did not have any man working for them who go to people's homes and ask questions.

God had supernaturally and divinely intervened by placing within me a holy unction to cry out to him. Now it might be assumed that this man simply left because there is another woman in the house. Personally, I do not believe this is the case. A man so possessed by devils could have easily intimidated both of the ladies, and taken advantage of them. Praise God for divine intervention and guidance.

The thief cometh not, but for to steal, and to kill, and to destroy: I am come that they might have life, and that they might have it more abundantly. I am the good shepherd: the good shepherd giveth his life for the sheep (John 10:10-11).

*50. Cockroach City

At this time, our apartment was overflowing with cockroaches. They were all over the place. We had inherited them like all the other previous tenants. This apartment complex was notorious for cockroaches. Fumigating an apartment did not seem to work because they would just run from one apartment to the other. All the renters were simply just chasing these cockroaches back and forth between each other's apartments.

We were simply rejoicing in the fact that we had a roof over our heads. Before the Lord had opened the door for this apartment, we had been staying in a tent with other people. However, if you can do something to change the circumstances—without murmuring and complaining—by all means, do it!

One day, faith was quickened in my heart to deal with these nasty little insects. So, I took my wife's hand and told her we needed two pray to the heavenly father about this situation, and then to agree in a prayer of faith to get rid of these ugly little bugs. She wholeheartedly agreed with me. Together in complete agreement and faith we prayed, and then we commanded these cockroaches to get out of our apartment.

We told them to get out of our clothes and our possessions, and to be gone once and forever. We further commanded that if they did not leave immediately, in the name of Jesus Christ of Nazareth, they would die. After we finished praying and commanding, we lifted our hands and started praising God for answered prayer.

When we went into the kitchen the next morning there was not a single cockroach to be found anywhere (except in the sink, where a cockroach was laying on its back—dead). From that time until the day we left, we never saw another cockroach in our apartment.

God said unto them, be fruitful, and multiply, and replenish the earth, and subdue it: and have dominion over the fish of the sea, and over the fowl of the air, and over every living thing that moveth upon the earth (Genesis 1:28).

*51. I Quit

HOW I ENDED UP WORKING FOR KENNETH HAGIN!

I had been working for the Broken Arrow school district for about six months in 1978. During that time, I had shared Christ with all the other janitors at the elementary school. The man who was over me was a very large and nasty fellow. He seemed to be antagonistic against the things of God. I did not preach at him, but I did share as the Lord allowed.

These people spent a lot of time in the coffee room talking and backbiting. I would only go there to eat my lunch, and then only when needed. Then I would be back to cleaning. We all had a schedule to keep when it came to maintenance work and waxing and buffing hallways and classrooms. I was way ahead of my schedule and doing extra things just to keep busy. The reason I did this, was because I was working as onto the Lord, not unto men. Christ had a servant's heart, and it was my greatest desire to be just like Jesus. Ever since I've been born again wherever I have worked, God has prospered me. He has supernaturally elevated me into positions much faster than those around me! Why would this be? It is because I'm doing it heartily to the Lord and not for men.

We can see this in the life of Joseph before God elevated him into the second-highest position in Egypt. Well this attitude seemed to extremely aggravate my boss. At times, he would follow me around trying to intimidate and mock me. To be honest, it did not really bother me. I had been through so many rough situations that this was simply like a little aggravating fly buzzing around my head. I did not even go home and complained to my wife about this situation. It was nothing compared to the times when people had tried to kill me for my faith.

One day I went to work as usual, not knowing this would be my last day of employment with the school district, because God was about to elevate me.

I was waxing and buffing a classroom floor (and at the same time praying quietly under my breath0 when this man came storming into the room. He asked me what in the #@!#@ that I think I was doing. I just looked at him and kept working. He became more aggravated, yelling and screaming like he had lost his mind. (He was quite demon oppressed.) I knew he was living a perverted and very twisted lifestyle, because he talked and bragged about it. I had not condemned him, but simply strove to live a holy life in front of him and the others.

He finally got in my face and tried to push me around. As I was standing there, I heard the Lord say, it's time to quit; you have done all that you can here. Now, in the natural I really needed this job for my wife and I to keep going to Bible school and to pay bills and food. However, the Spirit of the Lord said to me, your job is done here.

I have learned through the years that if God tells you to do something, then you better do it, because He is my boss. Whenever I have ignored the voice of God, the results have always been tragic. So right on the spot I turned off the floor buffer, looked at this man and said," I quit!"

He said, "What?"

I said, **"I quit!"**

He said to me, "You can't quit!"

I said, **"Oh, yes I can, and I just did!"**

I walked right past him out into the hallway of the school. He was yelling and screaming at me as I walked down the hallway. I simply ignored him and kept walking. What was I going to do now?

I went home and told Kathleen what I had done. She took the news with a gentle acknowledgment that God would provide. That's one wonderful thing about my lovely wife. She has been in very difficult situations with me, and yet she just keeps on loving. God will give you the desires of your heart, especially when those desires are led and directed by his Spirit. I prayed asking the Lord if I could have a job working at the Bible school (Rhema) we were attending. It would be the perfect place to work because I wanted to be around Godly people and get more connected to the ministry.

Several days later as Kathee and I sat in class, there was an announcement over the loudspeaker the school was hiring people to work with their maintenance crew. My heart leapt for joy. Immediately after that class was out, I went to the main office and filled out an application. The next day, I went back to the office and they informed me that I had been hired. They wanted me to start that very day. Working for the Broken Arrow school district had prepared me for this job. If I had not quit when the Spirit of the Lord had quickened me, I would have missed this opportunity.

I worked right alongside of Dad Hagins older brother Dub who before he was born again used to drive the getaway car for gangsters. I also helped Dad Hagin move into a new house that someone had donated to him.

And Samuel said, Hath the LORD as great delight in burnt

offerings and sacrifices, as in obeying the voice of the LORD?
Behold, to obey is better than sacrifice, and to hearken than the
fat of rams (1 Samuel 15:22).

52. Blood on My Hands

Kathleen and I went back to Wisconsin for Christmas. While I
was there, the Spirit of God spoke to me very strongly to go
witness to a local neighbor boy named Billy, who was three years
younger than me. I was not in the least afraid to go speak to him,
but I was extremely busy and preoccupied. Now the Spirit of God
kept dealing with me strongly. I am so sorry to say that I did not
obey. My wife and I Left Wisconsin soon after and we went back
to Oklahoma.

I was speaking to my mother a couple of weeks later on the
phone and she asked me if I had heard about what happened to
Billy. The hair on the back of my neck stood up as she started to
tell me about it. There was a certain local pond, and entrance to it
was in a valley between two hills. There was an extremely sharp
and dangerous corner right there at the bottom of the hill. My mom
said Billy had been out drinking on New Year's Eve and was
coming home from a bar. It looked as if he was coming around the
corner a little too fast.

At the same time, there was another man who had been drinking
coming from the other direction. It was a head-on collision and
they were both killed instantly! Conviction overwhelmed me, not
just because I did not speak to Billy, but because the blood of two
men's lives were on my hands. Who knows, if I would've obeyed
God, Billy might have been touched by the Lord and given his
heart to Jesus. If he would not have been out drinking that night, it
may have prevented the terrible accident from happening.

Sometimes we do not realize the responsibilities that God has
placed within our hands, and how disobedience brings about so

much pain and sorrow!

My people are destroyed for lack of knowledge: because thou hast rejected knowledge, I will also reject thee, that thou shalt be no priest to me: seeing thou hast forgotten the law of thy God, I will also forget thy children (Hosea 4:6).

53. Learning to Be Quiet

I had led my whole family to the Lord but my mom. I had witnessed to her many times. She had seen the wonderful transformation of my life, and I had prayed for her once and her hip had been healed. Not meaning to, I began to harp on her. Then one day the Spirit of God arrested me and dealt with my heart to just love her and stop preaching to her.

We were able to spend a couple days with my mom in the summer of 1978, when we took a trip through Wisconsin as we were headed to Pennsylvania. She was doing laundry in the basement of her house where the washing machine and dryer were. I went downstairs to help her. As we were doing the laundry together, she started weeping out of nowhere. She was really broken up. I asked her what was wrong. She told me she could not be saved and she was going to hell.

I said, "Mom what are you saying?"

She replied, "Your father was married previously. He was in the military and had only been married three months when his wife ran off with another man. He met me a number of years later when I was only seventeen years old. He proposed to me. I married him and had you children. Your father was Catholic and I was Lutheran. He wanted me to become a Catholic, so I went to see the priest. He began to ask questions. When he discovered I was not your dad's first wife, he said because my husband had been married previously, that I was living in adultery with him. He said that even though his first wife ran off with another man, their marriage was not dissolved, therefore all of our children were bastards. The priest told me that I am going to hell."

All of this time I thought that her heart was hardened to the gospel, but rather her heart was broken because she did not believe that salvation was available to her. Because she was ignorant of the Scriptures, the devil had her by the throat. I shared with her what Jesus said about this situation, and talked about the truth of God's amazing love. She immediately and wholeheartedly gave her heart to Jesus Christ. I held her in my arms as she wept with joy. It was a wonderful conversion.

For whosoever shall call upon the name of the Lord shall be saved. (Romans 10:13).

CHAPTER SEVEN

Miracles in the Harvest Field

*54. Walking through the Fire

Red Hot Skillet (1980)

We ended up pastoring a little church in Three Springs, Pennsylvania. The parsonage that we lived in was very old and dilapidated. There was a large porch deck over a garage area. One day my wife was walking on this deck when she broke through the flooring. Praise God, she didn't get hurt. But, we understood that the church did not have much money. Also, the amount of fuel oil that we went through to keep the place warm was ridiculous. So, I decided to put a wood stove in the parsonage to help with the heating costs. I put it in the half-basement of the house since the floor of the basement was nothing but rocks and dirt.

The wood-burning stove was a long, deep, cast-iron outfit. Using an existing chimney in the basement, I connected the wood stove to this chimney. It was a very old system, however, with very little draft. That made it extremely hard to get it started with a good fire going. In the process of trying to maintain the fire, I would consistently somehow place my hands against the stove. I do not know how many blisters I got from that wood stove. It seemed as if I could not help but burn my hands! You would have thought that I would have begun to believe God for wisdom not to burn my hands but that's not what I did. Instead, I began to confess verses about the fire not being able to burn me.

Isaiah 43:2 When thou passes through the waters, I will be with thee; and through the rivers, they shall not overflow thee: when thou walks' through the fire, thou shalt not be burned; neither shall the flame kindle upon thee.

This went on for many weeks and sure enough, without fail, I would touch the stove by accident. But I was getting burned less and less. My hand or fingers would simply turn red. One day, I again touch the stove when it was literally glowing red. That's how hot the stove was. Instantly, my hand hurt. I put my other hand over the burnt part of my hand and commanded the pain to cease. I confessed that I would have no blister. From that point for I would be thanking and praising God that my hand was healed. Sure enough, the pain left, and my hand was only slightly pink.

I was cooking breakfast one morning, having just put oil in a cast-iron skillet. I was making eggs, bacon, and hash browns. As I was busy making breakfast, there was a knock on the door. When I opened the door, one of my parishioners named Paul was there. Paul and I were very good friends and would spend hours together praying and witnessing. He probably was fifteen years my senior. I invited him into the house and we began to talk about the things of God. I had completely forgotten about the cast-iron skillet on the stove.

The next thing that I knew, my wife was screaming. I went into the kitchen and saw that the oil in the skillet had exploded into fire, with flames reaching as high as the old kitchen cupboards. I knew if I did not move fast the whole house would go up in flames. The house was a firetrap waiting to happen. I was not thinking. I yelled for Paul to open the outside door as I was running for the stove and the skillet. I scooped the red-hot skillet up into my hands, spun around, and carried it out the door. Paul was standing out of the way and my wife was watching everything as it happened. I ran outside and flipped the pan upside down on the ground.

After a while the flames went out. I was standing and looking down at the cast-iron skillet when I suddenly realized what

I had done. I was in such a hurry that I did not even grab a towel or any kind of heat pads before I scooped up the frying pan. I had literally picked it up with my bare hands. I looked down at my hands in complete amazement. They should have been severely burned all the way to the bones. All that happened was that they became a little red. Not only that, but why didn't the flames of the burning oil not burn me? In just a brief period, all the pain and the redness in my hands were gone. If my wife and Paul had not seen me do it, I would truly doubt it myself. But God and his word is amazing!

Who through faith subdued kingdoms, wrought righteousness, obtained promises, stopped the mouths of lions, Quenched the violence of Þ re, escaped the edge of the sword, out of weakness were made strong, waxed valiant in fight, turned to fight the armies of the aliens (Hebrews 11:33-34).

*55. Success in the Projects

Kathee and I had a burden for souls. We prayed about what to do and where to go. To reach sinners, we knew we had to go where they were. There was a rather large town fifteen miles away. I knew we would have to believe for a bus, but so be it. We began to go door-to-door to the people in the low income housing projects in this town. They were basically African-American people. There were already two other churches running their buses through this area. We would simply go to each door, and knock on it. When a person opened the door, we introduced ourselves and say that if they had any needs, we would love **to pray** for them. We began to see wonderful results immediately. A miniature revival erupted in that community. People were getting saved and healed everywhere! They were also getting filled with the Holy Ghost.

One day I was out with another brother instead of my wife. As we were working our way down the street, I saw an African-American lady about five apartments ahead of us. She was hanging laundry out to dry on a clothesline behind her apartment. At that moment, she looked up and saw us. Our eyes made contact for a brief second, and she dropped her clothes and ran into her house. I knew something strange was happening. We continue going door to door.

We finally got to her door, which was just a screen door. I knocked on her door and a woman's voice yelled from upstairs. She said to come on in. I did not want to just step into her house, being a total stranger, so I yelled through the screen door and asked her if she knew who we were. She yelled back down at us, "Yes your men of God." We stepped into her house not knowing what to expect. She appeared at the top of the stairs with wet hair and completely different clothes on.

The next thing we knew she came down the stairs to the bottom step. The minute she got to the bottom of the stairs, she fell to her knees weeping and crying. She asked us to lead her to Jesus Christ. I led her into the sinner's **prayer** and then I perceived she was ready for the Holy Ghost. So, I **prayed** right then and there for her to be filled with the Holy Ghost. She began to speak in a brand-new heavenly language. We were awestruck by how God was moving. She later informed us what had happened. She said that when she saw us, she knew in her heart that she was not right with the Lord. She was convicted that she was filthy and lost. She felt so dirty that she said she had to go in and take a quick shower and put on some clean clothes. God was working so strongly in her that by the time we got to her house, she was ready to be saved and filled with the Holy Ghost.

Then he called for a light, and sprang in, and came trembling, and fell down before Paul and Silas, and brought them out, and said, Sirs, what must I do to be saved? And they said, Believe on the Lord Jesus Christ, and thou shalt be saved, and thy house (Acts 16:29-31).

*56. Victory over Tumors (1981)

I woke up one morning with tremendous pain in my lower abdomen. As I lifted my shirt, and looked down to where the pain was, I noticed there was a lump on my abdomen - about the size of an acorn. I laid my hands on it immediately and commanded it to go.

I said: "You are lying devil! By the stripes of **Jesus,** I am healed and made whole." After I'd spoken to the lump, the pain became excruciating, overwhelmingly worse. That whole day, I walked the floor, crying out to God. I praised Him and thanked Him that His Word is real and true. I went for a walk, on the mountain right behind the parsonage. It was a long day - before I got to sleep that night. When I awoke the next morning, the pain was even more severe! It felt like somebody was stabbing me in my gut with a knife. I lifted my shirt and looked … there was another lump.

So, now I had two lumps in my lower abdomen! I laid my hands on them and commanded them to go. Tears were rolling down my face, as I spoke the Word. I lifted my hands toward heaven and kept praising God that I was healed. Even though I did not see any change, I kept on praising God! All the symptoms were telling me that God's Word is a lie, and that I was not healed by the stripes of **Jesus**. But I knew that I was healed! It was another long day, and it seemed as if I would never get to sleep that night. The pain was continual and non-stop.

When I got up the next morning the pain had intensified - even more! Once again, I looked at my abdomen … and to my shock there was yet another lump! Now I had three of these nasty lumps! Each one was about the size of an acorn. I did not think that the pain could get any worse - but it did. Yet again, I laid my hands on these tumors and commanded them to go in the name of **Jesus**

Christ of Nazareth.

I declared that by the stripes of **Jesus** I am healed! All that day and night, it felt like there was a knife sticking in my gut. I lifted my hands, and with tears rolling down my face (again!) I kept on praising God that I was healed! By faith, I began to dance before the Lord. It was a victory dance! I continually praised God that I was healed by the stripes of **Jesus**.

I went to bed that night hurting worse than ever. All night long I tossed and turned, moaned, and groaned; yet all the time I persisted in thanking God that I was not going to die, but that I was healed! I got up the next morning and all the pain had gone. I checked my abdomen …all the tumors were gone! Furthermore, they have never come back!!

And he said, Let me go, for the day breaketh. And he said, I will not let thee go, except thou bless me. And he said unto him, What is thy name? And he said, Jacob. And he said, Thy name shall be called no more Jacob, but Israel: for as a prince hast thou power with God and with men, and hast prevailed (Genesis 32:26-28).

57. Singing in Arabic

During worship one Sunday morning in 1981, Kathleen began to praise God in tongues. It was a very beautiful language. I love to listen to my wife speak and worship God in tongues because she operates in the gift of diversity of tongues.

On that particular morning, we had a first-time visitor that we had never seen before. He looked as if he was from the Middle East. At the end of the service he came over to me with a look of amazement on his face. He asked me where my wife had learned to speak in such perfect Arabic. I informed him that she did not know how to speak in Arabic. He informed me that she had been singing in perfect Arabic. I asked him what she had said. He told me that she was giving praise and glory to God in the Arabic language.

And how hear we every man in our own tongue, wherein we were born? Parthians, and Medes, and Elamites, and the dwellers in Mesopotamia, and in Judaea, and Cappadocia, in Pontus, and

Asia, Phrygia, and Pamphylia, in Egypt, and in the parts of Libya about Cyrene, and strangers of Rome, Jews and proselytes, Cretes and Arabians, we do hear them speak in our tongues the wonderful works of God (Acts 2:8-11).

*58. When I Was Brought Back to Life (1980)

I woke up one morning extremely sick. My whole body ached from my head to my toes, even to the ends of my fingers. It felt as if I had been pulled through a knothole. I cried out to God and came against this satanic sickness. However, I grew worse, and worse all-day long. I had an extremely high fever with sweat just pouring off my body.

Kathee would pray for me throughout the day. I knew I had to shake this thing, whatever it was. So, I went outside and began to climb the mountain behind our house. Every thirty feet or so I would get so dizzy that I had to stop and put my hands on my knees with my head bowed to the ground. When this happened, I would pray hard. Dizziness and fatigue kept hitting me like the waves of the ocean. After a while I would begin to climb the mountain side again, and it wasn't long before I'd have to stop and bend over again. It felt like I would pass out any second, but I kept on declaring that I would live, and not die.

I think this is where many people make a major mistake: their faith is a passive faith; but biblical, God-given faith is not passive, but it is aggressive and violent. I finally made it up to the top of this small mountain. I remembered where there was a log lying on the ground, so I sat down next to it, and fell unto my back. I just laid there and prayed. When I say I prayed, I mean I kept praising God, thanking God that by the stripes of Jesus Christ I was healed.

Eventually, I pushed myself back up, and began to go back down the mountain. When I finally saw the parsonage, I was filled with great relief. I went into the house, feeling worse than ever. I asked Kathee to pray with me. She stayed and prayed at my side. I was burning up with a fever and I needed to get my clothes off. I went to our little bathroom and stripped down to nothing. I was going through terrible flashes. I lay on the linoleum floor hoping to absorb some of its coolness.

Then something frightening happened. I began to sense in a real way that I was going to die. It wasn't exactly fear; it was just something I knew. I cried out to Kathee to come to me. She came into the bathroom and sat down on the floor, putting my head on her lap, praying fervently for me. I could feel my life slowly ebbing out. The next thing I knew my spirit and soul were leaving my body. I was above my wife, looking down upon my body, with my head in her lap. She was crying out to God for me. For a while I simply hovered over the top of myself and my wife. There was no pain or sickness racking me anymore. There was just a total complete peace.

My wife must have noticed that I had died, and she began to command me to **LIVE in Jesus Name**! Suddenly, as she was commanding, I felt myself being pulled back rapidly into my body. It was like somebody had turned on a vacuum cleaner and sucked me back into my body. I came to my senses with my head in her lap. It felt like a cold wind was now blowing over my whole body me. I was totally, completely, and instantly healed! The fever and sickness was completely gone. If you ask my opinion of what happened on that day, I literally believe that I died, but my wife's prayers, and her taking authority in Jesus Name brought me back.

And as ye go, preach, saying, The kingdom of heaven is at hand. Heal the sick, cleanse the lepers, raise the dead, cast out devils: freely ye have received, freely give (Matthew 10:7-8).

*59. The Huntington County Fair

Revival at the Huntington County Fair 1981

My vacation time was coming up as a pastor and I had two weeks in the summer time. The Spirit of God had spoken to my heart Prophetically as I was in **prayer** to put a tent up at the Huntington County Fair. I began to investigate where I could get a tent. I was informed that another Christian group had a campground in Roxbury, Pennsylvania, and they would rent you a tent for a very good price. I was able to reach them and gave them the dates I wanted to rent their tent. I made arrangements to pick the rental tent up. The tent I was going to rent would seat two hundred people.

Next I contacted people in Huntington to find out who the coordinator of the Huntington Fair was. When I finally got his number, I called him up. He informed me all of the spaces were filled in advance for two years ahead of time. I was not worried because it wasn't my responsibility to make it happen. If I had truly heard from God, then all I had to do was my part, God would do the rest. I did not tell this person that they had to give me a place because God told me. I simply asked him to speak to the personnel who made these decisions. When he came back, he said they had an empty space they always kept open for people who wanted to have picnics. It was right next to the fire department's bingo stand. They said if we wanted to put up a gospel tent we could use that particular area. Praise God for His favor! God did awesome things under that tent.

The Lord's hand was on these tent meetings in the Huntington Fair. People came to me, wanting to be involved. God lined up some tremendous Holy Ghost preachers and singers. About 1/6 of the tent was used for a prayer area. I used tent curtains and strung them across behind a platform where we and others could **Pray** before, during, and after the services in privacy.

Our plans were to conduct services in the afternoon and evening. It would be just a week long. People began to gather in the mornings to pray, including a good minister friend of mine. He moved in gifts of the Holy Ghost in a wonderful way. As we were in **prayer,** the Lord quickened to my heart that the Holy Ghost was about to show Himself in unusual ways—that people would even begin to fall under the power of the Spirit as they were walking past the tent. I informed the volunteer workers who were with us to get ready for this to happen.

As I was ministering in the afternoon session one day, the presence of God began to manifest Himself in a precious way. I looked out and saw an older lady crumpled to the ground about thirty feet in front of us. I pointed her out to the workers in the tent. They ran out and brought her in. There was nothing physically wrong with her as far as we could tell. She did not understand what was happening to her, but the Spirit of God was convicting her heart to such an extent that she gave her life to Jesus on the spot and was wonderfully saved.

That was the beginning of a wonderful move of God in Huntington. This tent meeting later helped give birth to a church of now over three hundred people.

And said, Cornelius, thy prayer is heard, and thine alms are had in remembrance in the sight of God. Send therefore to Joppa, and call hither Simon, whose surname is Peter; he is lodged in the house of one Simon a tanner by the sea side: who, when he cometh, shall speak unto thee (Acts 10:31-32).

60. Falling under the Glory

The Lord's hand was on these tent meetings in the Huntington Fair. People came to me, wanting to be involved. God lined up some tremendous Holy Ghost preachers and singers. About 1/6 of the tent was used for a prayer area. I used tent curtains and strung them across behind a platform where people could pray before, during, and after the services in privacy.

Our plans were to conduct services in the afternoon and evening. It would be just a week long. People began to gather in the mornings to pray, including a good minister friend of mine. He moved in gifts of the Holy Ghost in a wonderful way. As we were in prayer, the Lord quickened to my heart that the Holy Ghost was about to show Himself in unusual ways—that people would even begin to fall under the power of the Spirit as they were walking past the tent. I informed the volunteer workers who were with us to get ready for this to happen.

As I was ministering in the afternoon session one day, the presence of God began to manifest Himself in a precious way. I looked out and saw an older lady crumpled to the ground about thirty feet in front of us. I pointed her out to the workers in the tent. They ran out and brought her in. There was nothing physically wrong with her as far as we could tell.

She did not understand what was happening to her, but the Spirit of God was convicting her heart to such an extent that she gave her life to Jesus on the spot and was wonderfully saved.

That was the beginning of a wonderful move of God in Huntington. This tent meeting later helped give birth to a church of now over three hundred people.

Then a cloud covered the tent of the congregation, and the glory of the LORD filled the tabernacle (Exodus 40:34)

CHAPTER EIGHT

Signs, Wonders, and Miracles

*61. Unbelieving Man Healed (1980)

One day as I was preaching in the tent, a man who looked to be in his mid-thirties was hobbling by really slow on a pair of crutches. He was not even looking in the direction of our tent, but was looking straight ahead, minding his own business. As I looked at him, the Spirit of God quickened the gift of faith inside of me.

When God quickens my heart in this way I do not even think what I'm about to do. I simply act upon the quickening and the witness in my heart. I found myself calling out to this particular man, speaking over the microphone system. Everybody could hear me within a hundred feet, if not further. Probably the whole Huntington Fair could hear us! (The fire department was really upset with us because we were disturbing their bingo games.) I called out to this man, but he ignored me. Once again, I challenged him to come into the tent so God could heal him. This time he looked my way but kept hobbling along. I called out the third time, encouraging him to come and be healed of his problem.

After the third time, he finally came into the tent. When he came to the front, I asked him if he had faith to believe that God would heal him. He looked at me as if I had lost my mind. He was probably thinking : *You're the one who called me up here. I don't even know what this is about. Everybody was staring at me, so I had to come!*

He did not respond to my question. I told him that I was going to pray for him now and God would heal him! I asked him again if he believed this. Once again, he did not respond. Then I laid my hands on him and commanded his leg to be healed in the Name of Jesus Christ of Nazareth.

After I was done praying, I told him to put down his crutches and start walking without them. He stood there staring at me. Everybody else was also staring at me. This was okay because the gift of faith was at work in my heart. I reached forward and took away his crutches. I threw them on the ground and spun him around. When I'm in this realm I'm not thinking, I'm simply acting. Then I pushed him, and he stumbled forward and began to walk toward the back of the tent. He was picking his legs high up in the air, high stepping it. When he got to the edge of the tent he spun back toward me. Tears were streaming from his eyes and down his cheeks. He came back toward me walking perfectly normal with no limp whatsoever!

I gave him the microphone, and asked him to tell us what did God do for him. He kept saying, "You don't understand" over and over. Once again, I encouraged him to tell us his story. I had him face the people in that tent and those outside of the tent who had been watching. He told us that last winter he had been walking on a very icy sidewalk and he lost his footing. Slipping and sliding, he fell forward onto the concrete and ice. He fell so hard on his kneecap that he had done something terrible to it. He could not move his knee whatsoever, and it was extremely painful. He went to the doctor's office and they x-rayed it. The x-rays revealed that his kneecap had literally been shattered and destroyed. In just two more days he was scheduled to have a major operation to replace his kneecap.

I encouraged him to go back to his doctor and get it x-rayed again, and to come back and tells us the doctors report. Sure enough, a couple days later he came back to the tent giving a wonderful testimony. He had gone to his doctor. He said when he walked into the doctor's office they could tell that his knee was normal. The doctor asked him what had happened. He told them about the encounter he had with Jesus at our tent meeting. They x-rayed his kneecap and discovered he had a brand-new kneecap!

Jesus Christ the same yesterday, and today, and forever (Hebrews 13:8).

*62. Conversion of an Atheist

During this week-long tent revival, there had been a tall, distinguished-looking older gentleman standing behind an oak tree. He would just stand there and watch what was going on. One afternoon after I had finished ministering I walked over toward him. As I began to approach him, he turned and began to walk away. I called out to him. Something inside of me would not let him go.

I introduced myself and he informed me that his name was George, and that he was the treasurer for the Huntington Fair. I tried to share Jesus with him, but he shut me down immediately, informing me that he was an absolute atheist. He said he did not believe in all of this "hoopla." I tried to share with him, but he was too intelligent in his own mind to listen to me. I became very quiet and asked the Lord what to do. Only one thing came to me. I said "George, will you do me just one little favor?"

He asked, **"What's that?"**

I said, "I want you to get alone, all by yourself, and **pray a simple little prayer.**

He said," **No, I'm not going to do that."**

I asked, **"Why not?** If God does not exist, it will not hurt a thing. All I want you to do is to pray this simple **little prayer.** Here it is. 'Jesus, if you are real, and you are the Son of God, please make yourself real to me.'"

He told me very forcefully that he would not **pray that prayer.**

Then I knew in my heart the Lord had him. I could see conviction all over him as he was standing there. I started laughing.

I said "George, what are you afraid of? It is a very simple **prayer**. Just ask Jesus to reveal himself to you if He is real."

Once again, he very boldly declared that he would not do it. I wrote down my telephone number and told him to give me a call when he had done it. As I walked away he was yelling at me "I am not going to do it."

Approximately two weeks after the Huntington Fair was over, our phone in the parsonage rang. I picked up the phone, and the first thing I heard was, "I'm not going to do it!"

I started laughing right at once. I knew the hook was set. Once again, I encouraged George to simply **pray that prayer** with sincerity.

Kathee sent George a letter explaining that she had accepted the Lord when she was eight years old, and yes, Christians did have a happy successful life, if they fully trusted in the Lord. She also encouraged George to **pray**.

In August, my wife and I left that little church and headed for Germany. When I got back from Germany, I walked into the church that had been birthed through the tent revival meetings. A very tall older gentleman came walking up to me and gave me a big hug. It was George! He had been gloriously saved and filled with the Holy Ghost, speaking in tongues. He became an elder in that church. My wife and I at times stayed in his beautiful log cabin house.

And when we were all fallen to the earth, I heard a voice speaking unto me, and saying in the Hebrew tongue, Saul, Saul, why persecutest thou me? It is hard for thee to kick against the pricks. And I said, Who art thou, Lord? And he said, I am Jesus whom thou persecutest (Acts 26:14-15).

*63. Over the Cliff

Kathleen and I had gotten up one morning to go to Huntington, Pennsylvania. Our son, Michael, had just been born. As Kathleen was getting ready to go, I was spending time in prayer and the Word. During my quiet time, I heard the Spirit of the Lord speak to me saying that on this day the devil would try to kill us in a car accident.

(Whenever I share these experiences, I want you to know that it is not like I go around all the time saying, "God told me!" I have discovered through the years that people who are constantly saying, "God told me!" are the ones who are simply hearing their own minds speak and claiming it is God. When God speaks you will know it because what He says comes to pass!)

We got into our automobile. Kathleen was holding Michael in her arms. I told Kathleen what I had heard the Spirit of God say to me. We held hands, bound the devil and agreed that no harm would come to us or to our new baby. The only problem is that we did not bind the demonic powers from causing us to have a car accident or tell them that they could not hurt our car. It was a rainy, dismal day as we took Route 655 towards Huntington. We ended up on a back country road (one of my famous shortcuts) to go over the mountain. There is a very sharp corner on this particular road.

I was busy talking to Kathleen and driving just a little bit too fast for the wet roads when, all of a sudden, a large farmer's work truck came around this sharp curve. The truck was partly on our side of the road and there was not much of a shoulder to move over onto on this narrow, mountain road. I swerved to miss him, barely getting around him. He had almost hit us. It seemed like we were going to be okay, but just then I hit a bad dip in the road and lost complete control of the car, skidding down the road side ways. We were approaching another sharp curve where there was a small cliff to the right on my wife's side. There were no guard rails there to protect vehicles from going over the side. There definitely should have been guard rails at that turn!

At that moment, we both entered that realm where time slows up. I vividly remember us going over that cliff sideways. The car began to roll down the cliff and I could see Michael flying through the air right above Kathleen's head. There is no way in the natural that he could have been rescued from slamming into the windshield or from bouncing around on the inside of the car like a ping-pong ball. I watched in slow motion as Kathleen reached up, put her left hand under his neck and grabbed his body with her right hand. She snatched Michael right out of the air as we were rolling down the cliff. It was supernatural!

We rolled down the cliff and ended up in a small stream. There were large rocks and boulders all around us. The car was sitting on its right side —the passenger side. Rocks pushed up against the windows. I had unbuckled myself from the seat belt and pushed my door up and away from me with all of my might to get us out of the car. After I got out, I reached in and took Michael and then helped Kathleen out of the vehicle. Amazingly, not one window of the car was broken or cracked. None of us had any wounds except for Kathleen, who had a scratch on her leg.

And the Lord shall deliver me from every evil work, and will preserve me unto his heavenly kingdom: to whom be glory for ever and ever. Amen (2 Timothy 4:18).

64. I Slapped a Woman

One day a woman came into our church who I had never seen before. When I finished ministering the Word, I gave an altar call for anybody who needed healing. This lady came up front. I began to minister and pray for people. When I came to her, I perceived that she had something wrong with her jaw. I was so deep in the Spirit that before I knew what I was doing, I slapped her face very hard with my right hand. The power of God hit her and she fell out under the power of the Spirit. I continued to work my way down the prayer line. Many times, it is not until after I finish ministering that I think back to what just happened and what I did. Now I realized with trembling that I had hit this visiting woman very hard in the face.

As I looked back over the prayer line I noticed she was standing up. I could see that tears were rolling down her face. The right side of her face was towards me, so I could not see if there were any marks on the left side of her face where I had slapped her. I was quite concerned about what I had done. For a while I tried to avoid her, but finally I took a deep breath and walked over to where she was standing.

When I came in front of her, I looked at her face intently. To my amazement there was not one finger mark upon her cheek. As hard as I had hit her with my hand, my finger prints should have been outlined on her cheek. She was still standing there crying. I very gently asked her what happened. She told me that she had an illness in her face and jaw, but now she was completely healed. I asked her out of curiosity if it hurt when I slapped her.

She replied in almost an offended way, "You slapped me?"

Embarrassed, I rephrased my question. "When I touched your face what happened?"

She said it was like a feather brushing her cheek. She went on her way completely healed.

And Jesus went forth, and saw a great multitude, and was moved with compassion toward them, and he healed their sick (Matthew 14:14).

CHAPTER NINE

Moving in the Miraculous

*65. Cancer Patient Raised from the Bed of Death
(1980)

One morning I received a phone call from my good friend, Paul. He told me that he knew of a man who owned a logging company and lumber yard who was about to die. They were waiting for him to expire any day because his body was filled with cancer. Most of it was concentrated in his chest and it had spread throughout the rest of his body. He was in the McConnellsburg hospital. Paul asked me if I would be willing to go pray for him. I asked him to give me one day to fast and pray for this situation. I spent the rest of that day in prayer, fasting, and in the Word.

The next morning Paul came to pick me up. We drove up to the McConnellsburg hospital, praying as we went. We walked into the foyer and up to the information desk. The nurse gave us the necessary information we needed. Paul said he would wait for me and that he would continue in prayer in the hospital's chapel. I found the room where they had put this gentleman, knocked on the door, and entered.

They had placed him in a very small room—just big enough to be a closet—that was off the beaten path, like they were just waiting for him to die. He was lying on a hospital bed and was nothing but skin and bones; he looked as if he had just come out of a concentration camp. His skin and the whites of his eyes were yellow. He was a rather tall man who looked to be in his late sixties. He was lying on his bed wide awake. I had no idea what his mental condition was. I began to speak to him and discovered he was totally aware of his surroundings, and actually, I was amazed at how clear and quick his mind was.

I began to speak to him by introducing myself. He almost seemed to take an antagonistic attitude towards me right away. I began to share Jesus with him, but as I was speaking to him, a smirk appeared on his face. He began to tell me stories of the things he had seen in church— supernatural things. He said one time he was in a wild church service where everybody was jumping and shouting. It was quite a number of years ago, and they did not yet have electricity in this church.

He said as he was watching people dance and shout, one of them jumped so high that he hit a lighted kerosene lantern, causing it to fall off of the hook. It came crashing down onto the floor and should have immediately broken into pieces and caught the building on fire. Instead, he said it almost acted like a ball. It never broke or went out but landed straight up. The people just kept on dancing and singing to the Lord.

After he told me this story he looked me right in the eyes and said to me, "If I did not get saved back then, what makes you think you are going to get me saved now?" I did not answer him. My heart was filled with deep sorrow and overwhelming love for him. I knew I could not help him, and if was going to get saved and be healed it was going to take God moving upon him supernaturally.

I stepped away from his deathbed, and I bowed my head and cried out to God. "Lord, touch this man, help me to reach him because I cannot do it within myself. Lord, you're going to have to touch his heart or he will lose his soul and end up in hell." As I was praying under my breath I sensed the awesome presence of God come flooding into that little hospital room.

Then the Spirit of the Lord rose up within me, and I walked back over to his bed. I began to speak to Elvin once again, but it was under a divine unction of great compassion. I know I did not say very much, but as I was speaking, all of a sudden out of the blue, he began to weep uncontrollably. In just a matter of seconds his heart was completely open to the gospel. He gave his heart to Jesus Christ right then and there. Then I laid my hands on him and commanded his body to be healed. I rebuked the spirit of death, and cancer in the name of Jesus Christ, commanding it to go.

When I was done praying, it seemed to me there was some immediate improvement in his countenance and body. I told him as I got ready to leave that I would visit him again in the hospital. After I left something wonderful happened, but I did not hear the story until later that day when I arrived home from the hospital. Immediately Elvin felt healed in his body. His appetite came back, and the yellow jaundice disappeared completely from his skin and from the white of his eyes.

The hospital personnel were amazed at this transformation. They took some new x-rays and discovered that the cancer he had in his body was almost totally gone. The cancer that was in his lungs which had been the size of a baseball was now the size of a cashew nut. In three days' time they released him from the hospital and sent him home. He was working at his sawmill with his son and grandsons within a week!

Jesus saith unto him, Rise, take up thy bed, and walk. And immediately the man was made whole, and took up his bed, and walked: and on the same day was the sabbath (John 5:8-9).

*66. The Name of Jesus

Power of God Came at the Name of Jesus (1980)

The Spirit of the Lord woke me up early one morning with a tremendous unction to pray. I went out into our little front room and began to pray in English and the Spirit. Before I knew it, I was lost in the Holy Ghost. When I finally quit praying, it seemed as if I had prayed for very brief time. I looked at my watch and to my amazement, **seven to eight hours** had come and gone. During that whole time my wife never bothered me, she is wonderful in that way. When I am trying to press my way into the things of the Spirit, she simply leaves me alone.

The next morning the Lord woke me early again in prayer. I travailed and interceded in the Spirit and English. I was praying like a house on fire with deep groaning's and urgencies in the Holy Ghost. When this burden partly lifted, it seemed as if I had prayed for only one or two hours. When I looked at my watch, another eight hours had come and gone! This continued for **seven or eight days where the Spirit of God rolled me out of bed with a deep unction to pray! Every time that I prayed it would only seem like an hour, and yet it was seven to eight hours had come and gone!** (I did not write down every day that this happened because I wasn't expecting it to happen.)

Right after this time of **Spirit-motivated intercession** we had a wonderful move of God. The local ministerial that I was a part of was conducting a week-long community revival in the little town's pavilion. They wanted ministers to volunteer to speak. I agreed to do one of the services. My wife, Kathleen, would lead the worship for this service and I would preach the message. A lot of the local community came to these meetings. I was there every night to support the other pastors. I think our night was the last service. Kathleen and I had both had been praying and fasting believing for God to do a mighty work. The host of the meeting opened with prayer and gave some announcements.

He introduced my wife and me as the pastors of the Three Springs Assembly of God. My wife did a wonderful job in leading worship. Then it was my turn. As I stood up to the pulpit, I sensed a great unction of the Holy Ghost to preach. I remember what I preached about The Name of Jesus. I'm not exaggerating when I tell you what happened. **The Spirit of God arrested everybody in that meeting**. It was like they were glued to their chairs. Their mouths were hanging open. The pastors looked like they were in shock. Then I gave an opportunity for people to be prayed for. The front of the pavilion filled with people wanting prayer.

After the service, the ministers came to me almost timidly. I was the youngest pastor among them. I was twenty-six years old at this time. Some of the older ministers seemed to be almost distraught. One of them said to me, **"No one ever taught me to preach like that!"** I told him it was the **Holy Ghost**. After that particular service people from the community began to flock to our church. People were getting filled with the Holy Ghost everywhere.

And with many other words did he testify and exhort, saying, Save yourselves from this untoward generation. Then they that gladly received his word were baptized: and the same day there were added unto them about three thousand souls (Acts 2:40-41).

*67. The Faith of Abraham

Bill and Pam attended our church. They had been married for over eight years and desperately wanted children. Both had gone through extensive medical testing to find out what was preventing them from getting pregnant. They discovered it was not just one but both that had situations in their bodies which would prevent them from ever having children.

Their hearts were broken because they loved children so much. They were in one of our church services when God started giving me prophetic words for people. I called them forward and told them I had seen a vision of them and within one year they would have a child and they would also be involved in children's ministry. They both wept openly and gave praise to God for the word. They knew that it was impossible medically for them to ever have children, but they took a step of faith. It was just like Abraham, who against hope, believed in hope to become a father of many nations.

Immediately they set aside one of the bedrooms in their house and got to work painting, cleaning, and fixing it up to be a beautiful nursery. Then they began to buy clothes for their new child which they believed to be on its way. Everything and anything they could think of connecting to their promised child, they acted upon. It was just about two months later that my wife and I went to Germany. When we came back from Germany we ran into somebody who knew this couple. They told us that everything I had prophesied by the Spirit of God about this couple happened. They had a beautiful baby boy within that year and were both teaching in children's church!

And being not weak in faith, he considered not his own body now dead, when he was about an hundred years old, neither yet the deadness of Sara's womb: He staggered not at the promise of God through unbelief; but was strong in faith, giving glory to God; And being fully persuaded that, what he had promised, he was able also to perform (Romans 4:19-21).

68. The Victory That Comes By Faith

One of the members of the church gave me a book to read from a well-known evangelist. This particular book was on the subject of faith. I was very interested in reading it because I wanted to see what he had to say on this subject as this was an area in my life where God had placed upon me a great demand. Over and over in the last seven years I had to move in faith in order to be healed, delivered, protected, set free, and for our needs to be met. As I was reading this book my heart was filled with sorrow. Some personal tragedies had taken place in this man's life and in the lives of those he had loved.

He had not seen his prayers answered the way he thought they should be. Based upon these experiences, he had been teaching a doctrine of faith which did not line up with the Bible. In the process of embracing his own self-made doctrine, built upon his experiences, he was cutting himself off from all that God had made available for him. Not only was he cutting himself off from wonderful experiences, but he was leading all of those who followed him into the same misguided and wrong philosophy.

I'm sharing this with you not to be critical of anyone, but Scripture says that if any man thinks he stands, let him take heed lest he falls. I'm sharing this to help people come into the place where they can experience a continual flow of the Holy Ghost and the miraculous. As I continued to read that book, the Spirit of the Lord spoke to my heart and said, that if this man ever fell, (not that he would fall into sin) it would be to prostitutes.

It is actually frightening when God begins to tell you specific things, especially when it comes to judgment or repercussions of disobedience. I told my wife what the Spirit of the Lord Had spoken to my heart. I am sorry to say that a number of years later it was revealed that he had fallen to prostitutes. Now what in the world would this have to do with this book? We need to connect the dots. What is the victory that overcomes the world? Read Hebrews chapter 11. Look at all of these great woman and men of God. How did they overcome? By faith! But faith in what, or whom? (Lord willing that's another book.)

For whatsoever is born of God overcometh the world: and this is the victory that overcometh the world, even our faith. Who is he that overcometh the world, but he that believeth that Jesus is the Son of God? (1 John 5:4-5).

*69. Going Deeper

We were preparing to leave the church that we had been pastoring for two years. Because the church was bringing in new candidates for examination, they did not need me to preach the Word to them any longer.

As a result, I was able to spend many hours memorizing and meditating on the Bible. A sense of great expectancy grew within my heart. The air was charged with the tangible power of God. I would walk the mountain behind our parsonage praying and meditating all day long. This continued for a number of weeks. At the time, I did not realize that I was about to step into a deeper realm of the Spirit.

My wife and I were scheduled to minister at a number of meetings, and I had been invited previously to minister at the Mifflin Full Gospel Businessmen's meeting located in Belleville, Pennsylvania. We arrived right before the meeting was to start. As I sat at a table with my wife, I remember that I felt no quickening of the Spirit of God on the inside whatsoever. One of the members of the organization came over and asked me if I would like to pray with some of the members before the beginning of the meeting. I consented to do so.

They were standing in a circle holding each other's hands. I simply stepped into this circle and took the hand of the man on my right and left. The men began to pray, and I prayed very softly, agreeing with them. During this time of prayer, I did not perceive in my heart that I should pray aloud. When we were done praying, the man on my right, an older gentleman, stared at me. He said, "What in the world was that?"

I said to him, **"What do you mean?"**

He said it was like a streak of lightning came out of my hand, and up his arm, through his face. You could tell that something radical had taken place. I told him that I had not felt anything.

That was the beginning of an unusual night. This same gentleman came to me at the end of the service, crying. He asked me to look into his eyes. I still remember to this day; his eyes were clear and glistening. He said to me, **"My eyes were covered in cataracts. The minute you touched me, the cataracts literally melted right off my eyeballs!"** Thank you Jesus!

Right up to the minute before I opened my mouth I had not felt a single thing spiritually. However, the minute I began to talk, the river began to flow. I do not remember what I said, but I do know I was speaking under a strong influence of the Holy Ghost. I flowed right into the gifts of the Spirit after the teaching of the Word. A very precise word of knowledge began to operate. I remember looking out over the people and beginning to call specific people out. Many of the women and men appeared to be Mennonite or Amish.

I began to point to specific people, and call them to come forward. As they came, I would tell them what it was that was going on in their bodies. When they would get within ten feet of me, they did not fall forward or backwards, but just begin to crumple. I never have seen anything like it! It was like they just simply, and very gently went down. As far as I know, all of them were instantly healed. I do not remember laying hands on anyone that night. The Father, Son, and Holy Ghost were in the house.

How God anointed Jesus of Nazareth with the Holy Ghost and with power: who went about doing good, and healing all that were oppressed of the devil; for God was with him (Acts 10:38).

70. Signs and Wonders

We were conducting special healing meetings in Huntington, Pennsylvania, where we had rented a large conference room at Juniata College. The meeting room had a concrete floor with no carpet. After I had ministered the message I began to move in the gifts of the Spirit. In this particular meeting I was quickened by the Spirit to have everyone stand facing the front in a long line. Quite a number of people had either been called out or wanted prayer. I specifically told the men that were standing behind these people not to brush against anyone's back. The reality of the presence of Christ was very strong. I knew that if someone brushed against these people, they would fall.

One of my coworkers accidentally brushed up against a young lady of approximately eighteen years of age. I was probably twenty feet from her. I saw the whole thing in slow motion. She began to fall forward. I went to move toward her, but I knew I could never make it in time. She fell forward with her hands at her side. I watched as her precious face slammed into the concrete floor. The minute her face hit the floor, it literally sounded like a pumpkin smashing and breaking in half and everybody gasped in horror. I walked up to where she was laying. Even though I had been in the Spirit, my flesh was filled with trembling. I was fully expecting there to be blood. As I looked around her head I did not see any blood! I knew I had to quickly step back into the Spirit. As I did, I had total peace, so I left her lying there. I started at the end of the prayer line, working my way down, one person at a time. We saw many wonderful things that night. God set many free.

After the service I looked for this young lady. She was standing about where she had originally fallen. I walked up to her very gingerly. I almost did not want to look at her face because I was afraid of what I would see. She was shaking a little and crying. When I came around to her front I looked at her face. To my amazement there was not one mark. In the natural there had to be some damage. We all heard her head when it hit the concrete. The room was filled with the sound of a loud thump. But here she was with not one mark on her face. I asked her what happened when she fell forward. She said that when she hit the floor it felt like as if she was falling into a bed of feathers!

And he went up unto them into the ship; and the wind ceased: and they were sore amazed in themselves beyond measure, and wondered (Mark 6:51).

*71. The Price of Disobedience

WHEN I UNDERESTIMATED AND MISUSED THE POWER OF GOD (1981)

Most times in our life as believers and ministers we are trying to believe God for more power, more authority, and greater manifestations. In the life of Christ, it was the opposite. There was so much power, authority, Spirit manifested in his life, he knew everything he said would happen. When you begin to walk in this realm is very important that you tiptoe. There's been a number of times in my life when I had tapped into this realm. What I said came to pass, whether I wanted to or not. Honestly! Let me share one such experience.

My wife and I were invited to minister at a woman's meeting in State College, Pennsylvania. On the way to this meeting, God began to supernaturally give me a message for this service. I have written over seven thousand sermon outlines through the years. Many of my sermons have come to me in dreams and visions. Numerous times I have simply preached what I saw myself speaking the night before from a dream I had received. These experiences are simply the quickening of the Spirit. We are all called as God's people to walk in His quickening.

The first Adam was a living soul, the second Adam is a quickening Spirit. In this experience, I saw a multifaceted diamond that filled the heavens. Remember, this all took place as I was driving. I was in two different places at once. I was driving my car with my wife next to me, and at the same time, I was in another world. As I looked at this multifaceted diamond, every one of its facets was a marvelous dimension of God's nature and character. I was overwhelmed with God's awesomeness and marvelous, never-ending possibilities. I wish someone would have recorded that sermon that day as it just flowed forth from heaven through me. When I had finished ministering the Word of God at this woman's meeting, I began to operate in a precise word of knowledge. (1981)

As I spoke forth what the Spirit of God showed me by a word of knowledge, I asked all the ladies that I had spoken to by the Spirit of the Lord to step out into the center of the room. The atmosphere Was Electrified by the Power of God to heal the sick. Approximately fifteen to twenty women (maybe more) were standing in the middle of the room waiting to be ministered to. The Spirit of God told me specifically:

"Do Not Touch Them. Simply Speak My Word."

I heard this very strong within my inner man, and oh how I wish I had listened to the voice of God. Now, there was one woman who was standing in front of all the rest. They were lined up in such a way that it looked almost like bowling pins set up at the end of a bowling alley.

At that moment, un-crucified flesh rose up in me and I disobeyed God. I was not just going to speak to them, but I would lay my hands on each one and they would be healed, and wouldn't I be something (Me, Me, Me)! That's why God cannot use a lot of people —because they start thinking that they are something special. I reached out Oh so very gently touching the very first woman on the forehead with just the tip of my fingers. My wife was there, and she can testify to this story.

The minute I touched this precious lady she flew back violently. She was literally thrown back as if a mighty power had struck her. She hit the ladies right behind her. Every one of these ladies flew back like the first lady and slammed into the others. They all fail violently to the floor. These precious ladies ended up on the floor lying on top of one another in less than three seconds. There were exposed legs sticking up in the air everywhere. I am ashamed to say that even some of their dresses were lifted above their waist with their undergarments exposed. When they all flew back it looked like a bowling ball slamming into the bowling pins as a strike.

At that very moment the Spirit of God spoke to me and said: because of your disobedience, not one of them had been healed. If I had obeyed God, every one of them would have been instantly delivered and healed. Now, instead of God being glorified, confusion had entered this meeting. I had misused and abused my position with God. To this day, I am ashamed that I didn't obey God that night. Just think if I would have listened to the Lord; those precious ladies would have all been healed instantly and God would have been glorified. I did apologize to those present.

My wife and I helped the ladies get back up and I told them I would like to pray for each one of them individually because they testified that none of them were healed. When you don't obey, there is a price to pay. Many ministers I think simply use the power of God to knock people down. But by faith, you need to direct that power of the spirit into their bodies to heal them. Kathleen and I prayed for each person but this time it was with what the bible calls "common faith" while before I had been operating in the gift of faith and healing.

And David's heart smote him after that he had numbered the people. And David said unto the LORD, I have sinned greatly in that I have done: and now, I beseech thee, O LORD, take away the iniquity of thy servant; for I have done very foolishly (2 Samuel 24:10).

CHAPTER TEN

Miracles in a Foreign Land

72. Sprechen Sie Deutsch?

We were getting ready to move from the parsonage of the church we had been pastoring. As I was in prayer one morning, the Spirit of God spoke to my heart, Go to Germany! It was very strong that I needed to go to Germany. When I shared this with my wife, without hesitation she agreed. We had to raise money in order to buy the tickets and go.

We put our car on the market, and sold it within a couple of days. That was a miracle within itself. That was the Sports Granada that I had outfitted with ridiculous equipment. It was an older gentleman that bought the car. We tried to sell whatever else we could. What we could not sell, we put in storage. We then bought round-trip tickets to Frankfurt, Germany. My wife Kathleen, Michael (who was now three months old) and myself caught a plane and landed in Frankfurt, Germany.

When we entered the airport terminal I did not know what else to do. This pattern is how God has led me the majority of my spiritual life. I do not try to figure out what to do—I simply take one baby step at a time. As I was standing in the terminal, simply being quiet and waiting to hear what the Spirit would say, the Spirit quickened my heart to go to the American military welcome center at the airport.

I remember walking towards the military welcome center with my wife and child. Standing right outside of the glass window office area was a gentleman who was dressed in military clothing. Because I had been in the navy and not in the army, I did not know their ranking system. This particular military man, who was an older Hispanic man, was some type of officer. I walked up to him and simply started talking. It turns out he was a sergeant, and he was stationed at the local American military base. He asked me what we were doing in Germany.

I told him that I was a minister, and how the Spirit of God quickened my heart to come to Germany to minister and that we had come by faith with no connections in the Christian community. He then informed me that he himself was a pastor and had connections throughout Germany. As I was speaking to him, God moved on his heart to help us! He also invited us to come and preach to his congregation. We had a wonderful move of God's Spirit in the church. Then the pastor helped us get the proper papers and ID's to go to any military base in Germany. The doors began to swing open for us!

And the angel of the Lord spake unto Philip, saying, Arise, and go toward the south unto the way that goeth down from Jerusalem unto Gaza, which is desert (Acts 8:26).

*73. Vision of Destruction

Our Nine-Month-Old Son Michael Would Have Burned to DEATH with Out an Open Vision! (1981)

While we were in Germany we bought a used Audi 100, with which we crisscrossed all over Germany, Holland, and the outskirts of France. One day as we were driving on the autobahn (German highway), I had an open vision.

Suddenly, right in front of my eyes I saw the back seat of our car exploding in fire, with our son Michael burning alive in his car seat. This was a very disturbing image. I remember shaking my head, thinking this can't be! I tried to ignore it for a little while, but I had the vision again! I told my wife what I'd seen. She informed me that she was also seeing the same thing; that is why she had her chair leaning back, so she could grab Michael. She also had been praying in her heavenly tongues.

We pulled off to the side of the autobahn immediately, and got out of the car with Michael. I began to search high and low over the car. As Kathleen held Michael I searched underneath, in the trunk, and inside out but I could find nothing wrong. Not knowing what else to do, we all got back into the vehicle, strapped Michael back into his baby seat, and went back onto the autobahn. Kathee kept her seat back as far as possible, and put her hand on Michael.

As we were driving, the same vision burst in front of my eyes stronger than ever. The vision was so real that I could barely see what was in front of me. Now, without any doubt, I knew something was going on. That God was trying to save us from a tragedy! At the same time my eyes began to water and burn from some nasty fumes. This time I pulled over to the side of the road as quickly as I could. I turned off the car and we evacuated the vehicle like it was about to explode. After I had got Kathleen and Michael far enough from the vehicle, I once again began to meticulously comb the car, which again came up with nothing wrong. The last thing to try was to pull the seat out of the back.

Since all American vehicles have their back seats attached, I wasn't sure how to do it. Yet to my surprise and delight, I discovered that the backseat was removable as I grabbed it. As I pulled it out, acidic fumes instantly overwhelmed me. Right underneath where Michael was sitting was a large twelve-volt battery! Acidic fumes were rolling out of its open caps at an alarming rate, bubbling and boiling. It was obvious that this battery was about to explode at any moment!

We managed to get the vehicle to a mechanic shop to be repaired. The mechanic told us that the alternator was putting out way too much amperage, perhaps due to some malfunctioning diodes. He also informed us that had we not stopped the car, the battery would have exploded into flames, and our precious little boy, Michael, would have been burned to death. Many believers die early and some from tragic deaths because they are not sensitive enough to the signs from the Spirit. They are not living within what I call the Realm of Faith and obedience.

He hath said, which heard the words of God, which saw the vision of the Almighty, falling into a trance, but having his eyes open (Numbers 24:4).

*74. Out in the Cold

We had been ministering in a church in the industrial part of Germany. God had moved in a wonderful way. The pastor and congregation did not realize it, but we had nowhere to go after this service. We did not have any more services lined up at the moment. I did not tell this pastor anything about our situation. I like the opportunity to watch God work. If I would have told the people our needs or what was going on, then most likely they would have responded out of compassion to help us. But I love to live on the forefront of watching God perform perfectly-orchestrated divine events. For this reason, Kathee and I did not tell anyone what was going on. We simply held hands together and **prayed**, asking God for somewhere to stay that night. After the meeting, a German woman in her 50's approached us very timidly. She informed us that her husband was working in Saudi Arabia for the oil industry and that she had an apartment in the area. She was leaving for Saudi Arabia the next day and was desperate for someone to stay at her apartment.

She asked us if we could possibly stay at her home until she got back within the next month. Remember, this lady had just met us and we were complete strangers to her. Not only that, but we were foreigners from America. Kathee and I both looked at each other, knowing once again the Lord had come through for us. We told her that we would be willing to do that for her. She also encouraged us to eat all of the food that there was in her house, and we were glad to accommodate her request!

I have been young, and now am old; yet have I not seen the righteous forsaken, nor his seed begging bread (Psalms 37:25).

*75. Dancing with Anticipation

We continued to minister in the local area where we were staying. Eventually we had also consumed all of the food in the sister's apartment as she given us the liberty to do. All of our finances were completely depleted. We did not even have any money for gasoline.

I got up early in the morning - as per my usual routine - it was time for me to talk to God: about our needs. We were in Germany at this time, doing missionary work. We were also completely out of food, money and gas for our car. Our one-year-old son was having to depend on mom for all of his nourishment. The apartment we were staying in, at this time, had a long hallway leading to all rooms: straight ahead was a very small front room (with sliding doors); on the right-hand was a small kitchen and on the left-hand was the bedroom.

I was in the front room praying and crying out to God. I never complain, gripe, or tell God what is wrong when I pray. Prayer, supplication, and thanksgiving are the order of the day. So, I was talking to the **Father,** in the name of **Jesus**, and I knew, that He already knew what we needed. Still, He tells us in His Word to let Him know what we need. After I was done talking to the **Father,** I stepped into the realm of praise and thanksgiving. I lifted my hands and began to dance before the Lord. My dance is not elaborate, orchestrated, symbolic or a performance. It is just me, lifting my feet (kind of kicking them around) and jumping a little bit - in a rather comical, childlike fashion. Some people really believe that they have to get into some kind of elaborate system of swinging their arms and bodies: I just keep it really simple, sincere, and from my heart.

While I was seeking God, my wife was in the kitchen, cleaning up. During me singing in tongues and dancing before the Lord, there was a knock on the apartment door, which I did not hear. My wife, however, did hear the knocking. She put down the dishes and headed for the door. Now, as far as we were aware, no one knew where we were staying. My wife opened the door to a tall, distinguished-looking, German gentleman. He informed her that he had been looking for us. He said he'd been actually hunting us down, because God had used us in a service where he'd experienced his first supernatural encounter.

My wife came to inform me about the gentleman at the door. So, I walked down the skinny hallway, to where this gentleman was standing, to speak to him. I did have a recollection of meeting him at a previous service; I'd prayed for him to be filled with the Holy Ghost and I remember him speaking in tongues. At the time, I had no idea of his background. He gave me quite an impressive resume of who he was; it turns out he was a professor at a local German college.

He shared with us how he had struggled to believe in the supernatural, because of his superior intellect, but when he came to the service I was ministering at, his world was turned upside down! He had experienced God! When he left that meeting, he said, the Spirit of the Lord was upon him. He also said the Lord spoke to him for the first time he could ever remember. The Lord told him specifically that he was to find me and give me a certain amount of money.

Ever since the Lord had spoken to him (a number of days

previously) he had been trying to find us. He had just learned of our address from someone at a church we had been ministering at. Now ... here he was! Standing at our door, during the exact same time when I had been praying— praising and thanking God for the finances and food we needed. Before he left, he handed us an envelope. When he'd gone we opened up the envelope and it was exceedingly abundantly above all that we could ever ask or hope for. We did not have any more financial worries or needs until we left Germany.

Jesus saith unto them, Fill the waterpots with water. And they Þ lled them up to the brim. And he saith unto them, Draw out now, and bear unto the governor of the feast. And they bare it. When the ruler of the feast had tasted the water that was made wine, and knew not whence it was: (but the servants which drew the water knew;) the governor of the feast called the bridegroom (John 2:7-9).

*76. Sliding Out of the Chairs

EVERYONE FELL To The Floor WEEPING as I Was Preaching! (1981)

I was ministering in a German-speaking church called The Industrial Center of Germany. This church was situated about five stories up in a high-rise office complex. They did not have a pastor in this church at the time. They had a board of elders, and I understood one of the men was an oil tycoon. He was the one who supported all the activities and outreaches of the church. I had an interpreter with us who was a famous German worship leader and singer.

When I preached at the church, I ministered a radical message on being one hundred percent, completely and totally sold out to Jesus Christ. I shared that there was a price to be paid to enter the deeper things of God and that you had to die to the flesh to live in the Spirit. Jesus gave His everything, and now it was our turn to give everything. About two-thirds of the way through this message, something amazing happened.

As I stood before the congregation to speak, the Holy Ghost began to move upon me in a mighty way dealing with the subject of being completely sold out 100% to Jesus Christ. The presence of God was manifested in a very strong and real way. Something amazing happened as I was about 35 to 45 minutes into my message.

All of a sudden, the **Spirit of God fell** upon that congregation in such a mighty way that everyone in that church **fell out of their chairs at once.** Instantly everyone in the congregation was on the floor weeping and wailing under the influence of the Holy Spirit. This was such a strange occurrence because neither my interpreter or I seem to be feeling or experiencing what everybody else was. This happened in such a synchronized way that the thought came to me that for some reason they had organized this as a church.

Because I no longer had their attention, I simply quit preaching, and got down on my knees, and started praying along with them. This continued for quite a while. Eventually, the weeping and crying stopped, and people began to get up and trickle away from the meeting. **No one was talking.** There was a Holy hush upon the whole congregation. One of the leaders of the church invited us with a whisper down to the next floor where there had been a meal prepared for us in the fellowship hall.

As we sat down to eat, I could tell that they were all looking at me in a strange way. As my wife and I ate the food that was prepared to for us nobody in the room spoke at all. I finally worked up enough courage to speak to the brother who was on my left. I simply asked the man if this happened very often?

He replied, **"Does what happen very often?"**

I said, **"Where all the people suddenly as one fall on the floor and start praying, crying and weeping?**

" He looked at me as if something was wrong. **He told me they had never seen or experienced anything like this before in their church services".**

This had been a divine move of the Holy Ghost that came about as I was preaching on being completely sold out to **Jesus Christ.** The end results of this meeting were that the leadership of this church was so moved that they offered my wife and me to become their pastors. They told us that our financial needs were not to be concerned about because one of the brothers was an oil tycoon. I told them that I could not speak German, and therefore I would not make a good pastor.

They said this would be no problem because they would provide an interpreter into I became fluent in their language. I got quiet before the Lord and asked him whether I should accept this offer? The Lord very strongly spoke to my heart and said: No, I have other plans for you, and as it is not for you to pastor this church. I informed them that I could not accept their offer, but that I was truly grateful and humbled by their request.

And why call ye me, Lord, Lord, and do not the things which I say?(Luke 6:46).

77. Open Doors

I was ministering in the industrial area of West Germany, close to Düsseldorf. The Spirit of the Lord was moving in a mighty way. The gifts of the Spirit were in manifestation. This particular church had a good core of believers. The man who was the head of this church was an American, named Brad, who was married to an English lady. They wanted us to continue working with them. We stayed in a small room of their house for a while. Brad had to go to Great Britain to do some meetings for about two weeks. He asked if I was interested in going with him. I told him I would pray about it. He said my wife and son would be perfectly fine staying with his wife and their children. The Spirit of the Lord quickened my heart to go along with him. We had a wonderful time of fellowship as we drove to Great Britain.

When we got to France, we had to catch a ferry. When I stepped onto the shore of Great Britain, I knew in my heart I would be back. This was just the opening of a great door to reach these precious people. During that two-week period, God did wonderful things. I did have some opportunities to minister. I also met a gentleman named Malcolm White who became a good friend of mine. Through the years, Malcolm traveled to America to minister to the different churches that I had started and pastored. He was to be a major key in opening up churches throughout Great Britain for me. I'm sorry to say Malcolm passed away a few years ago. I miss him sorely.

So far, I have been to Great Britain on five different occasions. I would travel from Wales all the way to Scotland and back down again. (I am a hyperactive kind of guy who hates sitting around.) Malcolm would arrange for me to be in twenty churches in twenty-one days. Many times these churches were many miles apart. I rode their train system from top to bottom, crisscrossing in every direction, visiting London, Scotland, Wales, and England. A little later in this book, I will share with you some of the astounding miracles that the Lord performed in this country.

And a vision appeared to Paul in the night; There stood a man of Macedonia, and prayed him, saying, Come over into Macedonia, and help us. And after he had seen the vision, immediately we endeavored to go into Macedonia, assuredly gathering that the Lord had called us for to preach the gospel unto them (Acts 16:9-10).

*78. Help Us, Jesus

After nine months in Germany with many signs and wonders,

the Spirit was tugging at our hearts to go back to America. The only problem is that we had ended up being involved with a ministry that wanted us to stay with them. They provided housing and food for us. It's not that they were controlling, but every time I would talk about leaving, they would convince me to stay. Don't misunderstand; they were beautiful people. It's just that it was time for us to leave! Please realize we were still a young married couple. My wife went through tremendous emotional stress because I was being wishy-washy. We had only been married for four years. During that time, it seemed as if I had always known what the will of God was, and now I was confused.

I finally realized I was out of the will of God and we just needed to leave. I did not want to discuss this with these people again, because I did not trust myself—they might convince me to stay longer. Their theology was that we needed to have a plan for every step we took. God doesn't lead me in that way. It is simply one little step after another, placing the future into His hands.

We were staying in this church's coffee and tea shop where the youth gathered and held special meetings. So, I woke Kathleen up early one morning. Michael was sleeping, so we bundled him up in some blankets. Then we, very quietly, tiptoed out of the facility. After we put Michael in his car seat, Kathleen sat behind the steering wheel. She put the car in neutral as I got behind the car and began to push it. Once the car was coasting and we were out of their compound and the parking lot, I jumped in and Kathee started the vehicle. She put it in gear, and away we went! Hallelujah! We were free from my indecision and wavering.

We followed the map back towards Frankfurt, Germany. We got on the Audubon, and I opened that little car up to eighty kilometers an hour. There is no speed limit on the Audubon, so we were slowpokes compared to everyone else. From Wesel, we had approximately a 280-kilometer journey to get to the airport in Frankfurt. As we drove along we both prayed that God's will would be done in this decision.

As we were driving on the Audubon, the car began to act very

148

strange. We had just begun the journey when the car began to slow down. I kept pumping the gas and the car would speed up. We had plenty of gas in the car so that was not the problem. Then the engine began to sputter and made loud knocking noises. There was something drastically wrong with our automobile. There was no way that we were going miss getting to the Frankfurt airport, because we needed to get back to America. Kathee and I began to command the car to keep running in the name of Jesus. By this time, everybody was passing us. The vehicle was slowing down to as little as ten kilometers an hour. Many times, it seemed to almost come to a standstill.

We laid our hands on the dashboard, commanding it to keep on running in the name of Jesus. Then the car would speed up again and I would put the pedal to the floor. We would hit up to 120 kilometers an hour and the cycle would start all over again—going back down to ten kilometers an hour, if not less. We kept speaking to that car all the way. I refused to pull off the road and turn it off. In the name of Jesus, we were going to make it to the airport! Smoke was pouring out of the back end of the vehicle. Kathy continue to pray quietly under breath.

This journey seemed to take days to complete, but of course it did not. We finally saw the exit signs for the American military base, where we knew someone we could leave the car with. As we pulled into the parking space in front of the military house of the people we knew, the car died completely. It was dead, never to live again. We heard later that they simply hauled it away and scrapped it. The engine had completely frozen up, and it was mechanically impossible for the engine to be repaired. Someone gave us a ride to the airport. We were just in time to catch a plane back to the USA.

And Moses stretched out his hand over the sea; and the LORD caused the sea to go back by a strong east wind all that night, and made the sea dry land, and the waters were divided. And the children of Israel went into the midst of the sea upon the dry ground: and the waters were a wall unto them on their right hand, and on their left (Exodus 14:21-22).

CHAPTER ELEVEN

The Faith That Brings Miracles

*79. A Boat of a Car

When we got back to the states, we ended up staying at Kathleen's grandma's house. We had no transportation and not a penny to our name. It was okay though because we were back home in the USA. On the way back to America, Kathee and I discussed what type of car we needed to get. We both agreed we'd need nothing fancy. I told her even if it's an old boat of a car, who cares? Godliness with contentment is great gain. So, we both agreed—with a little bit of laughter—to pray for an old boat of a car.

We held hands and simply spoke to the Father in the name of Jesus praying: "Thank you, heavenly Father, for providing us with a car. Father, we would be satisfied with just a big old automobile that would get us to where we needed to go, nothing fancy or expensive, something that can be given to us for free, amen. Thank you, Lord, for that vehicle." We did not tell anyone what we believed or prayed for. I am convinced that when your heart is in harmony with God, He will put in your mouth what you need to pray for.

We had been at Kathee's grandma's house for a day when she received a phone call. Her neighbors said that they heard that we were back from Germany and that we were staying with her temporarily. The neighbors said that the Lord spoke to them while they were in prayer. They were hesitant to even talk to us about what they thought they had heard the Lord say, and they seemed to be embarrassed by it. Grandma called for me and told me what was going on. I told her to let me speak to them directly. When I got on the phone, the gentleman told me that he wasn't exactly positive if he had heard the Lord correctly. He said while he was in prayer, God told him to give us a big old vehicle that had sitting out behind his house! He told me he did not think it could be God. But I told him it was. We hitched a ride over to his house, and there in his backyard was sitting the wonderful answer to our prayers—a big old boat of a car. We were riding in style...I think.

Who layeth the beams of his chambers in the waters: who maketh the clouds his chariot: who walketh upon the wings of the wind: Who maketh his angels spirits; his ministers a flaming fire (Psalms 104:3-4).

*80. I'll Buy That with No Money

Eventually, we ended up purchasing an old church bus. With all the scrap material I could find, I turned that bus into living quarters. Once I had everything installed, Kathee, young Michael, and I moved into our new home. The idea that had come to me was that we would go to different fairs and carnivals to hold tent meetings. Kathleen was in complete agreement with me, but we had one little problem. We did not own a tent, PA equipment, chairs, lights, or anything else to do with a tent ministry! I definitely was not going to ask anyone to help us with this equipment, God was our source.

Not only did we not have anything we needed to have a tent ministry, we did not have two pennies to rub together. In other words, we were flat broke. (As I think back to this time in our lives, I have to laugh. God is so good. He has such a wonderful sense of humor. All we have to do is look to Him). Well, I needed a tent to start with, so I went to prayer with supplication and thanksgiving. The Spirit of God quickened to my heart to get the tents from the Brethren denomination, where I had rented my last tent for the Huntington County Fair. I began to pray seriously what the Lord would have me to do. This is what came into my heart, call up the brother and Campground telling them that you want to buy tents.

I called up the Roxbury campgrounds and told them that I would like to purchase some of their tents if they had any for sale. They said that they would get back in touch with me. We had our old bus parked at Kathee's grandma's house during this time. Not long afterwards, I received a phone call from them on grandma's phone, informing me they definitely had some tents they would like to sell us. I set up a time when I could come down and pick these tents up. Kathleen had a nephew whose name was Gary. Gary's mother was a pastor and evangelist. Gary was about nineteen years old at that time (I was an old man of twenty-six, myself). I called Gary up and asked him if he wanted to go into the tent ministry with us. He said he would pray about it and get back in touch with me.

Gary called back that same day and said he was interested. I told him that I had to go to Roxbury to pick up our tents and asked him if he would like to go along with me. Kathee's grandma had a neighbor who owned a gas station and had a tire business. This gentleman possessed a large steel truck that he transported tires in. I asked if I could rent his truck. He said he would not rent it to me, but that I could use it.

On the day we were to meet with the personnel at Roxbury, Gary met me at Kathee's grandma's house. We both got into the big truck and were on our way. As we were driving and discussing spiritual matters, I told him there was something he needed to know. I told him when we get to Roxbury I did not want him to say anything about us not having any money to these people that we were purchasing the tents from. He looked over at me kind of strange, and asked what I meant. I told him I did not have a penny to my name.

With great surprise he said, **"What?"**
I told him once again, "I don't have any money to my name."
He asked what we were going to do then.

I said, "They don't know it yet, but they are going to give us these tents." PS: this was quickened in my heart as I was praying.

He said, **"They're going to do what?"**

I repeated my statement again, operating in the gift of faith and the word of wisdom. It was not just hoping, wishing, guessing, making a good confession, or coveting their tents. It was the gift of faith at work in my heart with the word of wisdom. I emphasized to him that he needed to be quiet about the finances no matter what.

We got to the campgrounds in Roxbury where they were waiting for us. They had gathered together a group of men to help pull the tents and all that went with them out of storage. I think there were about a dozen men. They opened the large doors on one of their storage buildings. Then the men would sweat and groan as they pulled a big canvas bag out of the storage barn. In those days all the tents were made of canvas and they were not easy to handle or put up. The tie down stakes and side poles were all brought out into the light.

Next came the center poles, which were made of heavy steel. They were extremely heavy and difficult to handle. Of course, then you had all of the side curtains. I'm just emphasizing this because there was a lot of work involved in bringing these tents out of the barn and loading them up. They would pull a tent out of one of their buildings and spread it out, asking me if I wanted to buy that particular tent. Each time I would say yes! By the time they were done there were five tents on our truck. I wish you could have seen Gary's face, he was very nervous. When the men had finished up loading all of the tents on our truck, I asked them how much I owed.

The truck itself was squatting because it was so full, and the tents were almost bulging over the side. When I asked him how much I owed them, one of the men said they had not yet discussed the cost per tent. I said okay, I would wait for them to let me know. These men went off together in a circle. After much discussion, they came back to me and told me that they had prayed about it and felt in their hearts they should give me these tents for free. Hallelujah! There was one other tent that was out in the field being used. It was a very large tent and some of the sections of that tent, for some reason, were loaded on our truck. They told me if I wanted the rest of that tent that it would cost me $250. Praise God, the Lord provided for that later, and we were also able to pick it up later.

Not because I desire a gift: but I desire fruit that may abound to your account. But I have all, and abound: I am full, having received of Epaphroditus the things which were sent from you, an odor of a sweet smell, a sacrifice acceptable, well pleasing to God. But my God shall supply all your need according to his riches in glory by Christ Jesus (Philippians 4:17-19).

*81. Black Ford Pickup

One night, Kathee and I were ministering at a Full Gospel Business Men's meeting in the northern part of Pennsylvania. The Spirit of the Lord had moved in this meeting in a most wonderful way. By the time we left the meeting, it was very late. We probably should've stayed overnight in a motel, but we had a meeting to go to in the morning. So we got into our old boat of a car, started it up, and were on our way home cruising along. The trip was probably over two hours long.

About an hour into the trip, I noticed that the temperature gauge was going into the red. I was so tired from ministering and preaching I just wanted to get home and go to bed. I just kept on driving and praying. Yes, I knew better! I just kept on driving and praying. It wasn't very long before the temperature gauge was pinned, but I just kept on driving and praying. Then the engine began to make funny noises. In my stupidity, I just kept on driving. This kept up for about a half an hour. Now the engine was making loud pinging sounds. My wife woke up and asked what was happening. I told her the engine was extremely overheated. We needed to command this car to keep running till we get home. Together we both agreed this car would get us home in the name of Jesus.

Mile after mile we kept speaking to the engine, "You will not freeze up, you will not stop running, and you will get us home!" Steam was rolling out from under the hood. I'm sure if someone had seen us that night going through their towns, they would have called the fire department. It was a very long drive and a very long night, to say the least. We finally made it to Kathee's grandma's house where we were going to spend the night, or should say the morning. When we pulled up to grandma's house, the old engine could not handle any more, and froze up on the spot. We were so happy God had gotten us home. (I just told you all of this to tell you the rest of the story!)

We were sitting there in this car rejoicing that we had made it home when the gift of faith rose up in my heart. When I told Kathee that we need a pickup truck, she looked at me funny. I explained that our motor home/school bus is what we used to haul our tents around with, and that we still needed a pickup truck in order to haul other equipment. She looked at me and basically said okay! I took my wife's hand and said I **would pray** and she could agree with me. I said "Lord, we would like to have a black Ford pickup truck. Lord, we need this pickup truck to have a 302 engine. And Lord, we need it to be an automatic. We also need this pickup truck to have a cap on its back so whenever we haul anything in the back, the stuff won't get wet."

When we finished **praying**, we began to praise God for the truck. (Remember prayer, supplication, with thanksgiving.) "Now thank you, Lord, for that black Ford pickup truck!" The next morning, we got up early to get ready to go to the meeting we were to be at. It was the church in Huntington, Pennsylvania, which had been a part of the tent revival we had conducted at the Huntington Fair. We were working directly with the pastor, who was a friend of ours, to evangelizing their local community. They had grown so fast that the little building which they had been meeting in could no longer hold them. At that time, they were using our largest tent for their meetings. It would seat over five hundred people. Of course, we had no way to get to this meeting. Kathee's grandma knew our needs, so she called up one of her neighbors to see if we could use their car. Thank God! They agreed to let us use it. This car was almost brand-new.

We arrived at the tent gathering before it began. I'm sure that everybody thought that God had blessed us with a new car. We did not tell anybody at the meeting that we had to borrow this car because our vehicle was shot. I think people are too quick to tell other people what they need. I love to keep my mouth shut and watch God work.

At the end of the service, when everybody was leaving, a couple walked up to us. The husband said that during the service he had looked over at us and had a feeling inside of him that they should give us a vehicle that they owned. He had shared this with his wife and she also had a witness. He told me they felt strange coming to me because they saw that we had a very nice car. I did not tell them this was not our car. I simply told them to obey God. I asked them when we could come and see this vehicle they felt led to give us. They informed us that they did not live very far from this meeting, and we could follow them to look at this vehicle. They thought maybe we would not even want it. I did not ask him what kind of vehicle it was. We said that we could follow them right then and there and take a peek.

After several miles, we pulled up in front of a farmhouse. There was no other vehicle sitting anywhere in sight. They told us the vehicle was behind the house next to their barn. We walked around the house and there next to the barn was a black Ford pickup truck, with a 302 engine, automatic, and with a cap. It was exactly what we had prayed and asked God for, not even eight hours previously.

Within two to three days, we were driving around in our black Ford pickup, with a 302 engine, automatic, and a cap on the back, and we did not have to pay a cent for it!

What things soever ye desire, when ye pray, believe, and ye shall have them. And when ye stand praying, forgive, if ye have ought against any: that your Father also which is in heaven may forgive you your trespasses (Mark 11:24-25).

*82. The Angels Catcher Mitt

My Family and I Were Saved from Certain Death by Angels While on a Motorcycle! (1983)

My wife and I were pastoring two churches. One church was in Gettysburg, Pennsylvania and the other one in Chambers-burg, Pennsylvania. My wife was about seven months pregnant with our second son, Daniel, when this event I'm telling you about took place. (I have three sons. From the first day that we were married, I always said to my wife, "Mike and his three sons.")

We were out one-day doing house visitation to some of our parishioners. This really sounds stupid, but it's true. My wife, my son Michael, and I were all on a Honda 450. Of course, I was in the front of the motorcycle driving. Michael, who was two years old, was in the middle. Close behind him was Daniel and Kathee. (Danny was still in a protective bubble called a womb). Thank God there was a sissy bar behind Kathee. We had been visiting a family from the church near Roxbury, Pennsylvania. After we had spent some wonderful time with this family, we got on the motorcycle and headed home.

We were now headed home on 997, or Black Gap Road headed for Highway 30. The sun was just beginning to set, and it was glaring in my eyes. I was looking for a shortcut that I knew about. This shortcut was a dirt road. (I'm notorious for my shortcuts). As I was going along, I finally saw it to my right, and so I thought. It was getting dark, in the last fading light of the sun was shining in my eyes so I could not see the road very clearly. I slowed up a little bit, and then turned off onto this dirt road was a shortcut, and would save me a little bit of time. I was probably doing about forty-five miles an hour. The speed limit through this area on 997 was fifty-five, and I usually always try to stay at the upper end, endeavoring to keep the law.

However, when I turned off on this shortcut, I discovered to my absolute horror and dismay that this was not the shortcut road that I was looking for. It was a very shallow area that was long and narrow created for semi-trucks to pull over in case of emergencies. Now right in front of us were three major obstacles: #1 a heavy-duty steel guard rail, #2 a large pile of big rocks, #3 and a large wooden light pole.

These obstacles were only about twenty feet in front of us. I knew instantly there was no way I could ever stop. Slamming on your brakes in the gravel in the dirt at 45 miles an hour, trying to stop within 20 feet, with four people on the bike is not at all a good idea. Even if I would have laid the motorcycle over on its side, we would still slam into these items at forty-five to fifty miles an hour.

It was clear with an overwhelming clarity that we were going to hit the rocks, guard rail, and telephone pole. I knew in my heart that in the natural my precious wife with our unborn child, and my two-year-old son Michael was possibly going to be not just extremely hurt but killed. I was not at all concerned about myself now.

Now, I did not even have time to put on my brakes because this happens so fast. I just simply cried out JESUS! (I know that what I'm about to tell you will sound insane, but this is what truly happened.) At the very moment I cried out JESUS, it felt like two large hands pressed against us on both sides, left and right. I mean literally I could feel tremendous pressure, (and yet it was soft and gentle) to the left and the right of my body. Now, we were still heading for the rocks, but then we instantly stopped, I mean

INSTANTLY. It literally felt like we had either run into a big, invisible, enormous heavenly fluffy pillow, or a very large and soft baseball catcher's glove. There was nothing visible in front of us to stop us. We simply ran into some invisible supernatural force.

We were completely stopped, and for a moment we were standing upright. We simply fell over on our right side. We fell over onto the gravel and rocks, but we really did not fall unto them. I know this sounds far-fetched, weird and strange. But it was like we fell onto another enormous heavenly and fluffy pillow! We fell into something extremely soft between us and the ground.

Now here we are laying in the dirt and gravel with an overwhelming peace, and even joy was upon us. What a miracle! Little Michael wasn't even crying; I think he was laying in between us sucking his thumb, as he liked to do. As we look back to the road, we notice there were no skid marks in the dirt whatsoever. It simply showed our tire tracks coming up to the place where we were, and then right there our bike stopped instantly. I looked at my wife, and she looked at me. We were both in shock, and yet great joy and peace came upon us. Then my wife informed me that just before we had arrived at this area on 997, she had seen two large pillars of light fire, one to the left of us, and one to the right.

Kathee's Interjection:

Right before the accident I remember going through a little town which had no lights, but I saw two pillars of white fire, one right to our left, and one right to our right. The pillars were like brilliant, white laser lights shooting towards the heavens. I realized at that moment that they were two angels of God! I began crying and praising God while on the back of that motorcycle even before the accident.

I was thanking God for His protection and goodness as we were headed down 997, with little Mikey sitting between my wonderful husband. I was still praising God when I noticed that we had turned off onto a dead-end path. I knew in my heart that we were going to crash. HOWEVER, I had and an overwhelming peace.

Everything happened so quickly that I knew God was indeed with us! The next thing I knew we were laying on the sand, gravel, and rocks. As we laid on the ground, the presence of God was so real and so thick that you could have cut it with a knife. Michael and I just laid on the ground crying, talking, and thanking God for his wonderful mercy and protection.

It was like we did not want to get up because it was such a holy moment. I do not remember for how long we laid there, but it was for some time. It was like we were just laying before the throne of our heavenly Father enjoying a precious moment with him.

And the angel of God, which went before the camp of Israel, removed and went behind them; and the pillar of the cloud went from before their face, and stood behind them: and it came between the camp of the Egyptians and the camp of Israel; and it was a cloud and darkness to them, but it gave light by night to these: so that the one came not near the other all the night (Exodus 14:19-20).

83. No Midwife

Kathee was due to give birth to our second son, Daniel. When she gave birth to Michael, it was so fast that she almost did not make it to the hospital. I did not make it for my first son's birth because I had been driving a church bus to pick up people for our Sunday morning service. It actually was her fault that she gave birth so fast, because she was aggressively quoting scriptures in order to have an easy birth. I actually asked her to stop believing so strong. But she just kept it up.

Kathee's Comments:

When I became pregnant with our first child, I had picked up a Christian book about home births. The book did encourage home births, but it was so much more than that. It was a wonderful book that explained many aspects about the development of the child within the womb and about the mother's emotional, hormonal, physical, nutritional, and spiritual needs. The secular books that our doctor had given us, only instilled fear; whereas this book presented God's wisdom, knowledge, and peace concerning childbirth.

For our second child, I wanted to try home birthing. After all, going to the hospital to give birth is a young practice; midwives have been around for centuries. Plus, after nearly not making it to the hospital for the first child, Michael agreed to try a home birth.

Confessing God's Word daily was very instrumental in our daily lives, especially during my pregnancies. However, as my husband said, he thinks that I overdid my confessions concerning having a quick, easy birth. I must admit, after nearly having our firstborn before I got to the hospital, and almost having this second in the toilet, I did begin to wonder. Since my husband loves to tell the stories, I will let him proceed.

Back to Mike:

The night prior to the morning that Kathee gave birth to Danny, we had received a phone call from our midwife, Martha. She asked whether it looked like Kathee might give birth. Martha told us that since there was snow and ice on the road that we'd have to make sure that we gave her plenty time to travel to our place. We both told her to not worry, and that everything would be okay, since there were no signs of labor pains yet. However, Martha would not have enough time, because Kathee was too quick.

Early in the morning, while it was still dark, Kathee woke up experiencing some contractions, and pondered whether to call the midwife. Kathee and I decided to go downstairs to the kitchen to call Martha. After calling our midwife, Kathee told me that she had to go to the bathroom.

We had two bathrooms in the old house where we were living, one upstairs, and one downstairs. The birthing room which we had set up was upstairs. The bathroom downstairs was out on a summer porch, so it would have been impossible to reach the birthing room from there if I needed to help her up the steps. Besides, that bathroom was extremely cold on this wintery December day. (The temperature had dipped down to sixty degrees below zero if you take in consideration the wind chill factor, just days after Danny was born!)

Kathee told me that she was going to go to the downstairs restroom. In my heart there was a quickening; I knew by the Spirit, to not let her use the bathroom downstairs. I said, "No baby doll, do not use the bathroom downstairs."

I think she complained a little bit, but then she went back upstairs to use the bathroom right off of the birthing room. She had a struggle to get up the stairs because her time was nearer than she knew.

No sooner had she sat down on the toilet when her water broke. She yelled to me, "Honey, I'm having the baby! "I can't get off the toilet!"

Needless to say, Martha was not going to make it before Daniel made his entrance!

Because Daniel's head had already started to push through, I ran over to her, and helped her to get up off the toilet. I had to get her to waddle over to the birthing bed. Since this was my Þrst experience helping to deliver a baby, I did not do everything exactly right. I propped her too high up in her bed.

Kathee's pelvis was aimed downwards; which made it very difficult for the baby to come forth. After I got her repositioned somewhat, she was able to deliver Danny, in spite of my fumbling "help." From beginning to end, it was probably twenty minutes before she gave birth. Martha came about three minutes afterwards.

We welcomed our new son, Daniel Judson Yeager, into this world. We had the very real touch of God's presence and peace upon us because we had been praying through the whole process.

Kathee's Final Remarks:

I would have never made it to the hospital to give birth, and we are so glad that our midwife came shortly after Daniel was born. Had she not showed up, we might have lost our little Danny, because he started choking on the mucus. The midwife was able to clear the blockage and save his life. (The next child we were more prepared because we had all the right equipment.)

God truly does watch over us! We were very happy that God helped us in the delivery and saving of our son. With grateful hearts, we sent out homemade birth announcements as our Christmas cards that year. We gladly declared from Isaiah 9:6, "Unto us a child is born. Unto us a son is given."

But thou art he that took me out of the womb: thou didst make me hope when I was upon my mother's breasts (Psalms 22:9)

CHAPTER TWELVE

Miraculous and Divine Guidance

*84. His Audible Voice

Right after my wife gave birth to Daniel, we had some good friends come and stay with us. They were our spiritual parents to an extent. Mary was helping my wife clean the house and care for Michael. I basically stayed out of their way. While they were cleaning the kitchen, I was upstairs in my **prayer** room spending time with the Lord in **prayer** and meditating on the Word. When I was finished, I got up and started to come down the stairs.

As I was coming downstairs, I heard the audible voice of God. This is what He said to me, and I quote, **"Go on TV!"** That's what I heard. The audible voice of God was so real, that I instantly fell to my knees. I said, "Lord, the church does not have the money to put me on TV!" Then He began to communicate with me in His still quiet voice. He spoke to my heart and said, **the church will not pay for your TV time. You will believe and trust Me for it!** I said, Yes, Lord! He then quickened to my heart that the first TV station I would be on would be Channel 25 out of Hagerstown, Maryland. The Spirit literally informed me about the specific time I would be on would be Sunday Mornings at 6:30 a.m. Once again, I told the Lord I would obey Him.

Now my wife is always very supportive of me. (Or maybe I should say she never tries to stop me!) She is a real trooper. In fact, she is so much of a trooper that she was up and about within twenty minutes of giving birth to Daniel.

After the Lord had finished speaking to me, I went downstairs to share this with her. When I told her this, she became very upset with me. I believe part of the reason is because financially we were already in need of some miracles. We did not even have money for fuel oil to heat our house. We probably only had enough fuel oil for one more day. She was so upset with me that she went and told Mary. (Mary, by the way is an aggressive pioneer woman. To date, Mary and her husband Paul have done many wonderful works in other countries and in America. She is a mother of the faith. I'm sure it did not help that my wife was distraught and had just given birth to Daniel.)

When I entered the kitchen, Mary cornered me. She tried to speak some sense into me. She basically skinned me alive! Of course, I didn't blame Mary or my wife, but I had heard from God! Later that day as I was praying, a brother who had been saved and filled with the Holy Ghost in our church, Andy, knocked at our front door. He was self-employed and he had been cleaning up people's properties. He asked me how Kathee and I were doing, and how was our newborn son? He then informed me that he had two fifty-five gallon barrels of fuel oil on the back of this truck and wanted to know if I knew anyone that needed heating oil. I said, "Yes, Andy, we do!" He backed his truck up, and put the fuel into our fuel tank.

Humble yourselves therefore under the mighty hand of God, that he may exalt you in due time: Casting all your care upon him; for he careth for you (1 Peter 5:6-7).

85. Just for You

After hearing the Lord telling me to go on TV, the very next day I called Channel 25, WHAG in Hagerstown, Maryland, asking to be transferred over to their sales department. When someone else answered the phone, I told this person that I was interested in purchasing a half-hour slot on their channel. I did not tell them what day of the week or time I wanted. I simply said that I was going to produce a half-hour program. (How I was going to produce these programs I did not know). The sales personnel was a lady who informed me that they did not have any time available, and did not know when another slot would be available. I asked her if she would go to their programming department and discuss with them if there was anything they could do. She said she would, even though she thought it would not make any difference because they had no time available.

Approximately three days later, the sales personnel called me back, telling me that they had called a special meeting to discuss my request. She informed me that normally they do not have their TV station on the air until seven o'clock on Sunday mornings, but they had unanimously agreed to bring their station on the air at 6:30 a.m. just for me! From the very first day of our broadcast we had a tremendous response. All the finances that we needed to stay on the air came in.

Eventually, we were on seven TV stations one day a week. Then I was on with Dr. Lester Sumrall's network five days a week. Dr. Sumrall later came to our church and ministered for us. Until the day Dr. Sumrall died, my ordination papers were with him and his ministry.

But he that shall endure unto the end, the same shall be saved. And this gospel of the kingdom shall be preached in all the world for a witness unto all nations; and then shall the end come (Matthew 24:13-14).

86. Tonight or Else

I was ministering in our church in Cashtown, Pennsylvania one Sunday night, when a young couple walked into the back of our facilities. They came in and sat down. I noticed right away that they were not communicating with each other, or anyone else for that matter. They sat and listened intently to my sermon.

At the end of the message, the Spirit began to quicken me. As I looked at this couple, the Lord began to reveal to me things that I had no way of knowing. When I gave a call for people to come and get prayed for, they came up front. As they stood in front of me, I had a vision of them in their house, specifically it was in their kitchen in the afternoon, having a terrible fight.

The wife had grabbed a frying pan and was trying to hit her husband with it. I saw them discussing what they were going to do. They had decided to come to our church service tonight, and if God did not do a miracle for them, they would get a divorce. I told them exactly what I saw in the Spirit. They both began to weep! Right then and there they gave their hearts to Jesus Christ. They were both filled with the Holy Ghost and became some of the best workers in the church.

And he departed, and began to publish in Decapolis how great things Jesus had done for him: and all men did marvel (Mark 5:20).

87. Prodigal Son Coming Home

One day I was in downtown Gettysburg, taking care of some business. As I was walking across the square, I looked over to the other side of the square and immediately the Spirit caused me to look at a tall African-American man. The minute I put my eyes upon him, the Spirit quickened me to go speak to him.

I did not have any idea what I was going to say to him. I just knew I was to go to him. That's how the Spirit of God leads, one baby step at a time. As I walked up to him, the word of the Lord came to me. He was standing there minding his own business, as I stepped right in front of him. When I had his attention, I told him that he was a backslidden preacher and that he was a Jonah. I told him that the Lord had revealed to me that God was calling him to come back to the work of God to fulfill his calling. God was not yet done with him. This was the first and last time I had ever seen this man. Before I left, he was standing on the square of Gettysburg with his hands lifted high towards heaven. He was weeping and praising the Lord.

And the son said unto him, Father, I have sinned against heaven, and in thy sight, and am no more worthy to be called thy son. But the father said to his servants, bring forth the best robe, and put it on him; and put a ring on his hand, and shoes on his feet: And bring hither the fatted calf, and kill it; and let us eat, and be merry: For this my son was dead, and is alive again; he was lost, and is found. And they began to be merry (Luke 15:21-24).

88. Divine Down Load of Engine Schematic (1985)

We owned a 1979 Cadillac Seville with fuel injection. My engine had started giving me major problems, with loss of power. I went to a local mechanic to happen examine my engine. He informed me that it was a hydraulic lifter that had collapsed. At the time, I did not have the money for a mechanic, so I decided to fix this fuel injected complicated engine myself.

I pulled the Cadillac into my little old garage, which had a dirt floor, and proceeded to tear the engine apart piece by piece. Valve covers, intake manifold, rocker arms, wires, electronic pieces all the other parts were scattered everywhere throughout my garage. What a mess!

Eventually, I was able to get to the hydraulic lifters and discovered the one that was collapsed. I went to pick up a new lifter at an automobile supply store where they had available. At the same time, I decided to replace all of the lifters at once. When I got back to my garage, I just stood there staring at my car, and all the parts scattered everywhere. Now I really was in a jam because I had no idea how to put the engine back together again, with all of its intricate parts. I did the only thing I knew to do. I cried out to God for mercy, I prayed: "Heavenly Father, please help me, in the name of Jesus, to get this car back together again."

This was the only vehicle we owned. Amazingly, knowledge entered into my brain at that very minute of how to do it step-by-step. It was like this divine download of the engine schematic flooded into my mind. If this had not happened to me, I would not believe it either. With this schematic in my mind it was as easy as one, two, and three.

Through this whole process I followed what I saw on this schematic in my mind. The peace and the joy of the Lord was his flowing up out of my heart. There was absolutely no confusion or question what to do. It was like the Holy Ghost was telling me step by step along the way what needed to be done. Now, I did not have a mechanics book next to me. It was a divine schematic in my brain.

To my amazement, when I was finished I had used every single part that was there in the garage. As I looked at the engine, everything seemed to be exactly where it needed to go. I closed the hood of my car, jumped behind the steering wheel, put the key into the ignition, turned the key, and it started right up and ran beautifully! Praise God for supernatural divine downloads.

Shall receive any thing of the Lord (James 1:5-7)

CHAPTER THIRTEEN

Miraculous Provisions

*89. Dangerous Chemicals

My Son Healed of an Incurable Affliction (1987)

When Daniel was little, he loved to put things in his mouth. While he was in the back seat of my sister's car, he found a can of DW 40. He was always inquisitive and nosey (and still is to this day). When he discovered the can of chemicals, his curiosity and the desire to put things in his mouth got the best of him. He sucked on the end and the cap popped off, so not only did he ingest the DW 40, but it also leaked all over him. By the time we realized what had happen, he was having a hard time breathing. I prayed over him, but he didn't seem to be getting any better. This chemical is not something to mess with!

Kathleen and I got someone to watch Michael while we took Daniel to our doctor right away. Informing the doctor what had happened, he strongly suggested x-rays, so we gave our approval. Lung problems have been a generational curse in my family, and I did not want Daniel to go through the same misery that I and other members of our family had gone through. My mother eventually died from medication related to her lung problems.

When the x-rays came back, the doctor's prognosis was not very encouraging. He showed us the x-rays. The chemicals he had gotten into were very dangerous. The x-ray showed that the chemicals were lining his lungs. Our doctor informed us that there was nothing that anybody could do for him. He also told us that he would always have breathing problems because of these chemicals in his lungs.

We thanked him for his help, paid the medical bill, and left his office. From then on it was a fight for his life.

Many times, late at night I would hear him struggling to breathe. Immediately, I would get up and take him into my arms, and begin to pray over him. I kept commanding the chemicals to come out of his lungs in the name of Jesus Christ of Nazareth. I would keep praying with him in the midst of it thanking, and praising God that he was healed, until he could be breathing normal, and then I would put him back to bed. This went on for many months. I began to notice that after each episode it would happen less and less. It has been over 20 years now since he has had an attack. Thank God, he's completely healed!

Now when the sun was setting, all they that had any sick with divers diseases brought them unto him; and he laid his hands on every one of them, and healed them (Luke 4:40).

*90. Hold on a Little Longer (1986)

"Mike and his three sons." I had been declaring this for the last six years. Early one Sunday morning, our midwife Martha called us to ask if it was okay for her to go away for the day. She said that she had to go out of town; I think for 吶 class reunion. She called just to double check and make sure that Kathleen was not going to be having the baby that day. As recounted in my last book, she had missed the birth of my second son, Daniel. I asked Kathee, my wife, what she thought. She informed us that there were absolutely no contractions whatsoever. She told me to encourage Martha to go ahead and enjoy herself at the reunion.

That morning we arrived early at church to practice for worship. Halfway through worship practice, Kathee's contractions started. Being a trouper, she kept practicing and then even led worship. When she had finished singing, Kathleen came to me saying that her contractions had begun. What I did next I believe was the Spirit of God. I told her to sit on the front row and to cross her legs until I was done ministering. She did exactly what I asked her to do. In this situation she should have protested (especially considering how fast she gave birth the last two times), but she sat there perfectly still until I was done preaching and praying for people. We had a family we knew take our two sons home with them. Kathleen and I then went home.

When we arrived home, she laid down on the birthing bed; however, something seemed to be wrong. Her water would not break. This went on for possibly forty-five minutes. I finally got on the telephone with the midwife. She told me that I would have to break the placenta. Right after I got off the phone, we cried out to Jesus together. At that moment while we were praying, her water broke and our third son, Steven Joel Yeager, came forth.

Kathee's Comments:

I expected that my contractions would start when we told Martha that she could go to her reunion. Mike and I had all the right equipment this time, so I wasn't worried. It seemed that our children wanted to arrive on church days and Steven was no different! I started having contractions during Sunday morning worship practice, but I kept focusing on what needed to be done. When I told Mike after worship that I was in labor, he asked me to sit on the front row. I wondered if the baby would wait to come until church was over... I found that if I sat perfectly still, with a straight back, the contractions slowed down. Boy, was that hard to sit that way all during service.

When we got home, something did not seem right because my water had not yet broken. Mike left the room to call the midwife and while he was gone, I asked the Lord how long it would be until the baby came. He told me fifteen minutes. I had my eyes glued to the clock, telling myself it will only be fifteen minutes. Sure enough, Steven arrived in fifteen minutes and all was well!

*91. Doing It by Faith

Building A $1,000,000.00 Building with No Money by Faith

While I was in Great Britain, the elders of the church in Gettysburg, had made a deposit on ten-acres of land. I was twenty-nine years old at the time this happened. Now, this property was located seven miles west of Gettysburg, on Route 30. When I got back from Great Britain, they showed me the property they had placed money on. The farmer had given us a tremendous deal on this acreage. It was not long afterwards, however, that our church went through a terrible split. It always seems that at the worst possible moment, when things look the bleakest, God has me take a gigantic step of faith.

As I was in prayer one day, the Lord spoke to my heart to build a church that would seat eight-hundred people. The key to this miracle, is that I had heard the voice of God. It is not something that I simply grabbed out of nothingness, and decided to do myself. Now, currently, the size of our congregation was only about seventy people. On top of this, we had no money! I knew the members of our congregation well, and as far as I could tell, none of them were wealthy. When the Lord quickened my heart, I immediately acted upon on what He spoke to me. I checked into local construction companies: just to put up the exterior steel building, and pour the concrete floor, would cost more than $800,000. I knew in my heart that this was not the way to go.

There was a man in our congregation who represented a steel building company from South Dakota. We began to coordinate with his company for the purchase of the steel we needed. They provided us with all the blueprints that were necessary for the foundation. I located an architectural company in Hanover, Pennsylvania, that was willing to work with us. I drew up a rough, simple schematic of what we were looking for. With that drawing, they were able to provide for us the simplest blueprint possible, which would be approved by the state of Pennsylvania. We went through the proper process to get the right building permits from local, county, and state authorities. We had everything in hand to start the project. We had done everything we could do!

Now what? We had no money!

As I was in prayer, the Spirit of God quickened my heart to simply step out in faith and do it. There was a man in our church, Richard, who owned a backhoe. I approached Richard about what I wanted to do, and he said: "Let's do it!" We went out to the property and staked out where the footers and foundations were going to be. Then he brought his son, from Maryland, to dig the footers. We ended up with a 100 x 150-foot ditch. We prayed every step of the way. As the Spirit of the Lord quickened me, I ordered the building materials.

On the day we were to lay the blocks that the metal building would sit on, it was pouring down rain. The men of the congregation wanted to cancel the Saturday work party. However, I told them that God was going to make it possible for us to lay the blocks on that day. As we were on the building site, we cried out to the Lord, and immediately the rain stopped, and the sun came out! By the end of that day 500 feet of block had been laid.

For thou, O LORD of hosts, God of Israel, hast revealed to thy servant, saying, I will build thee an house: therefore hath thy servant found in his heart to pray this prayer unto thee. And now, O Lord GOD, thou art that God, and thy words be true, and thou hast promised this goodness unto thy servant (2 Samuel 7:27-28).

*92. My Life on the Line

The company providing the steel for our building called from South Dakota, telling us that the steel building was almost ready to be shipped. They said they could ship it: cash on delivery. When the building arrived, I would have to give them approximately **$49,000**. At the time, we only had **$1,000** in our building account - with no other means of finances. The representative from the steel company also informed us they could store the building for about $1,200 a month, or they could ship it out within six to eight weeks.

As I was listening to the man over the phone, I heard the Spirit of the Lord say to me: *"Tell them to send it!"* I became very still before the Lord, because I wanted to make sure that I had heard Him correctly. The Spirit spoke to me again: *"Tell them to send it!"* I told the man from the steel company to go ahead and send the building! He told me that would be fine, and they would prepare it to be sent. He also informed me that I'd better be aware that if the building arrived, and I did not have the money, I would be breaking interstate laws (I believe he said there were five of them) and I would be going to jail: because I was the one who gave the approval for the building to be shipped! I got very quiet before the Lord and asked Him again, *"What I should do?"* The Spirit, once again, confirmed and quickened in my heart, to have them send it. So, once again, I told the representative to go ahead and send it. He gave me another warning.

The **Gift of Faith** was operating in my heart. I knew that it was done. After I got off the phone, a desire came into my heart to give away the **$1,000** in our building account. I was not trying to bribe God to do something for us. The **$1,000** we had was not going to do a thing for us, so why not give it away - out of faith? We took that thousand dollars and divided it up into ten different checks, sending it to ten different ministries. That Sunday, I went before the congregation and told them this story. I told them the steel was coming, and if they wanted to, they could get involved. I also told them we had invested **$1,000** into ten other ministries. I did inform the congregation that if I was missing God, in this regard, I was going to have a prison ministry. I had put my life on the line …

Amazingly, I had no fear or anxiety whatsoever during the six weeks leading up to the steel arriving. Without any doubt, I knew the money would be there. The finances began to trickle in. To this day, I do not remember where it all came from. I did not beg, plead, or call anybody for money. I received a phone call approximately six weeks later from the representative of the steel company. They told me that they were loading the steel up on their big trucks, and asked, was I ready to receive it? At that point we were still extremely short of the finances we needed. I told them to go ahead and send it. Within three days the truck pulled onto our property.

I met the truck driver at the construction site and he handed me the paperwork. There were certain documents which I had to fill out. I started filling out the paperwork, knowing that I was still **$15,000** short of the **$49,000** that I had to pay them in just a few short moments. As I was signing the papers, one of the men from our church pulled into the parking lot. He drove his car right up to me with his window rolled down. I could see that there was something in his right hand; he handed a check to me for **$15,000!** Thank you, Jesus!

I would just like to take a moment and tell you that the people in this story, who gave of their finances, were operating in a higher level of faith than I was. That may sound strange … but it's not. We're always exalting those who believe for the money. But what about the ones who make these sacrifices to give what they have? I have been on both sides of this equation, more times than I can count. I have both given - until it hurt - and gladly received, with unspeakable joy.

Not that I speak in respect of want: for I have learned, in whatsoever state I am, therewith to be content. I know both how to be abased, and I know how to abound: everywhere and in all things I am instructed both to be full and to be hungry, both to abound and to suffer need. I can do all things through Christ which strengtheneth me (Philippians 4:11-13).

*93. Supernatural Education

We had approximately thirty volunteer men assembled, to help put the steel of the building up. Men who did not attend our church came to help us. The majority were not construction workers in any fashion of the word. The Lord had put in our hearts to use volunteers to get the job done. The man we had gone through, to purchase the steel building, was to oversee this work, and was there with us. He had been consistent all the time. He helped us do the footers and concrete piers, and he did excellent quality work. The large crane we needed to put all the steel up was on the property, with its operator. I think the cost of the crane and the operator was over $150 an hour. The big machine was idling and waiting to go to work. Everyone was standing there waiting to work.

We all bombarded the leader with questions and asked for directions. He had the blueprints in his hands, and every time he went to look at them someone would approach him. The pressure on him was overwhelming. It was easy to see that he was getting extremely frustrated. From what I understand, he had not put up a building like this before, and if he had it was many years ago. More and more people kept tugging on him. Next thing I knew, one of the brothers from the church said: "Pastor Mike! There goes so and so!" I looked to see where he was pointing. Sure enough, there was the leader, going down the road in his automobile. I did not hear from him, or see him again, for quite a number of years.

At the time of construction, it seemed as if this was a satanic attack. Actually, I can now say what Joseph said, that although this situation seemed as if it was meant for evil: God meant it for good. The Lord was stretching our faith. There I was, standing in front of all of the volunteer men, who were waiting to go to work. The steel was lying on the ground and the crane was idling. I can still remember walking away from everybody, looking up to heaven, and crying out to God. I said: *"Lord, please show me how to put this building up. I had never even built a doghouse, let alone a large steel commercial building!"*

At that moment, it was as if an invisible blanket came down upon me. Wisdom entered into my heart and I knew instantly what to do: moment by moment. I grabbed the blueprints, walked towards the crane operator, and began to tell him where to put the steel. The building began to go up! Through the process, we lost volunteers and gained volunteers. The Lord began to send us skilled labor. Not much of it … but just enough!

Except the LORD build the house, they labour in vain that build it: except the LORD keep the city, the watchman waketh but in vain (Psalms 127:1).

*94. Hernia Be Gone (1988)

*I Kept Radically SHOVING my intestines back into where they belonged with my fingers.

Day after day we were putting up the steel of our church in 1986. We only had the use of a crane for a day during its construction. We had the crane handle all the heaviest beams. All the rest of the steel had to be carried and placed into position by hand. I'm not a very large man, as I only weighed about 140 pounds at the time. I was pulling and tugging, walking on steel beams, and balancing precariously on large steel Beams over my shoulder, and being carried up against my gut.

One day, as I was trying to put a heavy beam into place, I felt something rip in my lower abdomen. Later that day I noticed I had a large bulge. I had torn loose some stomach muscles. I had a hernia! I did not tell anyone. I found a quiet place and cried out to God. I laid my hands over the hernia, commanding it to go in the name of Jesus Christ of Nazareth. I went back to work because the building had to be put up. Every day I kept on lifting heavy steel. The hernia did not go away so I kept looking to God, trusting, and believing. The only one who became aware of the hernia was my wife. Honestly, I do not even remember telling her.

Why would I not tell anyone? It wasn't because I was afraid that people would have a poor opinion of me because I wasn't getting healed. I Have never worried in the least about people thinking I did not have faith. Faith is the substance that is or is not. You can fake faith, but then it's not faith. The Bible says if any man has faith, let him have it to himself. In my heart, there was nothing I needed to prove. You see, my confidence is in Jesus Christ, the Heavenly Father, and the Holy Ghost! If I have to go to the doctor, or use medication, it's nobody's business.

For over two years this hernia remained with me. The problem is I really was not aggressively dealing with it, but had gone into a state of passivity. I knew in my heart that it was time to deal with this monkey on my back. I began to speak to this hernia aggressively telling it that it was gone. Commanding my stomach lining to be made whole.

The only problem is that the hernia had now come to the place of being almost Strangulated. It was quickened in my heart that I was going to have to get aggressive with this hernia. So, I would take my right hand and put my fingers against this hernia. Then I would SHOVE it back into where it belonged. As I SHOVED this hernia, I would be speaking to it. In the name of Jesus be healed! I commanded my intestines to stay where they belonged as I shoved up word.

"Strangulated hernia. This is an irreducible hernia in which the entrapped intestine has its blood supply cut off. Pain is always present, followed quickly by tenderness and sometimes symptoms

of bowel obstruction (nausea and vomiting). The affected person may appear ill with or without fever."

But Pastor Mike did you not know that you could die if this hernia got strangulated? YES, I knew this, but I also knew within my heart that By the Stripes of Jesus I Am Healed!

I cannot tell you how many times through the next two weeks that I kept SHOVING my intestines back up into my body with my fingertips. I would speak to it as Jesus told us to speak to the mountain. I told my stomach lining that it was healed. I told my intestines that they were healed. My body is the temple the Holy Ghost, and you have no right to be giving me any problems I would tell my intestines.

One Typical Night I Went to Bed and Got Up The Next Morning To A Miracle. The Hernia Was Completely Gone. Praise God, it has never come back! That has been over 30 years ago!

That ye be not slothful, but followers of them who through faith and patience inherit the promises (Hebrews 6:12).

*95. Commanding the Storm

Taking Authority Over a Dangerous Storm

One day as we were busy putting the steel sheeting on the roof of our new facility with a handful of volunteers, a violent wind storm blew in. It was coming over the top of the Allegheny Mountains, which are just two miles west from us. We could see very dark blue and purple clouds swirling violently and racing toward us. Lightning was striking everywhere in those clouds as echoes of thunder rolled across the valley. This was a fast moving thunderstorm system. If that storm was to hit us with its fierce winds, we would be in big trouble. I was on the top of the building with all of our volunteers. It seemed like all of us had stopped working at the same time. There were about fifteen of us there that day.

As I was looking at this storm, the Spirit of the Lord quickened me. Faith rose up in my heart. Every supernatural work of God is from His Spirit. I told them all to stretch forth their hands toward the storm. I pointed my hand with the rest of the men towards the storm. I declared, "In the name of **Jesus Christ** of Nazareth I rebuke this storm. I command it to split in half and go around us in the name of **Jesus Christ** right now!" Whatever God quickened to my heart is what I spoke at that moment.

When I knew it was done inside of me, I turned my back to the storm and went back to work. It seemed as if this same faith also came upon the other men. As far as I know, we all turned our back to the storm and did not look back. Why? It was because we knew in our hearts that this storm had to obey. I kept on working with the men until I saw flashing and movement to my left and to my right. I stood up and looked, and this violent lightning storm was on the north and south side of us. The storm was behind us and in front of us. It had literally obeyed us. It had split right down the middle, and had gone around us. When it reached the east side of us, it joined itself back together and went on its way. We just kept on with constructing our new facility that day.

Within five months of breaking ground we had our dedication service. This first phase of construction was 15,000 square feet. The next year we added 7,500 more square feet for our Christian school. The day the steel came in for that particular edition we were still $5,000 short. Once again a man from the church drove up and handed me a check for $5,000. At the time of this book being written, we have close to 40,000 square feet of building. To God be the glory!

And they came to him, and awoke him, saying, Master, master, we perish. Then he arose, and rebuked the wind and the raging of the water: and they ceased, and there was a calm. And he said unto them, Where is your faith? And they being afraid wondered, saying one to another, What manner of man is this! for he commandeth even the winds and water, and they obey him (Luke 8:24-25).

CHAPTER FOURTEEN

Miracles Just Keep Coming

*96. Go Tell My Children

I was standing in my office during **prayer** one day looking towards the east, which was nothing but my office wall. To my shock and amazement, Jesus Christ stepped right through the wall and into my office! This happened so fast that it frightened me. I was only about four feet away from this wall. When He stepped into my room, He did not say a word to me, but just kept walking right toward me.

Pauls Prayer: *Ephesians 1:17 That the God of our Lord Jesus Christ, the Father of glory, may give unto you the spirit of wisdom and revelation in the knowledge of him:18 The eyes of your understanding being enlightened; that ye may know what is the hope of his calling, and what the riches of the glory of his inheritance in the saints,19 And what is the exceeding greatness of his power to us-ward who believe, ….*

The next thing I knew, Jesus walked right into my body. It was one of the strangest experiences I have ever had. My body did not resist in the least. It was as if my body was made for Him to dwell in. It was almost like when someone comes home to their house, opens the door, and simply steps in. When Jesus stepped into me, His face would've been looking out of the back of my head. I know this is hard to believe, but I literally felt Him turn around inside of me.

His arms and hands went into my arms and hands. His legs and feet went into my legs and feet. The moment Jesus was in His proper position, I instantly grew a hundred feet tall! I was gigantic in size. My head and half of my body were outside of the building I was in and I was looking down upon everything. My whole being was filled with amazing power, authority, and knowledge. All the problems and difficulties of this world were to be laughed at compared to the One who was within me. All of creation itself could not compare to Him!

As fast as it had begun, it was over. The next thing I knew, I was back to normal size. Then the Spirit of the Lord spoke something to me that would change the course of my life forever. He said to me, Go tell my children who they are! They know not who they are! The reason so many Christians walk around defeated is because they've never had a quickening of the Spirit, which brings revelation of who Christ really is. They do not realize that the same Jesus who overcame principalities and powers, rulers of darkness, and spiritual wickedness in high places now lives in us. The very one who brought all things into existence now lives in side of us. Christ in us the hope of glory!

*97. Black Gold, Texas Tea

Oil Tycoon Wanted Our Land! (2007)

In 1986 we purchased ten acres of land, which was just cornfields when we purchased it. The purchase of this land was a miracle in itself, because at the time there was no indication that this land was for sale. This land was located right across from where our main church facility was. I just knew by experience the prompting and functioning of the Holy Ghost, that I was to check into the purchasing of these 10 acres. After making several phone calls and inquiries, I was given the name of the person who owned it. It belonged to a doctor who had passed on some years previously. I heard that his wife was still alive and was in possession of this piece of land. I called the number that had been given to me. It was this doctor's widow who answered the phone. I told her that I was interested in this piece of property. She told me that she was not interested in selling it, but she would like to meet with me in person. I told her that I would be glad to come and meet her.

I went to her house on the prearranged date and time. She was a wonderful little lady who had been involved in much charitable work throughout her life in the community. After we spoke for a while, she informed me that she had changed her mind and decided that she wanted us to have this land! She said that she would sell it to us for the same price her husband had originally bought it for years before. I encouraged her to not take less than what it was appraised at. I hate it when people take advantage of people, especially widows. She insisted that all she wanted was what her husband had paid for it. Not only did she want to sell the land to us for what her husband had paid for it, but she wanted to set up payments with us with no interest, in order that we would not have to borrow the money. This was God!

Within a year, the land was completely paid off. I went to bed late one night after a time of prayer and meditation in the Word, and as I was sleeping, I had this incredibly realistic dream in which I was walking over this particular piece of property, which was still a cornfield. As I was walking down the rows of this cornfield, I was lifted up off the earth. I was suspended in the air approximately one hundred feet above the ground. As I looked down on this cornfield, it was like someone then took a large invisible knife and cut it directly in half, like cutting a cake.

Now, below me and underneath the top layer of the ground was a large lake of black gold, Texas tea (oil). After this dream I had enough wisdom to keep my mouth shut and I only shared it with a small handful of people throughout the years. In the pursuing years I began to take some exploratory steps to discover whether or not there was oil on this property. From all the geological maps I could discover, and information I gathered, the indication was that there was oil underneath that 10 acres. We did eventually drop a one thousand foot exploratory well, which was not deep enough.

In my dream the oil seemed to be between three to five thousand feet deep. At the time that I had this dream, I did not realize that the first operating Oil Company in the world was in Pennsylvania in 1859. According to the records on August 28, 1859, George Bissell and Edwin L. Drake made the first successful use of a drilling rig on a well drilled specially to produce oil, at a site on Oil Creek near Titusville, Pennsylvania. It was considered the most important oil well ever drilled and was in the middle of farm country in North-western Pennsylvania. Of course, there are times and seasons for everything. The timing to sink this oil well had not yet arrived. I believe we are coming very close to the edge of completing the drilling for this oil well. Another amazing fact is that no one had previously kept the mineral rights of this property. The mineral rights now belong to the ministry with thirty acres of land attached.

One day a strange event transpired when an eccentric gentleman showed up at our property. It all took place in 2007 as we were about to auction off thirty acres of our land in order to pay bills. At the time, I did not realize that this man was an oil tycoon. This particular man had showed up the day before the auction saying he would like to look around. He seemed to be in his early to mid-60s. Oddly, he was wearing a pair of slippers on his feet with no socks and driving an expensive white Cadillac. He was being attended to by a very attractive woman. He asked me some simple questions, stating before he left that he would be at the auction.

On the day of the auction, I was standing about twenty-five feet in front of the auctioneer watching the auction when this man came up behind me and whispered in my ear. He said to me: if you release the mineral rights on this land I will keep bidding the price up. At this moment the property had been pitted up to $400,000. Of course it was on this particular piece of property that I had the vision of there being Oil! When this man whispered this in my ear I turned around and looked him in the face, and my heart was quickened. In my mind came the thought, "This strange gentleman must be an oil man. And for some reason he knows there is a lot of oil underneath the property." In my dream, this lake of oil was located under the ground where our radio tower is erected. It came in my heart to check out my theory with him by making him an offer, so I said to him: I will release all the mineral rights to the 30 acres except for the acreage right under our radio tower. Without hesitation he said no, he wanted all the mineral rights.

I repeated my offer to him once again and said that I would release all the mineral rights to the almost forty acres except for the acreage under the tower. His face turned beet red and in front of all those present, he started yelling at me like an idiot. I could hardly believe the way he was acting in front of all those people. I turned my back on him as he continued to yell at me and everybody stood there watching him. The very next thing I knew he stormed away from me getting into his white Cadillac with this blonde lady. He started up his engine, backed up spinning his tires and drove off the property. From that day to this, I have never seen him again. What about the oil well? We are still waiting on God to provide the finances and the right people to drill it.

And the LORD answered me, and said, Write the vision, and make it plain upon tables, that he may run that readeth it. For the vision is yet for an appointed time, but at the end it shall speak, and not lie: though it tarry, wait for it; because it will surely come, it will not tarry (Habakkuk 2:2-3).

98. Could You Please Hurry up

Our daughter, Stephanie, was born on February 18, 1988. She was born at home in McKnightstown, Pennsylvania. We had the same midwife as before, but this time Martha said she was not going to miss this birth. She was going to earn her pay for once.

Martha was a very godly woman who had been a missionary (and midwife) in other countries for many years. This may seem kind-of silly, but Martha and I got it into our heads that Kathee had to give birth on February the 18th. Martha wanted this because this was the time she had available. I wanted this because it was my birthday. God gives us the desires of our heart. We had three wonderful sons, but I was waiting for my daughter.

How did we know this was a girl? It was by the Spirit of God. We have never had any sonograms performed to discover the sex of our children before they were born.

Kathee's Interjection:

I began to have contractions around 12:30 a.m. in February 18, 1988. By 1:00 a.m. I asked God what time the baby would come. He said at three o'clock. All my other labors were quick, so I failed to ask if it would be a.m. or p.m. We called Martha, because we didn't want her to miss this child's birth. If I had only asked the Lord for details, I would have been spared having two people trying to hurry me, God, and the baby! Despite them trying to hurry me, the contractions resided after four something, and they allowed me to sleep from five thirty to ten in the morning. Hallelujah!

Back to Mike's Perspective:

The contractions stopped and then began again much later in the morning, proceeding all day long without really growing in intensity. It was completely different with our boys. The contractions came and the next thing we knew, they were in our arms. But the birth of Stephanie was a little bit obstinate. (That is still a little bit of her personality.) Martha finally came to the end of her patience, and said that she had to do something, so Martha broke the water sack, and still nothing happened.

Now Martha and I were getting even more in a hurry, so she wanted to give Kathee a shot of medication that would speed up the birthing process. I told her that Kathee was very sensitive to medications. We discussed this back and forth while Kathleen wished that we'd just go away. She believed that God would bring forth the child in His time. But Martha and I were the ones in a hurry, negotiating what we were going to do. Kathee gave up and let us have our way when Martha said that she would just give her one fourth of the normal dose. Within just a matter of minutes after she gave my wife a shot, Stephanie came forth like a rocket. Martha barely caught her!

Kathee's Fi'-al Note:

I am so glad that Martha only gave me one fourth of a regular shot! I had one long contraction that lasted for over twenty minutes! Our baby, Stephanie, had to be totally squeezed through!

Note: I never had any afterbirth pains with Stephanie, because I believed that God redeemed me from the curse of the law concerning pain. I had believed God to have no birth pain for all my children, but then I realized that I had believed the lie about afterbirth pain. Yes, I did experience the labor and pressure, but no pain.

Howbeit when he, the Spirit of truth, is come, he will guide you into all truth: for he shall not speak of himself; but whatsoever he shall hear, that shall he speak: and he will shew you things to come (John 16:13).

*99. Lack of Faith and Not of Money

I was walking the floor of our sanctuary one afternoon, crying out to God concerning the finances of the church. We had some overwhelming financial needs that were weighing heavily upon my heart. At the time we had twenty-one people working for the church. Of course, we had vehicles, insurance, electricity and utility bills. Plus, we were on seven TV stations, cable stations and satellite broadcasting. As I was letting my needs be known, God said to me:

"Your problem is not money or lack of finances. Your problem is a lack of faith! You do not need more money. You need more faith in Me!"

I took this to heart, and asked God to forgive me for complaining and whining. Just a couple of days after that, I was sitting in my office, with approximately $24,000 worth of bills in front of me. I piled all the bills in one spot, laid my hands upon the needs, and confessed every bill paid - according to God's riches in glory.

As I was praying, there was a knock on my door. I told the person who was knocking to come on in. One of the men of the church came into my office. He was a very quiet man, and we had never really spoken very much to each other. He seemed to be just a very nice, everyday kind of person. Out of the blue, he asked me: "Pastor, how much money do you need to bring all the bills up to date?" I said: "You mean to bring the bills current?" He responded, "Yes. To pay the bills up to date."

He pulled out a blank check, and began to write on it. The thought entered my mind that he was going to make a small contribution towards the bills. I told him it would take $24,000 to bring the bills up to date. He handed me a check and I thanked him for it. Then I took a peek at it. I looked up at him … and back down to the check again. He had handed me a check for $24,000! In a thousand years, I would never have guessed that this quiet man, who seemed to have no money, would have that kind of wealth available.

It took this man more faith to give that money than it did for me to receive it.

Thank God for obedient people that are willing to do what God says, no matter what it costs them. Many times, it seems to me, that we as ministers boast and brag about how we believe God for money, and yet never recognize that it took a lot more faith for the person who gave the finances, then those of us who have believed for them.

And he said, Take now thy son, thine only son Isaac, whom thou lovest, and get thee into the land of Moriah; and offer him there for a burnt offering upon one of the mountains which I will tell thee of. And Abraham rose up early in the morning, and saddled his ass, and took two of his young men with him, and Isaac his son, and clave the wood for the burnt offering, and rose up, and went unto the place of which God had told him (Genesis 22:2-3).

100. I should've Told Him

It was the Fourth of July weekend. I had stopped at the local convenience store to pick up some things to take to my wife's family reunion. Every Fourth of July all of her relatives on her mother's side would get together. We were running late, as normal. I was trying to get some things done before we left. As I entered into the convenience store, I saw the owner of the property standing behind the counter. I had spoken to him a little bit in the past, but not in great detail.

The minute I saw him, the Spirit of God quickened my heart to speak to him about Jesus. The only problem was that I was running extremely late. My wife and children would be upset with me if I did not get home soon. So I argued with God, and told him that as soon as I got home from my wife's family reunion I would stop and speak to him. Tremendous conviction began to flood my soul, but I ignored it.

You would think that I would have learned my lesson from the last devastating experience. You know the time that I was supposed to talk to Billy but did not. Billy had died shortly after in a head-on collision.

I went home and very quickly loaded up all of the picnic supplies and food, forgetting all about the owner of the convenience store. I got my family into the car, and we went to Kathleen's Fourth of July family reunion. Approximately four hours later that day we arrived back home. On the way home I decided to pull into the convenience store. When I pulled into the parking lot, I noticed there was something wrong. They did not have any business, which was highly unusual. There was not a vehicle in the parking lot.

A very bad feeling came over me. I walked up to their store doors. The doors were locked and to my dismay there was a notice on the door. It said, "CLOSED DUE TO DEATH IN THE FAMILY." That afternoon the owner of the store had died from a heart attack. I should have shared Jesus with him when the Lord had prompted me to earlier that day. Lord have mercy. The moment God speaks we need to obey!

For he saith, I have heard thee in a time accepted, and in the day of salvation have I succoured thee: behold, now is the accepted time; behold, now is the day of salvation (2 Corinthians 6:2).

CHAPTER FIFTEEN

Miracles in Everyday Life

101. Rolex Idolatry

We had a prophet come to the church for a number of services. On the day he was to leave our fellowship he said he needed to speak to me about something personal. We went into the sanctuary which was now empty of people. As I was standing there he removed a watch from his wrist, very timidly putting it towards me. I asked what he was doing. He said to me that it was his Rolex watch and the Lord had instructed him to give it to me.

Now I had never met this prophet before these meetings with him. In other words, I was a complete stranger to him. I told him I did not want his Þve thousand dollar watch. (He told me that's what it was valued at.) He insisted he had no choice but to give it to me. He did not seem extremely enthused about this. I got quiet before the Lord, asking Him in my heart what this was about. The Spirit of God spoke to my heart and told me that this man was in bondage to his watch and that he needed to be set free. The only way he would be free from this idolatry was to give the watch away. The Lord spoke to me very forcefully to relieve him from it.

I said "Okay, I will take your watch. The Lord just spoke to my heart and said you are in bondage to it and you need to be set free!"

He did not deny or argue with what I had just told him. He handed me the watch with a very depressed look, turned, and walked out the door of our church. I really did not want this watch!

You see I'm just not into jewelry or extravagant living. I never have been and never want to be. I contacted a local jewelry to try to sell it. I was going to use the money to spread the gospel. I told the jeweler the make and model of the watch. Now I do not know if the jeweler lied to me, but he told me that he could buy that same watch new for six hundred dollars and would then sell that watch for ten times the amount of money he paid for it. Because I could not find a buyer, I decided to wear it.

The first thing I had to do was have a link taken out of it. I put that link in the fancy box that the watch came in. Through the next year, I was extremely rough with that watch. I wore it just like I would a five dollar watch from a department store. I was doing some mechanical work and somehow, I scratched the glass. The links got all dirty and grimy. Then during moving I misplaced its box. I never have found it.

About a year went by. One day I was in my office and the church's phone rang. The secretary answered it. She knocked on my door to tell me that the prophet (who had given me the watch) was on the line and wanted to speak to me. The last time I had heard from him was when he had given me the watch. I asked the Lord what it was that he wanted. The Spirit spoke to my heart and said the man wanted his watch back. The Lord further said that he was still in bondage to it and he was going to ask me to sell it back to him for five hundred dollars.

I picked up my phone, and for a while we went back and forth with small talk. I finally asked him what I could do for him. He asked if I still had the watch he had given to me. I told him I still had it. Then he informed me that for the last year he had been looking high and low for a watch just like the one he had given me, but was unable to find one.

He asked if I would be willing to sell him back his watch. I told him that I would not sell it back to him but if he wanted to donate to the church, I would be glad to send it back to him. He asked me how much of a donation I wanted. I told him he would have to decide. After a couple of minutes, he asked me if I would take five hundred dollars for it. I said that would be just fine and I would pack up the watch and send it back to him immediately. I sent him back his watch, and he sent the church five hundred dollars.

I never heard from him again. I was questioning God why he had me get involved in this situation. What was quickened to me was that the Lord knew material things held very little value to me. Consequently, I would abuse, misuse, and mess up that man's precious watch. Once he got his watch back and saw the damage, he would be free from its power. In the end, he really did get set free from Rolex idolatry in a roundabout way!

But godliness with contentment is great gain. For we brought nothing into this world, and it is certain we can carry nothing out. And having food and raiment let us be therewith content. But they that will be rich fall into temptation and a snare, and into many foolish and hurtful lusts, which drown men in destruction and perdition (1 Timothy 6:6-9).

102. God Will Make a Way

The Spirit had quickened to my heart to open a food pantry for the local community and to send supplies and equipment to ministers in other countries. The Lord began to provide equipment, clothing, and supplies. However, we had a major problem in how to get the food, clothing, and equipment to these missionaries in other nations. There was a new couple in our church who had just moved into the community. They wanted to get together with me and share what was on their hearts.

When got together, they began to share their hearts with me about wanting to help missionaries and do missionary work. I informed them that we were on the same page. I explained how God was providing food, clothing, and equipment; but we needed a way to get all these supplies to the other nations. Also, we had no way to distribute it. They became extremely excited because the husband was a major in the military and worked at the Pentagon. He believed he could find a way legally to let the military ship everything we could get our hands on for free.

This was God! We agreed that his wife would go to work for us full time in this endeavor. We set up a special office in our church for them. He and his wife took this vision in hand and sure enough he had wonderful connections with the government. They were able to provide us with free shipping to Africa and other countries in large containers. In a very short span of time, ministers and ministries were coming to us to help them get equipment overseas. We eventually linked up directly with an international ministry that held this same vision. We were using pastors in these nations to spread the supplies to the needy.

We were so successful that a non-profitable foundation which helps needy children contacted us to collaborate with them. They told us that they heard we were able to get equipment and supplies to nations without it being stripped by wicked government officials or by criminals. We told them this was true because we used a network of pastors in these countries. They told us that they had medical supplies that were desperately needed in Romania, and they had no way to get the supplies to the small medical health centers without being robbed blind. They informed us that criminals would love to get their hands on these supplies. We asked him to give us some time to see what we could do.

After much work, the major and his wife were able to build a network of pastors that would help us distribute this medicine. We contacted the organization and told them we could help. They told us their medicine was valued at over five hundred thousand dollars. We were able to distribute this much-needed medicine through the pastors to the medical centers. They contacted us again not very long after that, telling us that they had another supply of medicine and asking us to help them again. This shipment was valued at the same price of five hundred thousand dollars. Once again, we were able to help them distribute this much-needed medication. As far as we know, all of the medication got through to those who needed it.

Then shall the King say unto them on his right hand, Come, ye blessed of my Father, inherit the kingdom prepared for you from the foundation of the world: For I was an hungred, and ye gave me meat: I was thirsty, and ye gave me drink: I was a stranger, and ye took me in: Naked, and ye clothed me: I was sick, and ye visited me: I was in prison, and ye came unto me (Matthew 25:34-36).

103. Stirrings of Revival

I came across a book that changed my life. It is about a mighty revival that God brought in an overseas mission. I was so impressed and convicted by this little book that I ordered the book by the case. I took this book and distributed it to the whole congregation for free. I also gave this book to all of our staff, including the teachers in our Christian school. I believe we even gave this book to the older classes in our Christian school. I began to preach along the line of repentance, prayer, and one hundred percent commitment to Jesus Christ; that there should be no hidden sin in our lives. The fire of God fell in our church. (Revival!)

The Lord started working in such wonderful ways that the teenagers in our private school started weeping and crying in the classrooms. We had to stop the classes when this happened. I walked into the sanctuary of the church one day, and there were all the teenagers lying on the floor weeping, crying, and calling out to God! This wonderful move continued for a short season.

Repent ye therefore, and be converted, that your sins may be blotted out, when the times of refreshing shall come from the presence of the Lord. And he shall send Jesus Christ, which before was preached unto you (Acts 3:19-20).

104. Christ, My Attorney

We had applied for an AM radio station in 1985. We were finally contacted by the FCC, which had accepted our application. In this process, the FCC opened the door for other broadcast companies to make application for the same frequencies. We were notified that twelve other broadcast applications had been filed on top of ours. Basically, what it amounted to was a lawsuit against us.

I spoke to some legal advisers who told us that if we wanted the station we were going to have to fight the other applicants. We were going to have to get the best attorney we could. There would be a court hearing, depositions, and all that goes along with the court case. Listening to their advice, I hired a very impressive law firm out of Washington DC. The problem was that something in my heart did not feel right about bringing in this law firm. Our attorneys began to send nasty letters to the opposition.

The opposition sent back nasty letters to our attorneys. It was beginning to look like it was going to be one long and fierce battle. Before we knew it, our attorneys sent us a twelve-thousand-dollar bill. Nothing had been accomplished yet. If anything, it had gotten worse. I knew another Christian man who was in the same situation in Frederick, Maryland. He ended up spending seventy thousand dollars, and still lost the fight, even though he was the first applicant for the frequency of the station he was trying to build. I began to seek the will of God pertaining to what was going on. I knew in my heart that God wanted us to have this radio station to spread His gospel.

As I was in prayer, the Spirit of God told me I needed to take charge of the situation, to step in and take care of it myself. I called our attorneys and told them I was going to deal with the opposition. They got rather feisty and told me if I did not have the money to fight a legal battle I had no right to own a radio station.

To be in the broadcast industry you needed to have the finances to back you up. I told them directly they work for me and I didn't work for them! They were to do nothing until they heard further from me. Amazingly, this expensive high-class attorney became like a meek lamb over the phone. He said that he would abide by my wishes.

Then I did research to discover the telephone numbers of every one of the applicants. I called up all the broadcasters involved and told them I wanted to meet them in Washington DC during the National Religious Broadcasters Convention. I told them we needed to get our attorneys out of this mess, and we needed to deal with this problem ourselves. Every one of them agreed to this meeting in Washington DC. I set up the time and location for us all to meet. My wife and I met all of the opposition in a hotel room. The Spirit of God quickened me with the legal and technical knowledge I had to have to resolve our problems. They all sat there and listened. We walked out of that meeting with our radio station and we have been broadcasting since December of 1988.

And God gave Solomon wisdom and understanding exceeding much, and largeness of heart, even as the sand that is on the sea shore. And Solomon's wisdom excelled the wisdom of all the children of the east country, and all the wisdom of Egypt (1 Kings 4:29-30).

105. Smooth as Baby's Skin

Terrible Warts Gone Over Night (1986)

A poverty-stricken couple began to come to our church. We watched as Jesus set this couple free from drugs, alcohol, violence, and immorality. We helped install a new bathroom in their little house. The wife became one of the main workers in the church. She was always there trying to help people.

One day they brought one of their young daughters to us. They told us she had a problem they did not know how to resolve. They had taken her to the doctor, but there didn't seem to be anything they could do. The girl was hiding behind them, so her mother brought her to the front. Then she had the girl hold out her little hand. It was terrible. Her little hand was completely covered with warts front and back. We are not talking about twenty or thirty warts. It literally looked like hundreds of warts. We laid our hands on her little hand. We then commanded these foul warts to come off her hand in the name of Jesus Christ of Nazareth, and for her hand to be completely healed.

As we looked at her hand, it did not seem as if anything happened. We told them that when you pray in faith, you must believe that those things you asked for in faith are done. We explained that what we need to do is begin to thank God that she is healed—that the warts are gone in the name of Jesus. Both the husband and the wife agreed that it was done. They took their little girl, got in their car, and left.

The next morning, I received a phone call from the mother. She was extremely excited and bursting with happiness. She told us that when her little girl went to bed that night nothing had changed. The warts were just as bad as ever. When she went to get her the next morning, every single wart was gone but one. They brought the little girl back to us to look at her hand. Sure enough, in one-night God had removed every single wart but one, which was in the palm of her hand! The skin on her hand was smooth and normal just like the other one, as smooth as baby skin. We declared that the last remaining wart would have to leave also!

And as he entered into a certain village, there met him ten men that were lepers, which stood afar off: And they lifted up their voices, and said, Jesus, Master, have mercy on us. And when he saw them, he said unto them, Go shew yourselves unto the priests. And it came to pass, that, as they went, they were cleansed (Luke 17:12-14).

106. Getting It Half Right

I was learning how to fly a single prop plane. I had already finished my ground school and was in possession of my student pilot license. I had just started my cross-country flights. I had been praying and thinking about how I could cover my cost and yet make money flying. Somebody shared with me that the flying school in Shippensburg was selling their Cessna 172 for a good price. I contacted the owners of this plane. It was in beautiful shape. I went through the process of purchasing it. I went to the airport in York, where I was flying out of, to see if they were interested in renting this plane from me once I purchased it. They said they absolutely were.

By the time everything was said and done, I had the financial backing for this plane, plus the airport was going to rent it from me. So, the end results were a win-win situation. I was going to have my own plane totally taken care of for free! Plus, I was going to be making good money from it. During this time, I was also in need of a pickup truck. I had sold my last truck and given the money to the church. I did not want a new truck, just one that would get me around. My wife informed me that her brother was selling his Ford pickup.

One day as I was in prayer, the Spirit of God spoke to me, and this is what He said: "if you buy this plane your whole family will die in it." The second thing he told me is that if I bought this pickup truck, I would not only lose all the money I invested in buying it, but that it would cost me more than what I invested into it. I knew the voice of God! I knew if God said that we would die in this plane if I bought it, we would die in the plane just as He had said. I did not care how good the deal was or how much money I could make off of it. I called the airport, and the owners of the airplane. I told them that I was not going to buy the plane, and that I was so sorry for any of their wasted time and energy.

201

I was confronted with what to do about my brother-in-law's pickup truck. For some reason I just did not want to let go of it. In spite of God telling me what would happen, I decided to buy it. I called up my brother-in-law and told him my decision to buy his truck. Amazingly, he spent a good amount of time trying to convince me not to buy it. I had made up my mind; I wanted his F-250 three-quarter ton pickup truck.

I bought his truck, and almost immediately the engine went bad, then the transmission went bad. After I had taken care of these two major problems I thought to myself, I better sell it before I lose all of my money. I put it up for sale as is. A young man came by really wanting my truck. I told him he was going to have to buy the truck as it was with no guarantees. He completely agreed. He bought the truck, and drove away with it.

Within three days, he was back on my doorstep mad as a hornet. He said the frame of the truck was bent and he wanted some of his money back. I reminded him that he had bought the truck as is with no guarantees. He said he did not give a flip, the frame was bent, and he should get back some of his money. I ended up giving him back some of his money.

When all was said and done, I lost more money than I had invested. It was the voice of God telling me not to buy the truck! Thank you, Jesus, that I did not buy the Cessna 172. If I would have, you would not be reading this book now!

Now when much time was spent, and when sailing was now dangerous, because the fast was now already past, Paul admonished them, And said unto them, Sirs, I perceive that this voyage will be with hurt and much damage, not only of the lading and ship, but also of our lives. Nevertheless the centurion believed the master and the owner of the ship, more than those things which were spoken by Paul (Acts 27:9-11).

CHAPTER SIXTEEN

Miracles of Provision and Deliverance

107. In the Land of the Britts

Crippled Women Healed in Great Brittan (1993)

I've had the wonderful experience of going to Great Britain (five times) from Wales and Scotland. I had the privilege of seeing many miracles and wonders on these five journeys. At one meeting where I was conducting a citywide healing service, there was a very heavyset lady in a wheelchair on the front row. This meeting was not held in a church, but it was a community center so that other churches would come together.

After I was finished ministering the Word of God about healing, the Holy Ghost quickened me to go over and lay my hands upon this lady. I had no idea what was wrong with her. As I laid my hands upon her, I commanded her to be healed and made whole in the name of Jesus Christ of Nazareth.

When I was finished praying and commanding her to be healed, I told her to get up out of her wheelchair and walk whenever she was ready. Then I took two or three steps back away from her. I saw faith flashing in her eyes! She began to push her large body up out of her wheelchair. When she was finally standing up on her feet, she began to move her feet forward one little step at a time. She was walking! It really did not seem that spectacular to me, but the congregation was amazed.

After the service, I discovered what had happened to her. She had been in a terrible car accident ten year previously, and both of her legs were extremely damaged to the point that they were useless. One leg was so mangled that the doctors had insisted on it being amputated. This precious sister refused to let them take her leg. She had not walked since the accident and now she was walking. Glory to God!

Jesus answered and said unto them, Go and shew John again those things which ye do hear and see: The blind receive their sight, and the lame walk, the lepers are cleansed, and the deaf hear, the dead are raised up, and the poor have the gospel preached to them(Matthew 11:4-5).

108. Got a Pastor Fired

I was preaching once in a very old rustic church in Wales. The church was filled with many elderly people the night I was there. I think they were celebrating eighty-nine years of ministry since the founding of the church. There were approximately thirty to forty people in the service. These people looked to me as if they could have all been there at the founding of the church. (Maybe they did not look quite that old.) Their pastor was a young Spirit-filled man who I had spent the afternoon fellowshipping with. That's where I made my mistake.

Knowing that this pastor was Spirit-filled and excited about Jesus, I reasonably thought that this whole church had come into the experience of the Holy Ghost. I was about to find out that I was wrong! A very strong stirring of the Spirit gripped my heart, I preached with fire and compassion in the Holy Ghost.

As I was finishing the message, the Spirit quickened me and the word of knowledge began to flow. As I looked over the congregation, I could see what was specifically wrong in people's bodies. This does not always happen, but it is wonderful when it does. I began to call specific people out of their chairs. They all seemed to be a little bit hesitant to come forward. I thought maybe they were simply timid. (The Welsh people tend to be that way.) I kept encouraging them to come as I called them. The first person I called was a little old lady. As she came towards me, she crumpled right to the floor about ten feet away.

This seemed to cause quite a commotion. These old men jumped up and began to hobble their way over to her. I told them that she was okay and that it was the Spirit of God upon her, making her whole. Then I called out another person to come forward. This man came hesitantly towards me. At about ten feet away from me, without me touching him, or waving my hands at him, he crumpled to the floor. The same old men who were trying to get this lady up divided into two groups now. One group came over to try to help the older gentleman.

As I continued to minister, more people were falling under the power. I was having a wonderful time. I was excited! God was really moving in a spectacular way in this meeting. But something seemed to be seriously wrong. After I was done ministering, it seemed like people were avoiding me like the bubonic plague. As I was getting ready to leave, I noticed that all of these old men had surrounded the young pastor.

I left the church shortly after the meeting. Someone later told me as a result of the move of the Spirit of God in this service, the board of that church fired the pastor. It turns out they had never seen a move of the Spirit. I really felt bad for this pastor being fired. I was told that the pastor had been hiding the fact that he was Spirit-filled because he did not want to lose the church. He eventually pastored a church that was hungry for the things of the Spirit of God.

Saying, What shall we do to these men? for that indeed a notable miracle hath been done by them is manifest to all them that dwell in Jerusalem; and we cannot deny it. But that it spread no further among the people, let us straitly threaten them, that they speak henceforth to no man in this name. And they called them, and commanded them not to speak at all nor teach in the name of Jesus (Acts 4:16-18).

*109. Where Others Dare Not Tread

To tell this story in it's the proper setting I need to give you some background information. I had been to the Philippines multiple times reaching out to the indigenous people. The areas I went were considered to be one of the most primitive and dangerous settings in the nation. When I go to the Philippines, I always worked directly with a Filipino Bible college in the province of Samar. I have been told that Samar is one of the most poverty-stricken parts of the Philippines and one of the most dangerous. Missionaries very rarely go there because of this. It is far away from all the modern conveniences of Manila. It is also inhabited by the New People's Army which is a Communist movement. The NPA are extremely dangerous.

I have personally known Philippine pastors who I have ministered with who have been killed by them. During my time in the Philippines, the natives have allowed me to use their motorcycles to go up into the mountains to preach to churches in the boondocks'.

On one of my missionary endeavors, I was just finishing three weeks worst of outreach when the Spirit of God quickened my heart to ask them a strange question. I said to them: Where it is the most dangerous place to go to in this province? They told me it was an island called Laoang. I asked him why? They told me that two American missionaries had gone to the island of Laoang, and had not come out alive. The NPA had slit their throats as they were there. There had been no missionary endeavor there for at least 10 years.

As they told me this story, I heard myself say out of the blue: that I needed to go and take this place for Jesus. As I declared this bold statement to them, there was an amazing peace within my heart! I informed them that the next time that I came back to the Philippines, that I needed to go to that island and preach the gospel. They asked me if I was serious.

I said absolutely! I told them I would give them the money that they needed to make the flyers and posters to spread the word that we were coming. Before I left, I was true to my word, and I gave them the money that was necessary to print flyers to distribute to inhabitants of the island.

About six months later, I arrived back in the Philippines with one of the men from my church who is now a pastor in the Phoenix, Arizona area. When we arrived in the province of Samar, the brethren informed us that the Communists were aware of us coming and were going to be waiting for us. I did not ask them to explain to me what they meant. I absolutely had no fear in my heart. It is hard to explain to people what it is like when you are operating in a gift of faith. It is not normal faith.

It is faith that makes you know that in Christ you cannot be defeated. In the operation of this faith, there is always overwhelming peace. It is the peace of God that passes all understanding. The minute you lose your peace, you need to stop and asked the Father what is wrong. This is a major way in which God leads and guides us is by his peace.

Isaiah 55:12 For ye shall go out with joy, and be led forth with peace: the mountains and the hills shall break forth before you into singing, and all the trees of the field shall clap their hands.

To get to this island, we were first going to have to go by land on a worn out concrete road that had been built right after World War II. We had to travel from Catbalogan City to the town of Catarman . Then from Catarman, we continued our journey another 40 miles to reach our canoes that were going to take us to the island. Altogether the journey was hundred and 14 miles.

Now, this may not sound like a long-distance when it comes to traveling in America, but that is a long way on a rough Filipino road. We finally reached a river called the Pambujan River.

To our dismay, the bridge was out. They were putting in a brand-new bridge which they had only begun. So we had to take a long alternative route to reach another bridge to get across this river. This river was over 300 feet wide. (I only mention this because it's an important part of my journey on the motorcycle) We stayed on this road until it ran into the Philippine ocean. From there we took two large canoes. Each canoe had an outboard motor on the back of them. We would have to traverse on the ocean over a mile to reach Laoang.

After all of our equipment and the people were loaded into the first canoe I found myself up front at the very tip of the vessel. During this time there was great excitement and peace in my heart to see what God was about to do. I was optimistic of God manifesting himself on this island that had been shut off from the gospel for many years.

I knew that God was going to have to perform miracles to keep us alive, and yet there was absolutely no fear within my heart, nothing but overflowing peace. As we were coming closer to the island, I could see that there were men lined up along the beach waiting for us. There was absolutely no fear in my heart as we approach the island. There were approximately 30 men who were standing there with guns and machetes in their hands. The Filipino brothers who were navigating the canoes kept the engines of the canoes running fast enough so the canoes would drive themselves up a little bit onto the dry shore.

As we approached the shore, I was so excited that I stood up to my feet, getting ready to leap out of this canoe towards these communists. It had to be the spirit of God with in me because no sane man would leap to his death. I almost felt like George Washington's famous painting of him crossing the Delaware River. The moment we hit the beach, I was up and out of that canoe. The Communists were standing there waiting to kill us.

The Spirit of God, the gift of faith, the peace of God was possessing me as I began to walk towards them very rapidly. I headed right for the center of this crowd of gun toting and machete-wielding communist.

As I reached them, something supernatural happened. It was like the Lord splitting the Red Sea, but instead of water, it was men who had murder in their hearts. They separated from left to right and allowed our team of men to walk right through the midst of them.

For God hath not given us the spirit of fear; but of power, and of love, and of a sound mind. Be not thou therefore ashamed of the testimony of our Lord, nor of me his prisoner: but be thou partaker of the afflictions of the gospel according to the power of God (2 Timothy 1:7-8).

*110. Guardian Angels

We Held Our Meeting That Night!

That night we held a crusade right in the middle of the village. As our worship team was singing, the Communists and pagan religious people were marching through our meeting trying to disturb what God was doing. We simply ignored them and kept on with the meeting.

There was a very large crowd that night, probably because they wanted to see a white man. It was very seldom when Americans or Europeans came into this area. The tourists flock to Manila and Mindanao. It had been 10 years since anybody missionary had even dared come to this island to preach Christianity. The last missionaries that had come they had murdered. Now here I was about to preach the gospel of Jesus Christ to them. A message that saves, heals and delivers just like it did in the days when Jesus walked in his earthly ministry.

After the singing had been finished, it was my opportunity to preach. It literally felt like the spirit of God was flowing through me like a mighty river of electricity and power. I preached under the unction of the Holy Ghost, not thinking at all what to say, but letting the spirit have his way. When I was done preaching, there was barely enough light to make out the crowd in front of us. They had lit some torches around the meeting area, trying to give as much light as possible.

Because I could not get down into the crowd to pray for them, I had to speak the word of healing and salvation over them. I began to command their bodies to be healed in the name of Jesus Christ of Nazareth. Every time I would speak something in the name of Jesus, the interpreter would translate me into their language.

Miracles began to happen the moment I said: In the Name of Jesus. One old lady who had been blind in one eye could now see. A little boy who had been deaf could now hear. It was too dark out for us to tell how many miracles happened that night, but to this day I have been told there is a thriving church there because of this meeting.

After this large meeting, we were led to a two-story shack. The precious brothers we worked with had made arrangements for us to be put into a two-story house. We would be on the second floor, while they were going to be on the first floor. I know why they did this! They were going to make the Communists have to kill them before they would let the NPA get to us. These were the kind of men that would give their lives without hesitation for the sake of the gospel.

It was late by the time we went to bed. They gave my friend and I some type of straw mats to lie on. We threw these mats on the wooden floor and tried to go to sleep. During the night, we could hear the Communists outside making a racket. The communist had surrounded our house with groups of men. They had started little bonfires around the house where we were staying as the communist sat or stood by their fires.

As I went to sleep that night, I saw two large angels like

pillars of fire in a dream with swords drawn standing over the top of the house we were staying in. They had started little bonfires around the house where we were staying as the communist sat or stood by their fires. As I went to sleep that night, I saw two large angels like pillars of fire in a dream with swords drawn standing over the top of the house we were staying in. When we woke up in the morning, it was very peaceful. And the Communists were gone.

The Spirit of the Lord is upon me, because he hath anointed me to preach the gospel to the poor; he hath sent me to heal the brokenhearted, to preach deliverance to the captives, and recovering of sight to the blind, to set at liberty them that are bruised, to preach the acceptable year of the Lord (Luke 4:18-19).

*111. Typical Missionary Journey

I arrived in the Philippines with some kind of stomach flu, or virus, and I became deathly sick. On top of the sickness, I was extremely tired because of jet lag. The trip over was a nightmare! I had used a foreign airline to get a low price, but you get what you pay for. It was a crowded flight, with babies crying and filling their diapers.

The air in the airplane was extremely hot and stuffy; it stunk so bad that I almost had to breathe through my shirt. The seats on the plane were very small and uncomfortable. The person sitting next to me was practically sitting on my lap! The journey was almost twenty-four hours long. When I arrived in Manila, I had to catch another small plane which would take me to the province of Samar, to the town of Calbayog City. I waited about four hours before I boarded the small plane to get to Calbayog. When I landed at the airport in Calbayog, I had to take what they call a Jeepney, which looks like a Willies Jeep, only it's about ten times bigger. I had to ride this Jeep, crowded with other travelers, all the way out to where I was to meet up with the believers I was working with.

There are no windows in the Jeepney - except for the very front windshield. Because of this, I breathed in diesel fuel for hours while traveling on rough, bouncy roads. Filipinos were pushing up against me all the way. I felt like an animal crowded in a cage.

After more than thirty hours without sleep my head was throbbing so bad I could hardly handle it. I felt like I was going to pass out at any minute. I was sicker then sick. Finally, after what felt like a never-ending nightmare, I arrived at Catarman, where I was scheduled to preach. In the natural, I was in no condition to preach or minister. Yet, I made it to my first meeting. The building had a tin roof, walls made of block, and the seats were wooden benches with no backs.

I almost fell over, right then and there, but I buckled down and gritted my teeth. When it was time for me to speak, the Spirit of God quickened my mortal flesh. I preached like a house on fire! For the next twenty days, nonstop, I preached every chance they gave me. My mind, heart, and body were energized and quickened by the Holy Ghost. This is the life of **Violent faith**!

James 1:2-4 My brethren, count it all joy when ye fall into divers temptations; 3 Knowing this, that the trying of your faith worketh patience. 4 But let patience have her perfect work, that ye may be perfect and entire, wanting nothing.

A Brief Description of Faith:

When God, His Word and His will are Supernaturally Quickened to you by the Holy Spirit! These realities become more real to you than anything in life. It is a revelation of who Jesus Christ & God, the Father really are! What They have done and Are doing. It is a quickening in your heart, when you know, that you know, that you know, that you know: if God is with you, then who can be against you? Christ Jesus, Himself, lives inside of you. Your mind, your will, your emotions, and every part of your being is overwhelmed with the reality of Jesus Christ! And you enter the realm where all things are possible! This is where, by God's grace, it is my hope and desire to take you.

*112. Driving under the Influence

Held Up By Angels On A Motorcycle under the Influence of The Holy Ghost!

We had left the island in the morning, and we were now holding meetings in a town called Pambujan, which was about 19 miles away. God was moving in a wonderful way. The Philippine brother who was over all of the work in this area is named Danny. He also had two other brothers, Jonathan and Hurley, who are also ministers of the gospel. (You can friend them on Facebook if you like). I personally knew their father, Reese Monte's (who has since gone home to be with the Lord), who was an amazing man of God who was instrumental in starting over five hundred churches throughout the Philippines islands.

The name of the organization was "Faith Tabernacle. These men are all apostolic in nature. If I understand correctly, Danny has been instrumental in starting over seventy churches. Now here I was ministering with Danny. Danny came to me late one night and said he was really homesick. He had never been away from his wife this long. We were approximately 32 miles from his home in Catarman.

This may not sound like a long-distance to you, but believe me with the road conditions, the weather, and the communist it was quite a distance, especially if you are going to travel in the night. Actually, in this area, I never saw any vehicles out on the road after the sunset.

Now I had earned a reputation for being good on a motorcycle. In all reality, though I wasn't very good on a motorcycle at all. It is simply that the Spirit of God would quicken me as I would take a motorcycle up into the mountains to preach the gospel to the natives. I'm kind of hyperactive, so in between Crusades and conferences. When everyone else was taking a siesta, I would find someone who was willing to go with me to interpret for me, and I would head up into the mountains.

We were deep in a heavily populated area where there was known to be anti-government radicals, Communists, the NPA, and it was extremely dangerous to be there and especially at night. Brother Danny came to me though one night asking me if I would be willing to take him home on a motorcycle that someone had driven who was on our team. It was a very rainy and foggy night. Now the motorcycle that was available was an old machine—I believe it was a Kawasaki 250. This motorcycle had some issues though. The headlights were very dim, and at times the shifting mechanism would fall off if you were not very careful.

When Danny asked me to take him home, the Spirit of God quickened my heart and said: take him. It was like when David had said he was thirsty for the waters of the well in Bethlehem. Three of his mighty men broke through the host of the Philistines and drew water out of the well in Bethlehem for David to drink. This quickening in my heart was so strong that without any hesitation I told Danny I would take him home to see his precious wife and children.

Danny informed me with almost a whisper that we must not stop along the way no matter what because the Communists would be out in full force. He also said we would have to to be very careful because the Communists (if they heard us coming) would stretch a thin cable wire across the road in order to kill us. I saw a video one time where this is exactly what they had done, and it was captured on film. The motorcyclist was cut right in half. It was not a very pretty image.

He also informed me that if they got their hands on us, we would be dead men. Even with this dire warning from Daniel, I had total and perfect peace. Actually, there was a divine excitement within my heart to go on this journey. This is not something you can explain to a person who has never experienced the quickening, moving, empowering presence of the Holy Ghost.

As we began this journey, we had made one major mistake. We forgot that there was road construction all along the way and that the main bridge was out. If we would have remembered, then we would've taken a long way around. As it was, we took the regular route that would've been the shortest route to Danny's home.

Now as I was driving the motorcycle, I could barely see where I was going. The rain and the fog were coding the shield of my helmet. The headlight was very dim almost nonexistent. I had to keep reaching up with my left hand to wipe my face shield to see where I was going. Danny was sitting behind me holding on tight as I was driving. I believe I was driving at approximately forty-five to fifty miles an hour.

After we had been on this rough construction road for several miles, I thought that I could see something very dark and threatening in the pathway ahead of us. In my mind it seemed to me to be an enemy and waiting, and yet I had total peace. I should have slowed down, but I just kept on going. The next thing I knew, Danny was yelling very loud in my ear with a great warning, "watch out."

I yelled back at Danny: Hold on, we are going to go through it! Whatever this object was, we slammed into it doing about 50 miles an hour. As it turned out, it was a very large pile of gravel and road material. We hit this very large pile of construction material which was almost vertically straight up. The bike without hesitation raced to the top of this pile of construction material and launched us up into the void of the night. During this event, Danny took his head and put it underneath my left forearm, under my armpit.

It turns out he had been in a terrible motorcycle accident before, and now he was trying to protect himself as much as he could from the disaster which was unfolding. In every scenario, this was going to be a major catastrophe. Not only would-would be killed or extremely hurt when we hit the concrete road but then the communist would be upon us. There was no hospitals or help that would be available for us. We Surely Were Dead Men!

Here we were launched up into the darkness of the night. As I was up in the air on the back of this motorcycle, it the truly felt like I was just sailing through the sky like when I used to fly airplanes. During this experience, I was supernaturally engulfed in an amazing bubble of peace and joy. I had absolutely no fear or anxiety whatsoever. I was operating in the REALM of the spiritual. It seemed like for the longest time we were not going to come down.

We were suspended in the heavens. Of course, we must've been sailing through the skies in an upward and downward flow. It was obvious when we hit the wet concrete roadway below us, that something would have to give. But when we make contact with the road, it was so smooth, so nonresistant, that it almost felt like putting on a pair of comfortable old bedroom slippers. This is the only way I can describe it. We did not skid, bounce, or slide in any sense of the word.

The only thing negative that happened when we met the road is that the gear shifter fell off the motorcycle. We were stuck in the Top Gear as we headed down the road. We had to stop and go back and look for it. We went all the way back to the pile of gravel we had hit and started from the pile working our way out in order to find the shifter. I did not think to measure the distance of our jump. We looked and looked, and looked with the dim headlight of the motorcycle. By this time, Danny was very concerned about the Communists seeing the headlight of the motorcycle and hearing its engine running, so we decided to leave the motorbike in top gear and leave.

As we were headed down the road at about four hundred feet away from the pile of road gravel, I saw something gleaming on the road in front of us in the rain. We stopped, and there was the shifting mechanism! We put it back on the bike and went our way. How far we flew through the night sky that night, only God Knows! Now if you think this sounds incredulous, weight two ye hear about the next part of this journey. Danny Monte's can verify every bit of this journey.

But they that wait upon the LORD shall renew their strength; they shall mount up with wings as eagles; they shall run, and not be weary; and they shall walk, and not faint (Isaiah 40:31).

*113. Over the River We Go

Over a 300' River, on Wet Slimy 18-inch Planks in the Fog, in the Night with the faulty headlight on a Motorcycle!

It seemed as if we had been on the road for a long time when we finally came upon the river. This river was over three hundred feet wide. It was a very deep and fast moving river that flows into the Philippine Sea. We forgot we had taken another way to get to the village of Pambujan. The reason we had to take another way is because the bridge was out. I believe God's hand was in this despite this very serious situation.

During the construction of a new bridge, the workman had driven wooden pilings down into the bed of the river in order to create a walkable system over the river. They had placed rough sawed planks upon these pilings. These planks were approximately eighteen inches wide and were loosely attached on these pilings. This footbridge appeared to be four to five feet above the river. These planks were extremely wet and slimy. I would not have wanted to walk on them in the daylight, let alone on a wet and extremely foggy night. To get to the beginning of the planks you had to go down a muddy embankment and back up a pile of dirt to get to the plank walk bridge. There was no way we could walk that motorcycle across this river.

When we found ourselves in this situation, Danny said to me: "What are we going to do?" The Spirit of God rose up in me, and I heard myself say "Hold on Danny!" When I hit the first plank of approximately 30 planks with my front tire of the motorcycle, I shifted into second gear. I watched as my bike sailed across the wet slimy plank in front of me. I gunned the throttle as I continued to drive the motorcycle over the wet, slimy, loose planks—not slipping one time.

If I would've gone to the left or to the right either way, we would have plummeted into the raging river, swallowed up into its strong current, never to be seen again. It was the Spirit of God that took us across that three-hundred-foot river in the rain and fog, on slimy wet 18-inch planks, over a precarious bridge that was only made for foot traffic during the daylight.

I'm telling you that if I had not been there to experience this myself, I probably would not believe this story. We sailed across that makeshift bridge all the way to the other side without one mistake or mishap. To make a long story short, the Lord saw us safely to Danny's house.

Years later I went on the internet to look at this river that we had crossed. The internet image had been updated in 2010. The new bridge that they were just getting ready to build at that time had been completed. You can see the alternative road we had to take another route until the new bridge had been built. I am overwhelmed at the amazing things I have watched God do.

For with God nothing shall be impossible. And Mary said, Behold the handmaid of the Lord; be it unto me according to thy word. And the angel departed from her (Luke 1:37-38).

*114. They were out to KILL us!

We had been ministering in the province of Samar. While we were there, a minister from Manila had been attending some of our pastor conferences. In the conference, I had simply stated that we were not afraid to die for the gospel. Whether it be by the Communists or any other physical or natural disaster, nothing would stop us from doing God's will. This particular pastor seemed to be enamored with the thought that we were not afraid of the Communists. That wasn't our message. We were not there to challenge the Communists or to Americanize the Philippine nation and its people. We were there to preach the gospel of Jesus Christ.

Because we needed to contact the airline three days in advance before we were to leave, we had to have someone in Manila let them know the date we were leaving. Our tickets were open ended, meaning we could leave anytime we wanted to, we just had to let them know three days in advance. This particular minister, who seemed to be enamored with our lack of fear, was headed back to Manila. We asked him if he would please let the airlines know when we were going to be leaving. He said he would be glad to do that for us. We gave him the dates that we were leaving.

There was unrest in my soul as we said goodbye to him. There was just something about him that made me extremely hesitant to trust him. When we were finished with our meetings in Samar, we caught a plane ride back to Manila. We called this minister, and he came and picked us up in his car at the airport. When we got into his vehicle, he began to talk right away about the meetings he had lined up for us. I asked him, "What meetings are you talking about? We are to be leaving tomorrow." I asked him whether or not he had contacted the airlines for us. He informed us in a hesitant murmuring way that he had not.

The red lights began to flash in my heart right away. It's like I heard the Lord say, get on a plane tomorrow, and get out of this nation. This man has set you up to be murdered. I leaned over and told my friend what the Spirit had spoken to me. He agreed with me one hundred percent. I told him that we were sorry, but that we could not accommodate him since we were leaving the next day. He looked back at us, and basically said that's impossible. You have to give a three-day notice. You might as well go ahead and minister at the meetings I have set up. We discovered later that he had been making outrageous statements about us, making it sound like we were there to challenge the Communists and were not afraid to die. Of course, the NPA would come to kill us, not because we were preaching Jesus Christ, but because this man made it sound like we were challenging them and their movement. I did not argue with this man any longer. We stayed at his house that night.

Early in the morning, we woke up and got ready to go to the airport. We discovered he had not taken us seriously about taking us to catch a flight. We insisted that he take us immediately. Finally, he grudgingly agreed. We had him drop us off at the airport and told him he could go home. He said he would wait for us because he knew it was impossible for us to leave. We went to the main office of the airline.

They informed us that our tickets could not be changed because we were flying economy and their plane had already been booked to capacity for the day. I very politely asked if there was someone higher up we could speak to. He took us to a gentleman. We explained to him we needed to leave. When he asked why, I informed him we could not give him a direct answer to his question, but we simply needed to leave. He asked us to wait a little bit for an answer. We stepped out of his office into the foyer.

After a little while, he called us back in. He told us that they were going to do it. Amazingly, they had bought us tickets from a much more expensive airline. He handed us two new tickets and told us that we better hurry to catch the flight, which was boarding at that very moment. As we ran to catch a flight, we saw the minister standing behind the rope line waiting for us. We waved goodbye to him as we headed to catch our flight home.

I know thy works: behold, I have set before thee an open door, and no man can shut it: for thou hast a little strength, and hast kept my word, and hast not denied my name (Revelation 3:8).

CHAPTER SEVENTEEN

We Need Miracles

*115. Where Is the Man I Married?

I began to grow a little bit cold and lukewarm in my spiritual walk with God. Now I still was very much active in the church, but I wasn't flowing in the Holy Ghost. My wife became very concerned about me. Unbeknownst to me, she began to pray and intercede on my behalf.

Kathee's Perspective:

My heart yearned for the man I married. Michael was not on fire for God like he once was. He had become burdened by the woes and cares of life and the church. He was miserable, and making us all miserable with him! My prayer to God was to bring back the man I had married, and make him more on fire for God. I began anointing everything that Mike touched with oil: his truck, his clothes, even his computer.

However, my prayers did not appear to be very effective, that is, until the day the Spirit of God came upon me! A supernatural spirit of travail overtook me. This time as I prayed, I anointed his pillows and things with my tears instead of oil. I had truly touched heaven, because that very night when Mike returned home, God was waiting for him!

Back to Michael:

When I came home from church, Kathee was already in bed asleep. I slipped out of my clothes and crawled into bed. The minute I laid my head upon my pillow, the overwhelming power of God's conviction hit me. It didn't seem fair! Kathee was sleeping peacefully, but I was about to lose my sleep, and so much more!

Immediately I began to weep and cry. The conviction of God so overwhelmed me, I had to get out of bed and begin to pray. I prayed all night long in this spirit of conviction. I kept praying through the next whole day. It was so strong upon me that I was not able to stop.

Not only could I not stop praying, but I had no desire for physical food. It wasn't as if I decided not to eat, it was because I could not eat. The only thing I could do was drink water and pray. This went on one whole day. After the first day it did not lift, but instead it increased. I went two days; then three days. This continued for the next forty days and nights. All I could basically do was pray and fast.

I do not want you to be led to believe that I did not drive my car, preach in the pulpit, check the mail, or do the necessary natural things; I did all those things. However, the Spirit of God was on me in a mighty way. Right after God dealt with me this way, we had a wonderful move of God in our home and church.

My little children, of whom I travail in birth again until Christ be formed in you (Galatians 4:19).

116. A Reprobate and an Outlaw

One Sunday morning, the Spirit of God moved in a powerful way. Many people came forward to be prayed for. In the prayer line was a young evangelist who had been attending our church for some time. This morning the spirit of prophecy was flowing. When I came to this young man, I laid my hands upon him, he immediately fell under the power of God. I continued to go down the line ministering to the people. When I was about three people down from him the Spirit of God took a hold of me. I found myself back at this man's feet. I ended up straddling him with my left foot on his right side, and my right foot on his left side.

Then I reached down and grabbed his shirt with my left hand. With my right hand I began to slap his face very hard. I must have slapped him at least five times, on both sides of his cheeks. When I was done slapping him, I went back to praying for the other people. After a brief period, the Spirit of God took me back to him once again. I spoke by the Spirit of God to him. The Spirit of the Lord told him, "Even as my servant has slapped your flesh, so you must slap your flesh. If you do not crucify your flesh, you will become a reprobate and a fugitive from the law!"

When the Spirit of God moves upon me that strong sometimes, I do not even completely remember the things that I say. After the service, I did not consider what had happened.

Three days later I received a phone call from one of the ladies in the church. She was weeping and said that her twenty some year old daughter had ran away with this particular evangelist, and that previously he had been having a sexual relationship with another lady in our church. I prayed with her over the phone.

Approximately one month later I received another phone call from this same lady. She informed me that this man had beaten her daughter, and that they had gone out one-night drinking, when they were pulled over by a policeman. This evangelist got in an argument with the officer, which ended up with him physically fighting this policeman. Before he knew what, he was doing, he had grabbed the police officer's revolver out of his holster and aimed the gun at the cop. He then left her daughter and the police officer, and ran for his life. Supposedly, he was headed for Canada. The last time I had heard, he was a fugitive of the law.

I therefore so run, not as uncertainly; so fight I, not as one that beateth the air: But I keep under my body, and bring it into subjection: lest that by any means, when I have preached to others, I myself should be a castaway (1 Corinthians 9:26-27).

117. New Work in Hagerstown

The Spirit of God quickened my heart to start a church in Hagerstown, Maryland. For three years I resisted this unction. I approached one of the godliest elders I had in our church, who happened to live in this area. I asked him if he would sincerely pray about helping me start this new church in Hagerstown. He came back to me and basically said that he really did not want to. He was happy and content coming to the church in Cashtown. Nevertheless, he would help start a church, if it was God's will. To this day that elder and his wife are still laboring diligently in the Hagerstown church, even though they are now in their nineties!

We began to conduct services in 1994 to start this church. At this present moment, they have a beautiful facility with a dynamic pastor. Furthermore, they have been blessed with a wonderful congregation.

And they, continuing daily with one accord in the temple, and breaking bread from house to house, did eat their meat with gladness and singleness of heart, praising God, and having favour with all the people. And the Lord added to the church daily such as should be saved (Acts 2:46-47).

118. Precise Prophecies and Testimonies

1.   In one particular service, there was a married couple who had come forward for prayer. The husband and wife were both working for a youth and children's camp ministry. He was a rodeo clown for the children's camp. As I came to this couple, the Spirit of God quickened me, and I told them that in three days he would

lose his job and position with that ministry. I also told them prophetically that at the time it would seem to be devastating, but that he should not despair, because God would open up new doors of opportunity for him and his family. Just as I prophesied, within three days he lost his job—he was fired! Yes, it was extremely devastating for them, but because the Lord had already told him that he was going to have a bright future and a new occupation, they were able to endure this trial. God supernaturally gave this man favor and he opened up another business that became prosperous.

2.   One of the mothers in the church came to the front for prayer. The Spirit of the Lord quickened me and I prophesied that all of her children would be saved. I also said and that her husband would also be saved, but it would be as if he was snatched from the flames of hell. A number of years later, she related to me that everything I said came to pass. Her husband ended up with cancer. He was not open to the things of God, but as he lay on the bed of death, he cried out to Jesus. He was gloriously saved, with a deep hunger for the things of God. Shortly thereafter, he slipped off into eternity. He had been snatched from the flames of hell. Here is her story in her own words.

Mary's Testimony :

My name is Mary J. Rockwell. I would like to share three quick testimonies in which I saw God move in powerful ways in connection to Pastor Mike's prophecy:

Testimony 1: Years ago my mother was very sick and in the hospital in New York state. I had asked Pastor Mike to pray for me prior to leaving Maryland to go see her. He told me when I saw her I was to pray over her and say, "I command all tormenting mental spirits to leave her now in Jesus' name."

When I arrived at the hospital three of her doctors told me that she was going to die. My sister had called a pastor and began planning for her funeral. She had not eaten for days and had huge bags of fluid in the whites of her eyes and all over her face and didn't even look human. She was hooked up to IVs and monitors. I waited until only she and I were left in the room. I pulled the curtain around us, put my hands on her head and prayed just as the Lord told me to. I clapped my hands when I said, "Now," and I felt a surge leave my hands and go into her body. The next morning I went in to see her. The IVs had been removed, she was eating, and all the pockets of fluid had disappeared from her face and eyes! The doctors were amazed. They released her that morning. She lived another three or four years.

Testimony 2: I had fallen and broken both my wrists. The doctor had put a cast on one but I wouldn't let him cast the other. I went to Pastor Mike's home and he met me in the driveway. I asked him to pray for my healing, so he did. I went home and within a week I felt that my wrists were healed. I told the doctor either he remove the cast or I would have my husband cut it off. The doctor had told me I would have to keep it on for several weeks, but he reluctantly removed it. That same week I painted three ceilings by hand. The Lord had totally healed my wrists!

Testimony 3: When my children were still in school, I went up to the altar for prayer. Pastor Mike prayed and said, "Your prayers have reached the very throne room of heaven. God said, " you will live to see all of your children serve the Lord. Your husband will be saved but he will be literally pulled out of the pit at the very end." My husband, at age seventy-two, contracted cancer from exposure to deadly chemicals while serving in the Marines in Vietnam. I had assumed that he knew the Lord. I prayed for him and said, "I could lay hands on you until you are bald, but you need to cry out to Jesus for yourself." He could not say the name, Jesus so I knew instantly that it was a demonic block.

I called a local pastor and was about to relate that to him when he told me that my husband's perception of salvation was wrong and he didn't believe he was really saved. He went to the hospital and prayed with him. My husband called me on the phone and said he had just received Jesus Christ as his Lord and Savior. His one regret was that he hadn't done enough for the Lord. The Lord had spoken to two young ladies who lived miles away from us to come and pray with him. When they came, my husband prayed for them and they wept and wept.

Three people who were there when Pastor Mike prayed for me called me on the phone and each of them reminded me of the prayer that Pastor Mike had prayed over me many years prior to that. Each of them inquired if my husband was saved and I told them it was just as Pastor Mike had prayed many years before. Since then, two of my four children are serving the Lord...two more to go!

Then Samuel took a vial of oil, and poured it upon his head, and kissed him, and said, is it not because the LORD hath anointed thee to be captain over his inheritance? When thou art departed from me today, then thou shalt Þ nd two men by Rachel's sepulchre in the border of Benjamin at Zelzah; and they will say unto thee, The asses which thou wentest to seek are found: and, lo, thy father hath left the care of the asses, and sorroweth for you, saying, What shall I do for my son? (1 Samuel 10:1-2).

*119. I'm a Dead Man

I was a Dead Man as I Flew My Plane into the High Voltage Lines (1990)

I was in the middle of receiving my airplane license. I had finished ground school and had completed all my cross country flying. One day I was at the York airport doing simple go-arounds (That's where you land and you just keep going after you land, and take back off again).

I later found out that the Spirit of God had quickened my wife and told her to pray for me. She had already been really upset at me for wasting all this money on flying. The Lord told her that if she did not forgive me and get her heart right, I was going to die. She repented, and cried out to God, and said, "Lord, I give it to you. Please protect him."

Everything seemed to be going okay as I did go-arounds, but as I was getting ready to land, the wind shifted to another direction. They called me from the tower and told me that they felt it should still be okay to stay in the same pattern one more time; and that the next time around I could land in the opposite direction. As I made my approach for the runway I began to meticulously go through all of the processes of making a proper landing: I lowered my flaps, turned on my carburetor deicer, and began to bring my airspeed down to where I would be landing at about forty mph. I was still about 30 feet above the runway. Everything seemed perfectly normal.

As I began to pull back on the yoke to flare the plane, suddenly, my speed indicator dropped to zero. As a young pilot, I did not realize what this meant. It was an indication that the wind was now coming in from behind me. This meant I had just lost all my lift. I dropped like a rock and my plane slammed into the runway. I hit the runway very hard. I pulled back on the yoke. The minute I slammed into the runway, I bounced back up into the air like a basketball. I made a terrible mistake: instead of going around, once again I pulled back on the yoke and tried to land my plane. Once again, I dropped like a rock, slamming just as hard into the runway as the last time. Not being very intelligent, I tried to land once again. This time when I bounced I was really in trouble.

Now my plane was completely turned away from the runway. There was nothing but a grassy field ahead of me with electrical power lines. I gave the little Cessna 152 full power. I kept my flaps down, in take-off position. Yet, I made another major mistake by keeping my carburetor deicer on. This means, I did not have the full horsepower of my engine. Now, I was headed right for the power lines! My airspeed was barely enough to keep me in the air. I knew that I could not turn away from the power lines. If I tried to turn away I was a dead man. Moreover, I knew that I didn't have enough skill to fly underneath them. In addition, I knew that I could not get over the top of them. If I pulled back too much on the yoke, it would cause the plane to go higher, but it would drop like a rock again, because my speed was way too slow.

At that very moment, I knew I was a dead man. My whole life flashed in front of me in a matter of seconds. My heart was filled with thankfulness and prayer to God for all the wonderful things He had done for me in my life, for giving me my precious wife and four beautiful children. The second thing that hit me was tremendous sorrow and regret: I would never see my beautiful wife, Kathleen, again in this world—I would never be able to hold her in my arms, never be able to hold my three sons and precious little girl to my chest.

I desperately wanted to get on the radio and tell the tower operators to tell my wife and my children that I was so very sorry and that I loved them beyond expression. I wanted to tell my wife and kids that I wished I could be there to see them graduate from school and one day get married—to see my precious girl walking down the aisle to stand at the side of her groom. But My time had run out. I did not have time to say my good-byes. I was headed straight for the power lines.

As I approached my certain death, these electrical power lines filled my eyes. It was if the wires were magnified in size. They looked to be six inches wide in diameter. They filled the windshield of my plane.

I realize that the wires are not anywhere near that size, but as I approached them, that's how I saw them. At that moment, all I could do was cry out for Jesus. The next thing I knew, I was through the power lines. **I went right through them!** I did not go underneath them, and I did not go over the top of them. As I flew my plane straight ahead, I was overwhelmed with amazement, thankfulness, and tremendous joy.

I kept rehearsing over and over in my mind what had just happened. Could it really be? Did I really go through the power lines? **I know I did**. I was headed right into the High Lines. Amazing! The tower kept calling out to me over the radio, "Mike, are you there? Are you okay? Please answer!"

They had, to some extent, seen what happened. When they finally got me to respond, all they could get out of me was, **"Thank You Jesus! Thank you, Jesus! Thank you, Jesus!"** The airport radio frequency at that time was also picked up by three other airports. All the traffic controllers and radio personnel on that frequency heard me say over and over, "Thank you Jesus!"

After I landed, the mechanical personnel took the plane into the hangar. They had seen me slamming into the runway three times. In their thoughts, there is no way that this plane did not have structural damage. They went over it with a fine-toothed comb. Amazingly, they came back with a report that everything was absolutely fine.

Kathleen's perspective:

My husband had disappeared early in the morning. He probably told me where he was going while I was still asleep, but I never remembered. As the day went on, I decided to call his cell phone to figure out where he was. After several futile calls, I called Debra, Mike's sister, who worked in our church office at the time. Upon hearing that he had gone for flying lessons, my anger began to rise. My thoughts were, *who does he think he is, going off and spending thousands of dollars on flying lessons, when we have enough bills to pay, and we need things for the house, the children, and me!*

Immediately, the Spirit of God arrested me and rebuked me. Within my spirit came, *which is more important, the money, or your husband's life?* Brokenness clenched my soul, and I quickly repented. Asking God to forgive me for my selfishness, I told the Lord that my husband was more important than millions of dollars, and that the money wasn't worth Mike's life!

The devil had lost the battle to keep me bitter and unforgiving and the unity between us, as husband and wife, was not broken. Directly, a spirit of fear tried to grip my heart, and I knew that fear was another tool of the devil to bring division and destruction. An urgency to pray and to stand in faith made me stop everything! To this day, I remember where I was sitting when I began to **pray**: right at our kitchen bar. As I sat on the bar stool reiterating my repentance of selfishness, I implored the Lord to spare Mike's life, keep him safe, and bring him back to me and the children. Little did I know that I was truly pleading for my husband's life!

Through my tears, I remember boldly declaring, "Lord, you've given Your angels charge over us, to keep us in all our ways, even in our stupidity." My declaration continued, "In our pathway is life and there is no death. So, Father, I put Michael in your hands. I know you'll bring him home safely."
At this point, I made a covenant in my heart. I made my stand, "I trust You, Lord, because there is no one else to trust. If, I can't trust You to keep Mike safe, then I can trust no one. Thank You for bringing my husband back to me!" I refused to give into bitterness, fear, or worry. My hope was in the Lord who is always faithful.

The devil had lost the fight on my side to cause division, bitterness, anger, fear, and lack of peace. I did not fail to repent and intercede for my husband when the Spirit of God dealt with me. God's grace had helped me through the test. God's faith had brought victory and brought my husband home alive. When Mike came through the door of our home that day, he told me of his near-fatal flight.

My response was, "If the Lord hadn't dealt with my heart, you might have eaten those power lines!" I embraced Mike with a thankful heart and a grace in my heart towards the Lord's goodness and mercy. God surely knew what He was doing in both of our lives to keep us under His protection. If I had given into bitterness and fear, or failed to intercede and stand in faith, I may not have my husband today!

Be ye angry, and sin not: let not the sun go down upon your wrath: Neither give place to the devil (Ephesians 4:26-27).

CHAPTER EIGHTEEN

Miracles in the Now

*120. In the Junkyard

There was a local auto salvage yard that I would periodically go to purchase parts for my vehicles. The Lord put it into my heart to begin to go down there on a regular basis to witness to the owner and his son. This was a man who had a rough exterior, but on the inside, I could sense a unique and tender-hearted person. He was the kind of man that I could relate with.

You see, I was raised in a very rough and tumble world. My grandpa, which was a large tell man, (I do not know what happened to me, I am only 5 feet 8 inches) was the original Texas kid! Grandpa was born in the late 1800s. Up until he died in 1973, he had a famous reputation. You did not mess with him. I still remember him with his cowboy hat, chewing tobacco in his mouth, and a large stogie in his hand.)

Back to the salvage yard. I would try to go there at least once a week to just chat with the owner, Dale. It really did not seem like I was getting anywhere with him spiritually. One day I received a phone call from him, which was highly unusual because he never called me. He seemed to be rather upset and distressed. He asked if I could come by and see him. I told him absolutely, and that I would be right down. When I got to his place of business, he began to share what was going on.

He said that he had not been feeling very well lately, so he set up a doctor's appointment to go see what was wrong. When they were done with all the tests and examinations, the prognosis was not very good. They informed him that he had cancer, and not just any cancer, but a very deadly form of cancer. I believe it was in his bone marrow and throughout his whole body. They told him there was no hope and that there was nothing they could do for him. They would not even give him chemotherapy, or radiation. When he was done telling me this tragic news, he asked me what he should do.

I could tell he was extremely serious. He was ready to do whatever it took. I told him he needed to give his heart to Jesus Christ. I said to him, "Put your hand into the hands of Jesus, and no matter what the outcome of this situation is, you need to walk with God." At once, Dale gave his heart willingly and openly to Jesus Christ. (I could tell that his was a true conversion, and he immediately became faithful in coming to hear the Word at church.)

I laid my hands on him, and began to take authority over this spirit of cancer and death. I cursed it from its roots, and commanded it to go in the name of Jesus Christ of Nazareth. We proclaimed life and healing. I continued to pray as the Spirit of God spoke to my heart. Dale was in complete agreement.

When we were done, I told him, "God requires us to have prayer-supplication, and thanksgiving. Now you need to begin lifting your hands and praising God that you are completely healed and made whole, and thank God that the cancer is gone, and that you have been set free by the stripes of Jesus Christ and His precious blood." At that very moment, he felt something happen in his body. He told me he began to feel extremely good. He even went back to work. Then he set up an appointment to go see the doctors. Their prognosis was amazing! They said almost all of the cancer was completely gone. It was in complete remission. They had given Dale just a couple weeks to live, but now they were saying that the cancer was in total remission. This was to their total amazement!

I wish I could say this story ended well. It did in the sense that Dale is on the other side of eternity waiting for us now. I have seen this happen more times than I want to relate. God does wonderful miracles, and the medical world intrudes, stepping in to try to complete what God has begun. The doctors told Dale and his family that even though the cancer was in total remission, just in case, they would give chemo and radiation!

They would not help him before because they said he was completely lost according to their estimates. But now that God had intervened, the medical world wanted to help Dale. The chemo and radiation took dale's life. I watched as his hair fell out, and he became a shadow of the man he was! I saw Dale in the last couple of hours before he died.

He said goodbye to me. He said he was tired of fighting, and he just wanted to go home to be with Jesus. I hugged him goodbye with tears rolling down my face. The next time I see Dale, it will be a glad reunion day in heaven.

But I would not have you to be ignorant, brethren, concerning them which are asleep, that ye sorrow not, even as others which have no hope. For if we believe that Jesus died and rose again, even so them also which sleep in Jesus will God bring with him (1 Thessalonians 4:13-14).

121. Staying in God's Will

I was on the board of a ministry that had been started by John G. Lake's daughter and son-in-law, Gertrude and Wilbert Wright. How I ended up on the board of this organization is a very long story. I did not seek this position, but was approached by its president to join up with them. I was still in my young thirties. God was moving in such marvelous ways in my life that this particular brother had seen and recognized an apostolic call upon me.

We became very close friends until the day he passed on. The ministry organization would fly me out to the state of Washington to teach on the subject of being a visionary. I spoke with some very well-known ministers of large organizations. After being on this board for approximately five years, I received a phone call one day. Something tragic had happened in the president's life. He was going to have to step down from his position for a season. (They never did reinstall him.)

At the time, I think there were about a dozen of us on the ministerial board. We had eight hundred ministers that were ordained and licensed through our fellowship. The corporate board was in Kensington Washington, and when the president stepped down, those in Kennewick basically were going to take over. When they called me and informed me of what was happening, they were implying that the board members there were going to start making all the decisions, and that they would tell us what the end results would be.

The Spirit of God quickened my heart, and I told them that they needed to have a gathering of all the board members, and that they did not have the constitutional authority, according to our letters of incorporation, to make these decisions on their own. I informed them that they needed to have a gathering of all of the board members to make these decisions. I and the other board members flew out to Washington, and we all gathered at the main office of the corporation. All of us sat around a large table and began to discuss what had happened, and what needed to happen.

You could feel the tension in the air. The room was filled with men who had their own agendas. I saw clearly by the Spirit that this was going to be a power struggle. There were men in this meeting who were not concerned about the former president or his restoration. I saw the spirit of greed and power radiating from them. The Spirit of God came upon me. I did not want to assume control of this gathering, but I was not going to sit by and watch the enemy destroy everything that John G. Lake's daughter and son-in-law had worked for. By the Spirit of the Lord, I began to deal with some major problems of those who were on this board. I told them judgment must begin in the house of the Lord, so let's deal with the issues of our hearts. This word was not received well by those who were greedy for control. I know without a shadow of doubt that God was using me to bring correction. Before I left Kennewick it seemed like there had been some major steps towards resolving the foreseeable problems. It had been agreed upon that the former president would be restored within a couple years after proper counseling and guidance. As I stated earlier, it never happened.

I left Kennewick and flew back to Pennsylvania. I was sitting in my office one day when the Spirit of God spoke to my heart very strongly, telling me that those who were appointed to elect a temporary new president were discussing about making me the president over this ministry. The Spirit of the Lord also informed me that if I took this position I would be out of the Father's will, and that pride would fill my heart and it would be to my destruction. At that very moment the fear the Lord came upon me, almost as strong as it did on the day that I was going to take my life. It shook me so much to the core of my being, that I immediately wrote a letter of resignation to the fellowship. From that day until now I have never gone back or contacted them.

Years later, a good friend of mine who was on that ministerial board was talking to me. He asked me, "Mike, why did you resign from the board? Do you know that we were about to make you the president of our organization?" I told him that I knew by the Spirit of God, that they were going to offer me that position, however, the Spirit of the Lord told me not to take it. I told my friend that I could not trust myself to resist the temptation of accepting the offer. Therefore, I had to resign. Many men are destroyed because they step into positions that God has not called them to walk in. It is either not His timing, or it is not His will for their lives.

Let every man abide in the same calling wherein he was called (1 Corinthians 7:20).

*122. Epileptic Seizure (1992)

My wife and I were shopping at a Lowe's building supply store, when all of a sudden, we noticed some commotion at the front of the store. It was at one of the checkout counters. The girl working behind the counter had gone into an epileptic seizure. A small crowd had gathered around the countertop, but nobody was trying to help her. Everybody was standing and staring as she fell to the ground, kicking and squirming. Somebody was calling 9-1-1 to get help.

Now, I'm the kind of guy who cannot just be a spectator. So, I walked up and said: "Excuse me," as I pushed my way through all of these people. I said, "Please, let me through, I am a doctor." This was the absolute truth, as I have a Ph.D. in Biblical Theology and a Doctorate of Divinity. I told the people standing there that I could help. I went over to the countertop, having to lean over it to see what was going on. This girl was on the floor thrashing away in a seizure. I simply leaned over the top of the counter, placed one hand on her arm. I whispered real quietly, "In the name of Jesus Christ of Nazareth, you lying devil loose her, and come out of her now!"

Immediately, her eyes stopped rolling; the convulsions stopped, and she got up from off the floor. But, when she stood up, it was not to thank me for helping her. With a demonic snarl, she began to curse and swear at me for taking authority over these demonic spirits. It could have become a brutal battle, but the Spirit quickened me to walk away. This was not the time or place. Plus, the Holy Ghost revealed to me that this girl had invited these demons into her life - to draw attention to her. It saddens my heart over how many people are embracing their infirmities, depressions, and oppressions to use them for their own benefit - either in the form of sympathy or for financial gain.

Timothy 1:7 For God hath not given us the spirit of fear; but of power, and of love, and of a sound mind.

Daniel 11:32 And such as do wickedly against the covenant shall he corrupt by flatteries: but the people that do know their God shall be strong, and do exploits.

Matthew 10:8 Heal the sick, cleanse the lepers, raise the dead, cast out devils: freely ye have received, freely give.

*123. Brain-Quickening Experience

My family and I were ready for vacation. We wanted to go somewhere and get refreshed spiritually. Because of the fact that we do not watch TV, we really did not know about the different ministries. We were encouraged to go to a well-known minister in Ohio who had a camp meeting every year. Supposedly, they had wonderful and amazing meetings. We bundled up the children and packed everything for one week of vacation.

We were on our way for an exciting and spiritual vacation, or so we thought. We arrived in Ohio just before the camp meeting was to start. We entered the parking lot of this large and impressive church, which had acres of parking. The worship and praise was wonderful and exciting with lots of enthusiasm. But pretty soon our joy was brought down a couple of notches. What caused this unexpected disappointment was how they aggressively went after raising money.

I never have been one for all of this hype and high-pressure tactics for money. It is not because we're not givers; many times we have given up to ninety percent of our income on a regular basis. To be honest with you, I've known some of the top money raisers in the religious world. One of the best-known money raisers years ago was ministering in our church. When he began to make wild promises to our congregation about how wealthy they would become if they would just give a certain amount of money, I basically had to put a stop to it. I took him out to eat and I tried to talk some godly wisdom into him. For over two hours I began to show him with the Scriptures that he was getting the people to be involved in idolatry and spiritual gambling. I showed him that he was taking advantage of people in their desperation, and this was absolutely against the teachings of Christ.

I thought he had received what I said, because of the conviction that was evident upon him. So, a year later when he was coming through our area wanting to speak at our church again, I decided to give him another opportunity; which was a big mistake. Praise God we had a heavy snowfall during the week he was to be with us, and very few people came to this meeting. I'm sorry to say that he was worse now than ever. He even was extremely upset because our turnout was so small.

Back to Our Ohio Vacation:

After the first night of meetings in Ohio, we went back to our hotel extremely disappointed. The next morning I said to the Lord, "Father, help me to keep my heart right with You. I do not want to be judgmental of these people." Once again, right after the worship, tremendous pressure was applied to the people to give in order to get back something from God. I sat there deciding to grin and bear it. After this fund-raising endeavor, there were some other announcements and activities with special singing and testimonies. Then once again, they started raising money.

This time I said, "Lord, if they raise money one more time, we are walking out of here and going home." A well-known speaker got up ministering a powerful message on how to win your whole household to the Lord. Now this was exciting what he was preaching, I could really get into this. He was ministering out of the book of Acts chapter 16 verse 31. But to my extreme disappointment, when he declared that if you wanted this scripture to work for you, then you were going to have to sow a seed of $16.31 for every person you wanted to be saved. Surely people had enough spirituality not to fall for this trickery. Yet that was not the case, people fell for it.

I could no longer take this manipulation and trickery. We got up, left, and I packed up my wife and children to go home. We checked out of the hotel and drove all the way back home to Pennsylvania. As I was driving home, in my heart I was complaining about these people.

Then the Spirit of the Lord spoke to me, not agreeing or disagreeing pertaining to these people. The Lord began to bring discipline into my life about my own spiritual condition. He basically told me that I was a "favorite scripture" preacher, and that I really did not know his Word the way I should. I was so convicted by this confrontation from God that I made a commitment that when I got home I would begin to pour myself into the Bible like I should. I was going to spend hours in God's Word and prayer.

I informed my staff (I had twenty-one people working for me) that I would begin to give myself to long hours of prayer and the Word. I began with the book of Ephesians, and started with the very first chapter. I not only wanted to memorize it, I wanted to get it deep into my heart. It took me close to three weeks and countless hours to memorize. **This was violent faith at work within my heart**.

The next mountain I climbed was the book of Galatians. As I memorized the Scriptures and chapters of the Bible I experienced tremendous headaches. But … I kept working at it because I knew that without pain - there is no gain!

Once I had conquered the book of Galatians, I moved on to Philippians. As I got into the second chapter of Philippians, something Supernatural took place. I had what the Bible calls an 'Open Vision.' This happens when you are wide-awake and everything disappears - except what God is showing you.

Right there in front of me was a large body of crystal-clear water: pure blue with not one ripple on it. It stretched as far as the natural eye could see; in every direction. The room I was in had all but disappeared and there was nothing but a gigantic, blue lake. I lifted up my head and looked into a beautiful, light-blue, cloudless sky. I saw a large, crystal-clear raindrop falling down from the heavens in slow-motion. I watched in amazement as it slowly tumbled down towards the lake. When it hit the surface of the water it caused ripples to flow forth.

The ripples flowed from the center of the water, where the drop had hit, and began to grow in size and intensity. Then ... all of a sudden, the vision was over. It ended as quickly as it began. I stood there in amazement, not understanding what had just happened. I knew this experience was from God, but I did not know what its significance was.

I knew in my heart that eventually God would show me what the vision meant. You see, when the Lord gives me a supernatural visitation, I do not lean on the understanding of my natural mind. I just simply give it to the Lord, knowing that in His time He will show me what He meant - or what He was saying.

When the vision ended, I picked up my Bible to get back to memorizing the Scriptures and I immediately noticed there was a change in my mental capacity. It seemed like my brain was absorbing the Word of God like a sponge. Amazingly, within one hour, I'd memorized a whole chapter - as if it were nothing! To my total surprise I'd developed a photographic memory! Before the vision it took me days to memorize a chapter, and now I could memorize a chapter in one hour!! I continued to memorize books of the Bible until there were ten books inside of me. This is not including the thousands of other Scriptures that I continued to memorize when dealing with certain subjects (I have videos on YouTube where I quote whole books of the Bible by memory).

Why would God open up my heart and my mind the way He did to memorize the Word? The Word of God has the capacity to quicken our minds and mortal bodies. God's Word is awesome, quick and powerful. There is an activation of the things of the Spirit when we begin to give ourselves one-hundred percent into whatever it is God has called us to do. There is a dynamic principle of laying down our lives in order to release the aroma, the presence, and the power of heaven.

I'm sorry to say that I became so busy with running the church, a Christian school, a small Bible college, a radio station, TV broadcasting and construction projects and twenty-five churches in the Philippines - not including other aspects of being a pastor - that I did not continue to memorize the Bible. I know within my heart that if I'd continued a complete diet of God's Word and saturated my whole being with the truth, I would have been able to accomplish a thousand times more than what I have. Thank God that I'm still alive, that I still have breath, and this opportunity is still before both you and I.

Even though I did not continue to saturate myself with the Word of God, through the years, I have continued in His Word daily. You see, I've had an insatiable hunger for the Word of God ever since I was saved. Because of God's Word in my heart, the Lord has allowed me to write over seven-thousand sermons and forty books. I have also been able to do many things that I have never been taught or trained to do.

Furthermore, during all these activities I earned a Ph.D. in Biblical Theology and I received a Doctorate of Divinity. I believe it is all because of the divine, supernatural visitations and quickening's of God's Holy Spirit. The reason I believe we do not experience more visitations is because of a lack of spiritual hunger, prayer, and God's Word hidden in our hearts. If we would hunger and thirst, God would satisfy these desires.

And the king communed with them; and among them all was found none like Daniel, Hananiah, Mishael, and Azariah: therefore stood they before the king. And in all matters of wisdom and understanding, that the king enquired of them, he found them ten times better than all the magicians and astrologers that were in all his realm (Daniel 1:19-20).

*124. Broken Busted Foot Instantly Healed

One day I had to climb our 250-foot AM radio tower to change the light bulb on the main beacon. However, to climb the tower, I had to first find the keys; which I never did. Since I could not find the keys to get the fence open, I did the next best thing—I simply climbed over the fence.

This idea turned out not to be such a wonderful idea after all! With all my climbing gear hanging from my waist, I climbed the fence to the very top. At this point, my rope gear became entangled in the fencing. As I tried to get free, I lost my balance and fell backwards off the fence. Trying to break my fall, I got my right foot down underneath me. I hit the ground with my foot being turned on its side and I felt something snap in the ankle. I knew instantly I had a broken foot, my ankle.

Most normal people would have climbed back over the fence, go set up a doctor's appointment, have their foot x rayed, and then placed into a cast. But I am not a normal-thinking person, at least according to the standards of the modern-day church. When I broke my foot, I followed my routine of confessing my stupidity to God, and asking Him to forgive me for my stupidity. Moreover, then I spoke to my foot and commanded it to be healed in the name of Jesus Christ of Nazareth. When I had finished speaking to my foot, commanding it to be healed, and then praising and thanking God for the healing, there seem to be no change what so ever in its condition.

The Scripture that came to my heart was where Jesus declared, *"The kingdom of heaven suffereth violence, and the violent take it by force!"*

Based completely upon this scripture, I decided to climb the tower by faith, with a broken foot mind you. Please do not misunderstand, my foot hurt so bad I could hardly stand it. And yet, I had declared that I believed I was healed.

There were three men watching me as I took the Word of God by faith. I told them what I was about to do, and they looked at me like as if I had lost my mind. I began to climb the 250-foot tower, one painful step at a time. My foot hurt so bad that I was hyperventilating within just twenty to thirty feet up the tower. It literally felt like I was going to pass out from shock at any moment. Whenever I got to the point of fainting, I would connect my climbing ropes to the tower, stop and take a breather, crying out to Jesus to help me. It seemed to take me forever to get to the top.

Even so, I finally did reach the very top of the tower and replaced the light bulb that had gone out. Usually I can come down that tower within 10 minutes, because I would press my feet against the tower rods, and then slide down, just using my hands and arms to lower myself at a very fast pace. However, in this situation, my foot could not handle the pressure of being pushed up against the steel. Consequently, I had to work my way down very slowly. After I was down, I slowly climbed over the fence one more time. I hobbled my way over to my vehicle, and drove up to the church office. The men who had been watching this unfold, were right behind me.

I hobbled my way into the front office; which is directly across the street from the radio tower. I informed the personnel that I had broken my foot, showing them my black and blue, extremely swollen foot. It did not help that I had climbed with it! I told them that I was going home to rest. At the same time, however, I told them that I believed I was healed.

Going to my house, which is directly across from the main office of the church parking lot, I made my way slowly up the stairs to our bedroom. I found my wife in the bedroom putting away our clothes. Slowly and painfully I pulled the shoe and sock off the broken foot. What a mess! It was fat, swollen, black and blue all over. I put a pillow down at the end of the bed, and carefully pulled myself up onto the bed. Lying on my back, I tenderly placed my broken, black, and blue, swollen foot onto the pillow. No matter how I positioned it, the pain did not cease. I just laid there squirming, moaning, and sighing.

As I was lying there trying to overcome the shock that kept hitting my body, I heard the audible voice of God. He said to me: "What are you doing in bed? God really got my attention when I heard him with my natural ears. My wife would testify that she heard nothing. Immediately in my heart I said: Lord I'm just resting. Then He spoke to my heart with the still small voice very clearly: Do you always rest at this time of day? No, Lord, I replied. (It was about 3 o'clock in the afternoon)

He spoke to my heart again and said: I thought you said you were healed?

At that very moment the gift of faith exploded inside of me. I said, "Lord, I am healed! Immediately, I pushed myself up off of the bed, grabbed my sock and shoe, and struggled to put them back on. What a tremendous struggle it was! My foot was so swollen that it did not want to go into the shoe. My wife was watching me as I fought to complete this task.

You might wonder what my wife was doing this whole time as I was fighting this battle of faith. She was doing what she always does, just watching me and shaking her head. I finally got the shoe on my swollen, black, and blue foot. I put my foot down on the floor and began to put my body weight upon it. When I did, I almost passed out. At that moment, a holy anger exploded on the inside of me. I declared out loud, "I am healed in the name of Jesus Christ of Nazareth!" With that declaration, I took my right (broken) foot, and slammed it down to the floor as hard as I possibly could.

When I did that, I felt the bones of my foot break even more. Like the Fourth of July, an explosion of blue, purple, red, and white, black exploded in my brain and I passed out. I came to lying on my bed. Afterward, my wife informed me that every time I passed out, it was for about ten to twenty seconds. The moment I came to, I jumped right back up out of bed. The gift of faith was working in me mightily. I got back up and followed the same process again, "In the name of Jesus Christ of Nazareth I am healed," and slammed my foot down once more as hard as I could! For a second time, I could feel the damage in my foot increasing. My mind was once again wrapped in an explosion of colors and pain as I blacked out.

When I regained consciousness, I immediately got up once again, repeating the same process. After the third time of this happening I came to with my wife leaning over the top of me. I remember my wife saying as she looked at me, "You're making me sick. I can't watch you do this." She promptly walked out of our bedroom, and went downstairs.

The fourth time I got up declaring, "In the name of Jesus Christ of Nazareth I am healed," and slammed my foot even harder! Once more, multiple colors of intense pain hit my brain. I passed out again! I got up the fifth time, angrier than ever. This was not a demonic or proud anger. This was a divine gift of violent I-will-not-take-no-for-an-answer type of faith. I slammed my foot down the fifth time, "In the name of Jesus Christ of Nazareth I am healed!"

The minute my foot slammed into the floor, for the fifth time, the power of God hit my foot. I literally stood there under the quickening power of God, and watched my foot shrink and become normal. All the pain was completely and totally gone. I pulled back my sock, and watched the black and blue in my foot disappear to normal flesh color. I was healed! Praise God, I was made whole! I went back to the office, giving glory to the Lord and showing the staff my healed foot.

Who through faith subdued kingdoms, wrought righteousness, obtained promises, stopped the mouths of lions, quenched the violence of fire, escaped the edge of the sword, out of weakness were made strong, waxed valiant in fight, turned to fight the armies of the aliens (Hebrews 11:33-34).

CHAPTER NINETEEN

Demonstration of the Miraculous

125. C-Band Uplink Satellite System

As I was memorizing scriptures one day, my fax machine began to print a page. I picked up the fax, not yet knowing who it came from. It was a picture of a very large, thirty foot satellite uplink system. I discovered that it came from a good friend of mine who lived in Ohio. A lot of our TV equipment had come from him; which he provided at tremendous discounts. I have no idea why in the world he would fax this information to me. Not in any stretch of the word was I looking for a C-band uplink satellite system. However, the minute I looked at the fax, the Spirit of God quickened within my heart, and said, buy this system.

I said to the Lord, Why, Lord?

He replied, because you are going to be transmitting my word across America, twenty-four hours a day by satellite."

I asked, Lord, why would you have me do this?

He responded, because you have been faithful in hiding My Word in your heart.

Now the original value of this thirty-foot Vertex uplink dish, with its pedestal and transmitter building, had been valued at over $250,000. That cost is not including all of the equipment that would have to go with it. It was located in State College, Texas, at the Westinghouse factory, where they had been using it for teleconferencing.

I have always hated raising money. I'm not good at it, and do not like it. I told the Lord, Lord I do not want to raise this money!

He spoke to my heart saying, You will not have to. I will move upon the hearts of the people, and all the money will come in, as you share with them what I am speaking to you now.

I went before the congregation the next Sunday and shared with them the experience that I had, exactly the way the Lord told me to. Almost nonchalantly, I told them that if they would like to donate towards this project they could. The finances began to come in, just as He told me they would!

And they came, every one whose heart stirred him up, and every one whom his spirit made willing, and they brought the LORD'S offering to the work of the tabernacle of the congregation, and for all his service, and for the holy garments. And they came, both men and women, as many as were willing hearted, and brought bracelets, and earrings, and rings, and tablets, all jewels of gold: and every man that offered an offering of gold unto the LORD (Exodus 35:21-22).

*126. A cross Dry Land

When God told me to buy a **C-band uplink system** (originally $250,000) that my friend had faxed to me. I contacted the broker and made arrangements to purchase the uplink system. As the money came in through the following weeks, we wired the money into a Westinghouse account. During this time, we also applied for our C-band uplink license through the FCC. Westinghouse sent us the blueprints we needed to begin to prepare and pour the foundation. I think there was over fifteen yards of concrete alone that we needed to pour. That was not including the precise placement of hundreds of rebars, which needed to be placed into the concrete pad - before we could pick up the dish.

Westinghouse informed me that where the satellite uplink system was located was a very wet area, and if there was any type of water on the ground when we tried to take a crane or an 18 wheel truck back into that area, it would sink - up to its windshield. They insisted it must be a very dry time before I could pick it up. I shared this with the whole congregation, so that we could believe for the dry spell that we desperately needed. As we came into the fall, rain began to fall heavily all the way from out West to the East Coast. It rained, and rained, and rained!!

On the Saturday, right before Thanksgiving, the **Spirit of the Lord spoke to me** - out of nowhere - and told me it was time to go get the uplink system. **I knew it was the voice of God,** so I contacted the men in my church who had volunteered to help pick up the equipment. (What I'm about to share with you could be a book in and by itself, so I will try to keep it brief.)

The men I had contacted to help me go pick up the system, challenged me a little about going. Nevertheless, they had been with me through numerous life storms, and they knew that I could hear from God. I told them to come to the Sunday morning church service and be prepared to leave right after the service. We had a Dodge Caravan, that six of us could cram into, with an attached covered trailer that would carry our air compressor and tools.

That Sunday morning, I informed the congregation of our intentions to go pick up the satellite uplink system. Some of the people became extremely upset - since it had been raining for weeks on end. After all, I had verbally told them that we could not pick up the system unless we had a thoroughly **dry season**. On top of that, we were still $8,000 short of the money we needed to complete the transaction! However, I told the congregation that I knew in my heart that the Lord had spoken to me, so we would be going.

We are talking close to a 1,400-mile trip. If I had not heard from heaven correctly ... we were in big trouble! As we pulled out of the parking lot that Sunday afternoon, it was cold, wet, and raining everywhere. All through the day we drove in the rain. We did not stop through the night, but drove straight through to the next day. As we pulled into State College, Texas, it was still raining. I told the men, even though it's the end of the day, let's go look at the **C-band uplink system**. We followed the directions to the Westinghouse factory. As we pulled onto the property, something really strange seemed wrong with their yard. All of their grass was **brown and dead**. We pulled up to a parking spot right outside of the main office; then we went inside to introduce ourselves to the personnel.

There was a woman behind a glass sliding window at a countertop. We commented to her about the grass being brown and dead on their property. She told us it was the strangest thing that they had ever seen or experienced. It had rained everywhere else in their area, but not one drop of rain had fallen upon the Westinghouse ground. There was absolutely no explanation for it. At least that's what they believed, we knew different! We were smack-dab, right in the middle of the will of God and God had kept their land dry.

I beseech you therefore, brethren, by the mercies of God, that ye present your bodies a living sacrifice, holy, acceptable unto God, which is your reasonable service. And be not conformed to this world: but be ye transformed by the renewing of your mind, that ye may prove what is that good, and acceptable, and perfect, will of God (Romans 12:1-2).

*127. All Things According to His Will

The Westinghouse factory informed us that the C-band uplink system was around the back. However, it was going to take special equipment to dismantle this sophisticated piece of equipment. One company had told them it would take about a week to dismantle, with the cost of $40,000. Well … we were all just a bunch of country hicks with an air compressor and regular tools! They also informed us we would need a large crane, with a specially-designed truck, to carry the equipment. In addition, it would be impossible during this particular week, because it was Thanksgiving. They also informed us that they would need to have all the money wired into their account – in advance - before we would even be allowed to touch, let alone disassemble, the system.

I told them this was acceptable to us, because we needed a good night's sleep anyway, and we would be back early in the morning to dismantle the system: in order to have it shipped to our facility in Gettysburg, Pennsylvania. Some of the men asked me what we were going to do, because we did not have the money, the equipment, nor did we have the truck. I told them everything was okay.

The gift of FAITH was at work in my heart

I called up the church office, just to double check about the $8,000 that we still needed, and they informed me nothing had come in, yet.

Even though I had been informed that the $8,000 we needed still had not come in, we were up bright and early. We headed out to have a good breakfast before arriving at Westinghouse. I called up our church office, after 8:00 a.m. EST, to ask if the money was there yet. They said: **"No Pastor, there is no sign of it ... and we don't know what to tell you."** I told them that it was okay. That we did not need the money until we got to the factory to pick up the equipment.

We arrived at the factory, walked up to the front office counter, and informed them that we were ready to begin dismantling the uplink satellite system. They said that there was still a problem - with us being short $8,000. I told them to access their account and they would discover the money had been wired. The lady went to her computer and came back a few minutes later and said, **"Yes, it had just been wired." Hallelujah!** The money had been wired to

Westinghouse's account! To this day, I am not certain where all the money came from, but God had supplied.

We drove the minivan and trailer to the uplink system. It was one *big* satellite dish. (You can come and see it at our church.) I had all the men gathered together in a circle, holding hands to pray. I prayed that God would give to us a spirit of wisdom and understanding in the knowledge of what we needed to do, and how to do it, quickly and speedily - with no damage to the system! After we were done praying and thanking God, I discussed with the men what needed to happen next.

The Spirit of God came upon all of us. I began to watch the men crawl over the satellite dish; like a well-organized and experienced team. It was so amazing, that the personnel, technicians, and scientists came out of the Westinghouse factory to watch us. They were snapping pictures as we were working! They were absolutely flabbergasted and kept talking about how it was supposed to take a week for the dish to be disassembled and packed - not two days!

As our men were working, I began to make phone calls. The Lord provided a crane company to come for the day. Of course, once they arrived they tried to charge us way more than what they agreed upon over the phone. But God gave me gentle, holy boldness to deal with it. So, they eventually came back down to their original verbal agreement. I then contacted a trucking terminal out of Houston, Texas and told them the kind of truck we were looking for. They informed me that they did not have that type of truck available; and they did not know where to send us to find one. Not only that, but there was nobody there, being only a couple of days before Thanksgiving. I asked them to please just go ahead and look around.

The man on the phone said: "Hold on! There's a man and woman standing outside of my office right now. I need to ask them what they want." To his amazement, they were a married couple looking to carry a load back East. He put the man on the phone with me. Amazingly, it was exactly the kind of truck we desperately needed! The couple arrived with the truck and backed up to the large satellite dish. The truck did not sink down in the least, because the ground was so dry, and hard. The panels of the uplink dish were all stacked off to the side, so we only needed the crane for one day. All the crane had to do was load up the main pedestal and the transmission shed.

The next morning, we came back to finish the packing. We had a wonderful time-sharing Christ with the married couple that owned the truck. I am convinced that both are probably saved now, because we asked if we could pray for them before they left with our equipment. I saw the gift of faith come upon them as we laid our hands on them.

We loaded the truck and found that the transmitter building itself was too tall to fit under the bridges. Not only was the equipment too high to fit under bridges, and overpasses, but our satellite equipment succeeded the legal weight limit of what the truck was allowed to carry. We told the couple that we did not know what we could do, but that we'd certainly be praying for them. The driver informed us not to worry about them getting our equipment to us.

How he brought our uplink system to Pennsylvania is another amazing story in itself. As he was driving his truck on the main highways, he would slow down as he approached a bridge, and let the air out of his air shocks. He'd crawl slowly under the bridge and would speak to other truck drivers by CB, those who were ahead of him, to find out if the weigh stations were open. If they were open, he would pull over until they had too many 18 wheelers to inspect, and then he'd pass by safely. He did this all the way from Texas to Gettysburg, Pennsylvania!

When the uplink dish finally arrived, we had a crew of men and women ready. The huge concrete slab, which was over three feet deep, and the rebar that was needed in the concrete was cured and ready. Within three days we had this system installed, ready to operate, and ready to broadcast. However, the time to broadcast was not immediate.

And he that searcheth the hearts knoweth what is the mind of the Spirit, because he maketh intercession for the saints according to the will of God. And we know that all things work together for good to them that love God, to them who are the called according to his purpose (Romans 8:27-28).

CHAPTER TWENTY

Conclusion

I have shared with you from my heart some of the experiences that the Lord has allowed us to experience. I know that what I have shared could never capture fully what took place in my journey to heaven. Plus, the visitations of angelic beings of protecting us, teaching, and giving us instructions, or all of are other supernatural experiences. But I pray that the Lord will use these experiences to touch your life in some degree. The harvest is truly great, but the laborers are few. I hope this book would become a catalyst that God could use to bring about a supernatural, enabling encounter with Him. If there was ever a time the body of Christ needs to be active, it is now.

"No man that warreth entangleth himself with the affairs of this life; that he may please him who hath chosen him to be a soldier"(2Tim.2:4).

You see, God is not a respecter of persons. But every one of us has a different job, a different position, a unique place within the body. Do not believe or accept the lie that God does not have a specific purpose for your life. After God created the heavens and the earth, He put in to place a new law. God made it so that man became the gateway, channel, and avenue by which He would move, rule, and reign. There is an overwhelming amount of Scriptures that clearly proclaimed this a mazing truth. Hebrews chapter eleven reveals the names of twenty-two people God used to bring about His ultimate purpose and plan. The entire Bible is a declaration that it is now through man that God steps into the midst of humanity. God is looking and searching for men and women who will agree with His heart.

"And God blessed them, and God said unto them, Be fruitful, and multiply, and replenish the earth, and subdue it: and have dominion over the fish of the sea, and over the fowl of the air, and over every living thing that moveth upon the earth" (Gen. 1:28).

"For the prophecy came not in old time by the will of man: but holy men of God spake as they were moved by the Holy Ghost" (2 Pet. 1:21).

The heavenly Father stepped into this world through Jesus Christ to deliver, heal, save, and set men free. He was the physical embodiment of all that the heavenly Father is. He is the answer and solution to all of the world's problems.

"Neither is there salvation in any other: for there is none other name under heaven given among men, whereby we must be saved" (Acts 4:12).

Now it is our turn to be surrendered and submitted to the heavenly Father, His precious Son, and the Holy Ghost. We were made to be possessed, inhabited, filled, and under the influence of the Three in One. God has given to us the opportunity to be coworkers in the harvest field. Let us go forth in His mighty name. By His divine grace, power, authority, and His name may we go forth to set the multitudes free!

Note to Sinners and Backsliders

For those who possibly are not right with God, the stories I have just shared with you truly happened to me. The Bible says that:

"By faith Noah, being warned of God of things not seen as yet, moved with fear, prepared an ark to the saving of his house; by the which he condemned the world, and became heir of the righteousness which is by faith" (Heb. 11:7).

God is moving in my heart with tremendous love and fear for you and for all of those who might not love God. I beg you and plead with you, in the name of Jesus Christ of Nazareth, to turn from your selfish, sinful, wicked ways and claim a new life in Jesus Christ. Or you will go to a burning hell. Once you have crossed the dark river of death, never more will you see a flower or green pastures or rolling oceans. Never will you again enjoy a glass of clear pure water or the simple pleasures of life. You will never again enjoy the sweet communion with those you love and know. But you will be lost forever in the endless ages of eternal darkness and fire.

Darkness and pain, torment and sorrow will be your eternal destiny. Shaking hands with a preacher will not save you. Putting your name on a church membership list will not do it. Giving money to a ministry or doing good deeds of any kind will not get you to heaven. We must repent of willful, known sin, and we must have a Godly sorrow for our actions. We must ask God, out of the depths of our hearts, to forgive us. And no matter how great our sin is, if we are sincere and no longer want to stay in our sins, God will deliver and forgive and accept us. Oh, sinner, be warned while there is yet time, and the eyes of the Savior still plead, and Jesus still beckons. Leave the broad and wide path of a selfish life, which leads to hell. And walk upon the straight and narrow way, which leads to heaven.

Remember how the demons cried out and asked Jesus whether He had come to torment them before their time? Are we so foolish as to not be moved by the realities of hell or to make light of them?

Christianity consists of a new heart and a new life, dedicated and committed to not sinning. It is living for the glory of God. If your heart and life has not been changed by God, if you are still living in open rebellion and known disobedience to the Word and will of God, and you are not concerned about it, you have no right to assume you are going to heaven.

The devil and his demons will have the right to grab you by the hair, by your arms and legs, and pull you to hell with them. Sin is worse than hell because sin made it necessary for Jesus to create such a place called hell. It is the ultimate conclusion of a sinful life. Please, flee from sin! Flee from living for yourself. Flee from being self-pleasing, self-serving, self-loving, and self-centered. When you die, it will be too late to turn away from your sins. All opportunity to turn to God ends at death. Unless you turn from your selfishness and run to Jesus Christ and believe on Him who is our only hope, you will curse God eternally. And you will never die to the pains, agonies, terrors, horrors, and sorrows of hell. You will never experience the glory of heaven.

"Many will say to me in that day, Lord, Lord, have we not prophesied in thy name? and in thy name have cast out devils? and in thy name done many wonderful works? and then will I profess unto them, I never knew you: depart from me, ye that work iniquity" (Matt. 7:22).

I pray with all of my heart that this experience God allowed me to have will cause you to look to the loving Savior who poured out His lifeblood for you and who was nailed to the cross for your sins. He lovingly and longingly desires you to become one of His children. Won't you believe upon Him today? Call out to Him today. He will in no way cast out any who come to Him. Please, please turn from your wicked, evil, and self- centered ways. Love Him who first loved us. Let God give you a new heart and nature, a heart that loves, serves, and follows God. I hope to see you in heaven!

How to Live in the Miraculous!

This is a quick explanation of how to live and move in the realm of the miraculous. Seeing divine interventions of God is not something that just spontaneously happens because you have been born-again. There are certain biblical principles and truths that must be evident in your life. This is a very basic list of some of these truths and laws:

1. You must give Jesus Christ your whole heart. You cannot be lackadaisical in this endeavour. Being lukewarm in your walk with God is repulsive to the Lord. He wants 100% commitment. Jesus gave His all, now it is our turn to give our all. He loved us 100%. Now we must love Him 100%.

My son, give me thine heart, and let thine eyes observe my ways (Proverbs 23:26).

So then because thou art lukewarm, and neither cold nor hot, I will spew thee out of my mouth (Revelation 3:16).

2. There must be a complete agreement with God's Word. We must be in harmony with the Lord in our attitude, actions, thoughts, and deeds. Whatever the Word of God declares in the New Testament is what we wholeheartedly agree with.

Can two walk together, except they be agreed? (Amos 3:3).

For the eyes of the LORD run to and fro throughout the whole earth, to shew himself strong in the behalf of them whose heart is perfect toward him (2 Chronicles 16:9).

3. Obey and do the Word from the heart, from the simplest to the most complicated request or command. No matter what the Word says to do, do it! Here are some simple examples: Lift your hands in praise, in everything give thanks, forgive instantly, gather together with the saints, and give offerings to the Lord, and so on.

I can of mine own self do nothing: as I hear, I judge: and my judgment is just; because I seek not mine own will, but the will of the Father which hath sent me (John 5:30).

4. Make Jesus the highest priority of your life. Everything you do, do not do it as unto men, but do it as unto God.

If ye then be risen with Christ, seek those things which are above, where Christ sitteth on the right hand of God. Set your affection on things above, not on things on the earth (Colossians 3:1-2).

5. Die to self! The old man says, "My will be done!" The new man says, "God's will be done!"

I am crucified with Christ: nevertheless I live; yet not I, but Christ liveth in me: and the life which I now live in the flesh I live by the faith of the Son of God, who loved me, and gave himself for me (Galatians 2:20).

Now if we be dead with Christ, we believe that we shall also live with him (Romans 6:8).

6. Repent the minute you get out of God's will—no matter how minor, or small the sin may seem.

(Revelation 3:19).

As many as I love, I rebuke and chasten: be zealous therefore, and repent.

7. Take one step at a time. God will test you (not to do evil) to see if you will obey him. *Whatever He tells you to do: by His Word, by His Spirit, or within your conscience, do it.* He will never tell you to do something contrary to His nature or His Word!

For whosoever shall do the will of my Father which is in heaven, the same is my brother, and sister, and mother (Matthew 12:50).

Then went he down, and dipped himself seven times in

Jordan, according to the saying of the man of God: and his flesh came again like unto the flesh of a little child, and he was clean (2 Kings 5:14).

FROM OUR BOOK: God Still Does Miracles

#58 Men, woman, children COULD NOT MOVE or SPEAK for 2 1/2 hours

My family and I traveled out West ministering in different churches and visiting relatives in Wisconsin. We were invited to speak at a church in Minneapolis, Minnesota. The pastor actually had two different churches that he pastored. One of these churches was in the suburbs, and the other one was in the heart of Minneapolis. The larger of the two churches was in the suburbs. I was to minister at the larger church first, and then immediately go to his other church downtown. The whole congregation was in the same service that morning. There were approximately 140 to 160 people including women, men, children, and babies in the sanctuary.

As I began to speak, I found myself unexpectedly speaking on the subject of: **The year that King Uzia died**, I saw the Lord high and lifted up, and his glory filled the Temple, which is found in the book of Isaiah! The unction of the Holy Ghost was upon me so strong, that it just flowed out of my belly like rivers of living water. To this day I do not remember exactly everything that I said. As I was speaking, I sensed an amazing heavenly touch of God's presence upon myself and on everyone in the sanctuary.

The spirit of God was upon me in a mighty way, and yet I was aware of the time factor. In order to get to pastor bills sister church downtown Minnesota, I was not going to have time to lay hands on, or pray for anyone. If God was going to confirm his word with signs following, then he would have to do it without me being there. It turns out this is exactly what God wanted to do! When I was about at the limit of the amount of the time allotted to me, I quickly closed with a prayer. I did not say anything to the pastor, or anyone else as I grabbed my Bible to leave the sanctuary. My family was already loaded up and waiting for me in our vehicle. As I ran out the door I perceived something strange, awesome and wonderful was beginning to happen to the congregation. There was a heavy, amazing and holy hush that had come upon them.

By the time I arrived at the other church, their worship had already begun.as I stood up to the pulpit to minister God's word, the Holy Spirit began to speak to me again, with a completely totally and different message. God did wonderful things in the sister church downtown that afternoon as I preached a message on being radical sold out and committed to **Christ. Everyone ended up falling out of their chairs unto the floor to their faces, weeping and crying before the Lord**. This is not something which I have ever encouraged any congregation to do. I have seen this happen numerous times where I simply have to stop preaching because the presence of God is so strong, and so real that people cannot stay in their seats. I stopped preaching, getting on my face, and just waiting upon God, as he moved upon the people's hearts.

After that service we went back to our fifth wheel trailer at the local campgrounds where we were camping. Later in the day, I received a phone call from this pastor. He was acting rather strange and speaking very softly in a very hushed manner.

He asked me with a whisper: does that always happen after you are done preaching? I said to him, tell me what happened**? He said as you were headed out the door, I began to melt to the floor, I could not keep standing, and I found myself pinned to the floor of the sanctuary**. I could not move or speak. Now all of the children (including babies) were in the sanctuary with the rest of the congregation. He said he personally could not move for 2 ½ hours. During this whole experience of 2 1/2 hours he did not hear another sound in the facility. For over 2 1/2 hours he just simply laid there not being able to move or speak a word under the presence and mighty hand of God. After 2 ½ hours pastor Bill was able to finally move, and to be able to get up. He had thought for sure that he was the only one still left in the church. Everybody must have gone home a long time ago, and that he was there by himself.

But to his complete shock and amazement everybody was still there, laying on the floor. Nobody could move or speak for over 2 1/2 hours! Men, women, children and even the babies were still lying on the floor, not moving, talking, or crying! God was in the house!" The tangible overwhelming solemn presence, and holiness of God had come to their church!

Pastor Bill asked me to come over to his house in order that we could talk about what happened that day in his church service. My family and I arrived, with him inviting us inside. He asked if this normally happened wherever I went. I informed him, no, but many wonderful and strange things do take place. That it did not always happen, except when I got myself into a place of complete absolute surrender and submission to **Jesus Christ**. This submission included not putting **ANYTHING else but the WORD of God into my heart.** That when I simply seek the face of God, by pray, giving myself completely to the word, meditation, singing and worship, intimacy with the **Father**, Son and Holy Ghost, that this was the results! God is not a respecter of people, what he does for one, he will do for others.

ABOUT THE AUTHOR

Michael met and married his wonderful wife (Kathleen) in 1978. As a direct result of the Author and his wife's personal, amazing experiences with God, they have had the privilege to serve as pastors/apostles, missionaries, evangelist, broadcasters, and authors for over four decades. By Gods Divine enablement's and Grace, Doc Yeager has written over

30 books, ministered over 10,000 Sermons, and having helped to start 27 churches. His books are filled with hundreds of their amazing testimonies of Gods protection, provision, healing's, miracles, and answered prayers. They flow in the gifts of the Holy Spirit, teaching the word of God, wonderful signs following and confirming God's word. Websites Connected to Doc Yeager.

www.docyeager.com

www.jilmi.org

www.wbntv.org

Books Written by Doc Yeager:

"Living in the Realm of the Miraculous #1"
"Living in the Realm of the Miraculous #2"
"Living in the Realm of the Miraculous #3"
"Living in the Realm of the Miraculous #4"
"I need God Cause I'm Stupid"
"The Miracles of Smith Wigglesworth"
"How Faith Comes 28 WAYS"
"Horrors of Hell, Splendors of Heaven"
"The Coming Great Awakening"
"Sinners in The Hands of an Angry GOD",
"Brain Parasite Epidemic"
"My JOURNEY to HELL" - illustrated for teenagers
"Divine Revelation of Jesus Christ"
"My Daily Meditations"
"Holy Bible of JESUS CHRIST"
"War In The Heavenlies - (Chronicles of Micah)"
"Living in the Realm of the Miraculous #2"
"My Legal Rights to Witness"
"Why We (MUST) Gather! - 30 Biblical Reasons"
"My Incredible, Supernatural, Divine Experiences"
"Living in the Realm of the Miraculous #3"
"How GOD Leads & Guides! - 20 Ways"
"Weapons of Our Warfare"

"How You Can Be Healed"
"Hell Is For Real"
"Heaven Is For Real"
"God Still Heals"
"God Still Provides"
"God Still Protects"
"God Still Gives Dreams & Visions"
"God Still Does Miracles"
"God Still Gives Prophetic Words"
"Life Changing Quotes of Smith Wigglesworth"

Made in the USA
Monee, IL
05 March 2022